UNIVERSITY OF CAMBRIDGE
DEPARTMENT OF APPLIED ECONOMICS

MONOGRAPH 20

NEW COMMODITIES AND
CONSUMER BEHAVIOUR

UNIVERSITY OF CAMBRIDGE
DEPARTMENT OF APPLIED ECONOMICS

Monographs

This series consists of investigations conducted by members of the Department's staff and others working in direct collaboration with the Department.

The Department of Applied Economics assumes no responsibility for the views expressed in the Monographs published under its auspices.

The following Monographs are still in print.

1. The Measurement of Production Movements
by C. F. CARTER, W. B. REDDAWAY *and* RICHARD STONE
4. The Analysis of Family Budgets
by S. J. PRAIS *and* H. S. HOUTHAKKER (*Reissue*)
5. The Lognormal Distribution
by J. AITCHISON *and* J. A. C. BROWN
6. Productivity and Technical Change   by W. E. G. SALTER
Second edition, with Addendum by W. B. REDDAWAY
7. The Ownership of Major Consumer Durables   by J. S. CRAMER
8. British Economic Growth, 1688–1959
by PHYLLIS DEANE *and* W. A. COLE (*Second edition*)
10. The Economics of Capital Utilisation   by R. MARRIS
11. Priority Patterns and the Demand for Household
Durable Goods   by F. G. PYATT
12. The Growth of Television Ownership in the
United Kingdom   by A. D. BAIN
13. The British Patent System   1. Administration   by KLAUS BOEHM
14. The Wealth of the Nation by JACK REVELL
15. Planning, Programming and Input-Output Models
Selected Papers on Indian Planning   by A. GHOSH
16. Biproportional Matrices and Input-Output Change
by MICHAEL BACHARACH
17. Abstract of British Historical Statistics
by B. R. MITCHELL *in collaboration with* PHYLLIS DEANE
18. Second Abstract of British Historical Statistics
by B. R. MITCHELL *and* H. G. JONES
19. Takeovers: their Relevance to the Stock Market and the
Theory of the Firm   by AJIT SINGH
20. New Commodities and Consumer Behaviour
by D. S. IRONMONGER
21. The Return to Gold 1925 by D. E. MOGGRIDGE

NEW COMMODITIES
AND
CONSUMER BEHAVIOUR

D. S. IRONMONGER

Reader in Applied Economic Research
University of Melbourne

CAMBRIDGE

AT THE UNIVERSITY PRESS

1972

Published by the Syndics of the Cambridge University Press
Bentley House, 200 Euston Road, London NW1 2DB
American Branch: 32 East 57th Street, New York, N.Y.10022

© Cambridge University Press 1972

Library of Congress Catalogue Card Number: 75–163056

ISBN: 0 521 08337 0

Printed in Great Britain
at the University Press
Aberdeen

To HEATHER

CONTENTS

Part I. New commodities and the theory of consumer behaviour

Part II.   New commodities and the measurement of consumer behaviour

TABLES

FIGURES

FOREWORD

'There are nine and sixty ways of constructing tribal lays, And-every-single-one-of-them-is-right!'

Rudyard Kipling, *In the Neolithic Age*

Duncan Ironmonger's work on new commodities was started in Cambridge over a decade ago and as one who admired it at the time I have much pleasure in writing this foreword to the now completed book. I share the author's liking for quotations and so have added one of my own choice, which, *mutatis mutandis*, seems to me to sum up rather neatly the state of play in the field of econometric demand studies. A survey of postwar writings on consumers' behaviour shows that there is a great variety of possible approaches to the subject, all of them useful, many of them necessary; and it is not very difficult to see why.

The econometricians of a generation ago had to contend with a number of problems which, though still with us, have become less serious with the passage of time: limitations of data; a statistical methodology largely developed in connection with the experimental sciences; and computing facilities which, by present standards, were very feeble. In these circumstances it is not surprising that econometricians should, generally speaking, have adopted a partial, static formulation based on a simplified version of the underlying theory. The linear or log-linear Engel curve, derived from family budgets, and the single equation, derived from time series, with income, relative prices and a residual trend as the independent variables, are characteristic of this period.

The results of these studies were moderately encouraging: typically, income elasticities were found to be positive and of a plausible order of magnitude, the exceptions being clear instances of inferior goods; the own-price substitution elasticities were almost always negative; and the cross-elasticities suggested the presence more often of substitute than of complementary relationships. But it was usual to find significant residual trends, suggesting that changes in tastes and habits might be important factors; the demand for some commodities, in particular durable goods, could not be explained by a static formulation; and the partial nature of the analyses conflicted in some measure with the systematic theoretical framework, in which all commodities entered simultaneously. With the data available it was, and indeed still is, impossible to deal with all these problems at the same time; and so, as the prelude to a new synthesis, each problem must be attacked separately and studied in detail.

This book is a good example of how this should be done. The conventional theory assumed a fixed number of commodities and fixed tastes and habits on the part of consumers. That these variables might change was a fact too obvious to be ignored; but having been recognised, it was quickly swept under the carpet or, at best, handled by residual-trend analysis. In the pages that follow, Dr Ironmonger examines, both theoretically and empirically, the importance of new commodities and their influence on the tastes and habits of consumers. He points out that for some time managers and technologists have been concerned not only with better ways of making commodities but also with the need to make better commodities. He distinguishes between new, established and outmoded commodities and shows how this classification can be carried out by the simple device of lag-sequence graphs. A retabulation of time series of consumption drawn up on this basis, in place of the usual shopping-list categories, is highly illuminating and brings out the extent to which the change in the consumption pattern of British consumers over the inter-war years is attributable to the diffusion of new commodities.

The explicit recognition of the importance of new commodities calls for a new look at the conventional theory of consumers' behaviour and, in particular, at the relationships connecting goods, wants and utility. Dr Ironmonger develops the theory from this point of view, dealing first with the individual consumer and then with groups of consumers. His analysis leads him to emphasise discreteness and discontinuities, which can best be handled by programming methods. As he says in his conclusions: 'some consumers may be infinitesimal calculators; rather more, we expect, are linear programmers'.

Studies like the present one are both useful and necessary because they force us to take seriously, and enable us to correct, the over-simplifications of earlier work. They also help us to get our priorities right in working towards a new synthesis. For in largely non-experimental subjects like economics it is usually impossible to test very elaborate hypotheses and it is therefore essential that our models should reflect the important aspects of reality to the exclusion of the unimportant ones.

RICHARD STONE

Cambridge
January 1971

PREFACE

This study is presented as a contribution to the theory and measurement of consumer behaviour. The ideas in the book were formulated at Cambridge during the period 1957 to 1960 and incorporated in a doctoral dissertation submitted in 1961.

My earliest interest in the subject of consumer behaviour was aroused by Professors Donald Cochrane and Jean Polglaze in Melbourne in 1953. This interest was strengthened by work on the measurement of consumer expenditure at the Australian Bureau of Census and Statistics and under Professor Heinz Arndt in Canberra during 1955 and 1956. In 1957 I was fortunate in being able to go to Cambridge to begin work on the role of new commodities in the theory and measurement of consumer behaviour.

There were many people in Cambridge, particularly at the Department of Applied Economics, with whom I discussed my problems and from whom I profited greatly. I particularly wish to acknowledge my debt to my supervisor, Alan Brown of the Department of Applied Economics. Over a period of two and a half years I had the benefit of increasingly frequent discussions with him. His enthusiasm was a constant inspiration. After my return to Canberra in 1960, this enthusiasm was continued by Ivor Pearce of the Australian National University. Professors Brown and Pearce provided the personal encouragement a young research worker needs.

I also wish to acknowledge the assistance of the Department of Applied Economics and the Mathematical Laboratory of the University of Cambridge. In particular I wish to thank Mr Martin Fieldhouse and Dr Lucy Slater for writing the programmes concerned with calculating some of the linear programming examples in Part I and all the regression analyses in Part II. These programmes were run on the EDSAC II computer of the Mathematical Laboratory in 1959.

My thanks are also due to the Australian Public Service Board for their postgraduate scholarship; to the Australian Bureau of Census and Statistics for leave to take up the scholarship; and to my wife for sharing all the trials and tribulations throughout the period of research and the subsequent revision of the work for publication.

Finally, it is with gratitude that I record that this study would not have been possible had it not been for the wealth of knowledge about consumer behaviour provided by the researches of Professor Richard

Stone, A. R. Prest, A. D. Rowe and their associates. In the last paragraph of his monumental 1954 volume, *The Measurement of Consumer Expenditure and Behaviour in the United Kingdom 1920–1938*, Stone suggests that a successful study of the problems associated with the appearance of new commodities and the disappearance of old commodities would 'help to close a serious gap in the existing theory of consumer behaviour'. It has been my aim to bridge that gap, even though such a bridge is almost certain to be superseded by a new one.

D. S. IRONMONGER

Institute of Applied Economic and Social Research
Melbourne
August 1970

INTRODUCTION

What does the existing theory of consumer behaviour have to say about new commodities? How should the demand analyst approach the problems presented by new commodities? These are increasingly important questions for those interested in the measurement and prediction of trends in market behaviour. Closely allied to them are problems arising from changes in the qualities, i.e. characteristics, of existing commodities.

On the whole it is true to say that these questions have been neglected by the economists who have laid the foundation of the present theory of consumer behaviour and of its measurement. This neglect can be explained by the fact that the emergence of new commodities and changes in the character of commodities have become important for consumer commodities only in recent decades. Prior to this, innovation and technological change were largely confined to the means of production rather than the means of consumption. Inventors and innovators were concerned with making existing commodities more efficiently rather than with making more efficient commodities. As the foundations of the currently accepted theory of consumer behaviour were laid at this time, it is hardly surprising that these topics were neglected.

This work, on the other hand, takes the view that the introduction of new commodities and changes in the qualities of existing commodities are of considerable and perhaps increasing importance to the consumer. It is concerned with developing a theory which covers new commodities and quality changes explicitly in addition to covering the traditionally considered influences of prices and income. It also attempts to demonstrate some of the problems in the measurement of consumer behaviour when new commodities are involved.

These themes are dealt with in two parts:

    I. New commodities and the theory of consumer behaviour, and
    II. New commodities and the measurement of consumer behaviour.

In Part I the currently accepted theory of consumer behaviour is examined from the point of view that some of the principal questions that this theory must be able to elucidate are those relating to the introduction of new commodities and the frequent changes in the qualities of commodities which are prominent features of the consumer market. Four assumptions of the theory are investigated and it is concluded that the assumption that commodities serve directly to produce utility (happiness) is the essential feature of the theory which makes it difficult to adapt to the requirement of the analysis. The idea of separate wants and other discontinuities in the consumption process have been overlooked, or discarded, in a search for mathematical treatment of the theory. There are discontinuities in the way in which wants are satisfied, in the number and qualities of commodities and in the terms on which commodities are obtained which are not adequately treated by the infinitesimal calculus.

Then follow three chapters in which the theory of consumer behaviour is reformulated so that changes in the technique of consumption can be treated explicitly at the same time as changes in income and prices. This reformulation is founded firstly on the idea that commodities serve directly to satisfy various separate wants, and secondly on some fairly strong assumptions about the nature of the individual consumer's preference between these wants. The development of this theory proceeds through an analysis of the choice of an optimum budget by an individual consumer. This budget is found to be the solution of a linear programming problem. The consumer has to find a budget which maximises the satisfaction of his marginal want subject to the restrictions that his supra-marginal wants are satiated and expenditure does not exceed income.

To complete the theory of individual behaviour, the effects that changes in the consumer's tastes, changes in the qualities of existing commodities, the introduction of new commodities, and changes in income and prices produce in the individual consumer's optimum budget are examined.

Since it is the behaviour of groups of consumers which interests economists, the theory of individual behaviour is combined into a theory of group behaviour by making some assumptions about the distribution of the various factors determining individual behaviour. The forms of the aggregate Engel (income) curves and aggregate demand (price) curves are examined. Attention is paid to the way in which new commodities diffuse through groups of consumers and to the form these diffusion curves for new commodities can take.

Part I ends with two applications of the theory to the analysis of market situations. The first develops an interpretation of the effect of changes in the quality of a commodity which has a close substitute and the second examines some of the difficulties in estimating the parameters which control a sequence of introductions of related new commodities.

Part II begins by examining some of the difficulties that have been encountered in demand analysis. It is found that a major part of the explanation of the variation in consumption through time must be found in influences outside of prices and income.

It does not appear that many explicit studies of new commodities or of quality changes have been made and it is not generally realised how numerous and widespread new commodities and new forms of commodities have been. A survey of the changes in the range of consumer goods in the United Kingdom in the last hundred years suggests that new commodities have been of increasing importance. An illustrative timetable of the introduction of new consumer commodities is presented and for some new commodities estimates of the 'diffusion' duration have been made. These range from 90 years for tea down to 20 years for television.

Some new, established and outmoded commodities consumed in the United Kingdom in the period from 1920 to 1938 are selected and an attempt is made to isolate the growth and decline of the consumption of these commodities from the changes in consumption due to changes in prices and incomes. This is done by using the level of the consumption variable (lagged one period) as an explanatory variable. These results are compared with earlier analyses of these commodities and an alternative interpretation of the same regression model.

The main change in the work since the original 1961 dissertation has been the inclusion in Part II of a chapter on the extent of diffusion of new commodities in the United Kingdom (Chapter 9). In the original work this discussion was confined to an estimate of the extent of diffusion among food, drink and tobacco. The subsequent publication of data for other commodities by Stone and Rowe (1966) has made possible an estimate of the extent of diffusion for the entire range of consumer expenditure.

In Part I the theoretical arguments have been left as originally written and no attempt has been made to compare or contrast these arguments with the contribution of Ivor Pearce (1964) or the approach of Kelvin Lancaster (1966).

PART I

NEW COMMODITIES AND THE THEORY OF
CONSUMER BEHAVIOUR

1. THE SITUATION IN THE THEORY OF CONSUMER BEHAVIOUR

'The nature of Economic Theory is clear. It is the study of the formal implications of these relationships of ends and means on various assumptions concerning the nature of the ultimate data.'

L. Robbins (1932), 2nd edn 1935, p. 38

1.1 THE FOUNDATIONS OF THE THEORY

What assumptions should an economist make concerning the nature of the ultimate data about consumer behaviour? In starting to build a theory of this behaviour he would find it simpler to begin with the assumption of a given set of commodities. He would be likely to start with this assumption if he thought that, in the real world to which the theory was to apply, the number and quality of commodities were to all effect constant; also if he thought that he would not be called upon to analyse the effects of the introduction of an additional consumer commodity.

It seems fairly certain that the economists concerned with the foundation of the marginal utility theory of consumer behaviour recognised invention and innovation as forces confined more or less to producers' goods and the production process. Economic progress was regarded mainly as a process of improvement in the technique of producing existing commodities, rather than involving changes in the range and character of goods. Hence, from that historical viewpoint, it was justifiable to establish a theory of consumer behaviour which ignored the role of technical change in the consumption process.

For the most part, the existing theory has continued with this approach so that today, when the invention and introduction of new commodities are prominent features of the consumer market, the theory is not equipped to provide an analysis of these features, nor does it provide a framework for empirical measurement.

1.2 THE EXISTING THEORY

We may take the final form of the static equilibrium theory of consumer behaviour to be that presented by Hicks (1939) and Wold (1953). This theory is concerned with the situation which an individual faces in making a single act of choice.† It is static in the sense that all the

---

† 'A consumer with a given money income is confronted with a market for consumption goods, on which the prices of those goods are already determined; the question is, How will he divide his expenditure among the different goods?' Hicks (1939), 2nd edn, 1946, p. 11.

variables affecting the single choice are assumed to be constant and also in the sense that the quantities concerned need not be regarded as having a time dimension since there is just a single choice to be made. The theory then uses the comparative static method of comparing two isolated acts of choice in which one or more of the variables affecting the pattern of consumption are different, so as to obtain some behaviour relationship between the changes in prices and income and resultant changes in the quantities consumed.

This theory isolates as the influential variables the prices of the commodities available on the market and the income of the consumer who has to choose his optimum budget. There are, of course, many assumptions behind this theory, but there are four which appear to have particular relevance from the point of view of technical change in the consumption process.

Two of these are assumptions about the nature of commodities and two are assumptions about the nature of human desires. They are:
(i) commodities are fixed in number and have constant qualities
(ii) commodities are 'single-priced' or 'perishable'
(iii) commodities serve directly to produce happiness (or utility)
(iv) human desires are constant.
These will be discussed in detail.

1.2.1   *Commodities are fixed in number and have constant qualities*

In the existing static equilibrium theory it is assumed that the consumer has a finite and constant number of different commodities of constant quality among which he can choose, subject to his income restraint. This assumption is tied in with the static equilibrium nature of the analysis.

It might be contended that all that is necessary is for some extra bits and pieces to be added into the theory, without making any major change – some modification rather than a reformulation. A new commodity could perhaps be regarded as simply adding an extra dimension to the commodity space – a change from n to $n+1$ dimensions. Is it quite as simple as that? Since, when commodities enter directly into the utility function (i.e. commodities serve directly to produce happiness), the preference index or utility function is in the n-dimensional commodity space, this introduction involves at the minimum an extension of the function into the extra dimension so that the preferences between the new commodity and each of the n existing commodities can be defined. It is clear however that the new commodity may also change the preferences between the existing commodities. Thus in effect the introduction of a new commodity can change the whole preference system and is equivalent to a change in tastes. When commodities are assumed to enter directly into the utility function, it is impossible to consider separately the introduction of a new commodity. It must be regarded as a general change in tastes. The difficulty of dealing with the introduction of a new commodity under the existing theory is shown by Harsanyi (1954).

The assumption of constant qualities is something more than the necessary assumption that commodities are homogeneous. It is the assumption that the qualities that commodities possess do not change from time to time – and hence their 'powers' to produce utility for the consumer do not vary. However, we know that the objective characteristics† of commodities do change, say due to an alteration in the nature of the processes used in their manufacture or distribution. Unless these changes are imperceptible to the consumer or occur in characteristics that do not interest him, their powers to produce 'utility' will change. This is a change which has occurred externally to the consumer – something that has been forced upon him. Such changes may be more important to the consumer than a change in price.

This assumption of constant qualities was no doubt made by economic theorists because they believed these changes to be unimportant and infrequent, and perhaps also because of the difficulty of constructing a theory which contained the qualities of commodities as explicit variables.

Since the existing theory does not consider distinctions between wants but makes all commodities serve a single want, happiness, there is no place in it for considering changes in a quality of a commodity, such as the increase in the speed of a car, except as a (possible) change in its suitability to serve happiness.

This is unsatisfactory, since the only quality that commodities can be considered to have is a power to produce utility. It is more usual, and probably more useful, to regard most commodities as having several qualities. Then the strength or degree of each quality of a commodity can be regarded as affecting its usefulness in a different direction – i.e. its suitability for satisfying different wants.

As with the introduction of a new commodity, in the existing theory, changes in the qualities of existing commodities can change the entire preference system and are, in that system, equivalent to changes in tastes. In view of the changes in the number and qualities of the goods available to the consumer from year to year, it seems very desirable to be able to consider changes in the number of available commodities, or in a quality of an existing commodity, even within the confines of the method of comparative statics. Yet in its existing form the theory of consumer behaviour is unconcerned with these changes and contents itself with considering the effect of price changes and income changes.

† Such as shape, density, colour, toughness, viscosity, malleability, tensile strength, porosity, age, durability, purity.

1.2.2   *Commodities are 'single-priced' or 'perishable'*

The second assumption of existing theory is the assumption that commodities are 'single-priced'. This is an assumption about the terms on which the consumer obtains the use of commodities, and may be formulated as the assumption that the consumer's expenditure on a commodity is always proportional to the quantity consumed. Therefore the consumer has variable costs but not fixed costs.

In practice fixed and variable costs can and do occur in consumption where the consumer has the chance to obtain some commodities such as gas, electricity and telephone calls by paying a two-part tariff. The consumer obtains the use of durables on terms identical with the terms on which he obtains two-part tariff commodities. However the fixed and variable costs are not quite so clearly set out for durables as for perishables with zero fixed costs or for two-part tariff commodities where the fixed cost and the variable cost are easily calculable from the price quotations of the sellers. For durables, the relevant fixed and variable costs are less easily ascertainable. Nevertheless, with durables and two-part tariff commodities, the consumer is faced with costs which are fixed per period independently of the amount of use he makes of the commodity and costs which are proportional to the use he makes. Even with commodities which are usually classified as non-durable, but where the consumer keeps a stock, the consumer is involved in fixed costs in addition to variable costs.

Can the current theory cover the case where both fixed and variable costs occur? The utility function is maximised subject to the restraint that income is greater than or equal to the vector product of the prices of the commodities and the quantities consumed. This product gives the total variable costs. Now if there are fixed costs, income will have to be greater than or equal to the sum of variable and fixed costs. The latter will be the vector product of the vector of given fixed costs and a vector whose elements are one or zero depending on whether the commodity is included in the budget or not. Unless it is insisted that all commodities are included there will be discontinuities which will prevent the calculus method of maximising from leading to a solution.

In view of the fact that many of the new products introduced into the consumer market are durable commodities, it seems desirable to see whether a theory can be devised which incorporates fixed as well as variable costs.

1.2.3   *Commodities serve directly to produce happiness*

The consumer is regarded, in existing theory, as having a single desire, happiness or utility, which he attempts to maximise. Happiness is regarded as being a direct function of the quantities of the various commodities which he consumes. Each commodity is therefore regarded as serving directly to produce happiness, and consequently each commodity is regarded as producing utility directly.

The idea that commodities may only indirectly produce utility through first satisfying some particular separate wants has been dropped from the theory of consumer behaviour. In the development of the theory, the idea of separate wants – an intermediate stage between the dominant want, happiness, and the commodities consumed – has been lost.

This was not always so. Marshall began his Book III 'On Wants and Their Satisfaction' with a short study of the variety of human wants in which we can see that by the term 'wants' he means something distinct from the dominant want, happiness. He regards these separate wants as being satisfied by commodities. He discusses, in his chapter on wants in relation to activities, such wants as 'the desire for variety', 'the desire for distinction', and 'the desire for excellence for its own sake'. Marshall suggests that the commodities shoes, stockings, black coats and silk hats, satisfy a separate want, the need for dress. Likewise, he distinguishes the separate want 'shelter from the weather' in his statement 'House room satisfies the imperative need for shelter from the weather'.†

Marshall ends this chapter with a long footnote which records the work done on the analysis of wants and desires by Hermann, Bentham, Banfield, Jevons, Senior, Hearn, Carl Menger and von Thunen. Although Marshall was careful to make distinctions between wants at the beginning of his analysis, he soon dropped it and quickly translated a statement about separate wants into a statement about a single want, utility. This he does in the following statement:

'There is an endless variety of wants, but there is a limit to each separate want. This familiar and fundamental tendency of human nature may be stated in the *law of satiable wants* or of *diminishing utility* thus: The *total utility* of a thing to anyone (that is, the total pleasure or other benefit it yields him) increases with every increase in his stock of it, but not as fast as his stock increases.'‡

With the mathematical development of the theory of consumer behaviour stemming from the work of Pareto and Fisher in the 1890s and in the 1930s associated with the work of Hicks and Allen and the rediscovery of the work of Slutsky (1915), the distinction was dropped completely and commodities were invariably regarded as satisfying a single want. As this treatment made use of the infinitesimal calculus it

† Marshall (1890), 8th edn, p. 88.
‡ Marshall (1890), 8th edn, p. 93, Marshall's italics. In this passage Marshall not only jumps from a statement about wants to a statement about a single want, but also jumps from a statement about a discontinuous process to a continuous one.

was of course necessary to maintain various assumptions about the continuity of the functions introduced into the theory.

In this mathematical treatment it was assumed that the quantities of the various commodities consumed entered directly into the individual's utility function. As there was only one want, all commodities served to a greater or less degree in satisfying that want. Hence in this theory the phenomenon of substitution was all-pervading – all commodities were to some extent substitutes for all others.

The idea that some, if not most, commodities have several uses (i.e. are capable of satisfying several wants) was not made an integral part of the theory and is still usually dismissed as relatively unimportant.†
Again it is evident that usually several, though not all, commodities, are capable of satisfying some particular want of the consumer. It is fair to say that the currently accepted theory does not have a place for an explicit treatment of substitutes. This seems a regrettable omission.

As originally developed, the law of diminishing marginal utility seems to have been a law of priority among wants. The Robinson Crusoe type of analysis where a given annual supply of a commodity is allotted to diminishingly important uses‡ illustrates the existence of priority among the various uses – what may be termed the law of priority among wants, which states that the most important wants are satisfied before the least important. The present form of the law of diminishing marginal utility has neglected the discontinuous nature of the process of satisfying wants and has assumed that marginal utility decreases continuously. This assumption is to be found particularly in the mathematical treatment of the theory, where discontinuity would not lend itself to treatment by the infinitesimal calculus.

Together with continuity and the calculus has come the almost universally accepted statement of consumer behaviour that the consumer maximises his satisfaction at the point where the ratios of the marginal utilities of all commodities to their prices are equalised. This result comes directly from the application of the infinitesimal calculus and requires an assumption of continuity. It will be contended later that the abandonment of continuity can have some desirable results.

1.2.4   *Consumer's tastes are constant*

The fourth assumption of the existing static equilibrium theory is the assumption that the consumer's tastes are constant; that preferences for the various *commodities* are fixed in a definite position. However, the number and nature of commodities are constantly changing and

† See Hicks (1956), p. 36, for discussion on this point. 'But unless we are specially interested in the distribution among uses we need not show this distribution explicitly in our study of his behaviour.'

‡ For example, Menger's corn used for food, brewing and feeding a parrot, and Marshall's woollen yarn used for socks and vests.

somewhat independently of the factors such as age, sex, occupation and marital status, which are usually regarded as determining the consumer's fundamental tastes. Hence it seems desirable to have a theory which separates out changes in the number and quality of commodities from changes in his wants due to changes in the factors determining the make-up of the consumer's physiology and psychology. This can be done when the consumer is regarded as having many separate wants. Consumer tastes would then only have to cover his preferences between these wants and thus would provide a more constant frame of reference than in previous theory, since wants are more constant than commodities.

1.3 Summary

The present static equilibrium theory of consumer behaviour is deficient in several respects. Use is no longer made of the fact that the consumer has various separate wants. This is particularly relevant from the point of view of technical change in the commodities entering into the consumption process. Without some distinction between various types of wants, there is no place for considering a change in a quality of a commodity or the introduction of a new commodity to the market. Since such changes are occurring constantly in the market and can have an importance for the consumer as great as or greater than price or income changes, it seems necessary to have an explicit treatment of them.

New commodities and quality changes in commodities can be brought out of the pound of consumer tastes so that tastes can provide a more constant frame of reference than before. The current theory does not have a place for an explicit treatment of substitutes nor does it allow adequate consideration of commodities such as durables which involve both variable and fixed costs.

2. INDIVIDUAL BEHAVIOUR (1):
THE CHOICE OF AN OPTIMUM BUDGET

'The reality that determines the individual's behaviour is not formed by utility, or ophelimity, or any other single element, but by his wants, or his needs.'

N. Georgescu-Roegen (1954), p. 512

The aim of this chapter is to rebuild the foundations of the theory of the individual consumer's behaviour so that changes in the technique of consumption as well as changes in income and prices can be considered. The theory is simplified at the beginning. The most obvious simplification is to assume that certain of the relevant variables affecting his choice are fixed so that the conditions of choice become static in the usual sense. The comparative statics of changes in the conditions of choice are examined in chapter 3.

2.1 SIMPLIFYING ASSUMPTIONS
2.1.1 *Commodities*

The situation involves the choice of a set of commodities which the consumer and his family will use or consume in a period. The commodities available to the consumer will either be physical goods which will be eaten, drunk, worn, slept in, sat on, eaten from, lived in, etc., or they will be services which will be provided by other people. Commodities have two essential features: first, many have overlapping or similar functions and so the consumer must exercise some choice; second, income has to be given in exchange for them; that is to say they involve costs. Free goods are disregarded, though of course they do increase the consumer's happiness and they may affect his choice of costly goods.

The discussion is concerned neither with bargaining where the consumer has to make bids with the suppliers, nor with barter where the consumer's income is in the form of commodities which he produces and which have to be traded for the commodities which he wants to consume. The discussion deals with the case where the consumer has a money income and is faced with a set of prices and conditions on which he can obtain commodities for his own use. Initially his income and the terms of purchase are regarded as fixed quantities, and the discussion relates to single-priced commodities where the cost involved in consuming the commodity is proportional to the quantity consumed. Thus it ignores two-part tariff systems of pricing and durable commodities which are stored or used repeatedly and hence involve both fixed and variable costs. The theory is limited at first to single-priced perishable goods and services.

2.1.2 *Wants*

The consumer desires to have satisfying experiences and can achieve satisfaction by using commodities. The great number of wants that he wishes to satisfy arise from physiological and psychological needs.

What exactly do we mean by wants? What is it that the consumer desires? In one sense the consumer has only one want – happiness. On analysis this happiness is seen to be composed of many parts. It is these parts that will be referred to as wants. Warmth, shelter, entertainment, companionship, variety, distinction, knowledge, occupation, and freedom from thirst, hunger and pain are perhaps the main wants which comprise happiness. Although these wants are related they may be regarded as being separable. The main point is that they exist in the human mind and body independently of the means to satisfy them. Wants exist independently of goods and services.

Over the lifetime of the consumer or his family these wants change considerably in strength and priority. Initially the case where these wants are fixed is examined, though it is to be realised that this case may never occur in reality.

2.1.3 *The want satisfying powers of commodities*

Springing from the idea of differences between commodities and the idea of differences between wants, comes the idea that commodities have different want-satisfying powers. Some commodities satisfy certain wants but will not do at all for the satisfaction of others which, in turn, may easily be satisfied by the consumption of some alternative commodities. Essentially this idea of want-satisfying powers is the notion that commodities have different qualities. These qualities are partly due to the technical nature of the commodities themselves and partly due to the nature of the wants they serve and the consumer's valuation of their effectiveness in serving these wants. It is impossible to separate these two determinants of qualities since, although the technical characteristics of commodities are objective, each consumer's evaluation of them in relation to his own wants is subjective. Nevertheless these subjective qualities are the links between commodities and wants. To begin with, these qualities will be regarded as fixed and they completely specify the consumer's technology.†

† This corresponds to the term 'environment' used by Keynes (1930), I, 96.

3

2.1.4   *The knowledge of the consumer*

The consumer is regarded as having full knowledge of the amount of his income, the prices of all available commodities, his technology, and his wants. Perhaps it should also be said that the consumer is regarded as having no expectations or knowledge of future periods – he is only concerned with making a choice for the current period. This is of course quite unreal.

A beginning is made by examining the trivial case where the consumer has just one want and one commodity available to satisfy this want. This elementary case is so simplified that it does not represent an *economic* problem since no allocation of scarce resources *between* various uses is called for. However it serves to introduce the problem of choice and to define some of the quantities to be used in the subsequent analysis.

The discussion proceeds by including more commodities and wants in the analysis and, by keeping to minimal assumptions regarding the consumer's preferences, examines how far the problem of finding an optimum budget can be solved. This procedure reveals at just what stage the minimal preference assumptions need to be abandoned and when further ideas about the operation of preferences are needed in order to proceed.

2.2   THE SATISFACTION OF A SINGLE WANT

2.2.1   *One commodity*

Here it is assumed that the consumer has a single want, say, a want to assuage his thirst, and there is a single commodity, say, water, available for this purpose. Water is available to the consumer at a given rate of exchange in terms of units of money for a unit of water. The consumer has a limited money income.

Some symbols will prove useful as a shorthand.

Let x_j be the number of units of commodity j used per unit of time

z_i be the number of units of satisfaction of want i obtained per unit of time

w_{ij} be the number of units of satisfaction of want i obtained from consuming one unit of commodity j

p_j be the number of units of money that must be exchanged to obtain one unit of commodity j

and y be the number of units of money income available to the consumer per unit of time.

It is to be noticed that x_j, z_i and y are quantities per unit of time and w_{ij} and p_j are scale factors. In addition, it is assumed that none of these quantities is negative and further that p_j and y are positive.

Also the quantities x_j, p_j and y are measurable or objective whereas z_i and w_{ij} are immeasurable or subjective. The value w_{ij} is partly determined by the objective characteristics of the commodity and partly by the consumer's subjective valuation of those characteristics. It may be called the 'i-th quality of the j-th commodity'.

Let us return to the problem where $i = 1$ and $j = 1$, y and p_1 are given quantities, and x_1 is a variable to be determined. Because of the restraint of income and price x_1 must lie within the limits

$$0 \leqslant x_1 \leqslant \frac{y}{p_1}$$

If we assume that w_{11} is a constant† then z_1 is a variable lying within the limits

$$0 \leqslant z_1 \leqslant \frac{w_{11}y}{p_1}$$

since $z_1 = w_{11}x_1$

In order to represent the manner in which the consumer determines the actual quantity of water to consume, it is necessary to introduce a function to represent the consumer's happiness, satisfaction or total utility. This is needed even in the 'one-want one-commodity' case where the only question to be decided is the level of consumption.

If it is said that in this case the consumer will choose some particular level of consumption, then the existence of some form of utility function is implied. On the other hand if it is said that the consumer has in mind some form of utility function, then the consumer will be able to make some logical choice between the various levels of consumption open to him. Both approaches have been subject to much discussion centering on terms such as 'consistency', 'rationality', the 'uniqueness of the utility function', and the 'constancy of tastes', while all the time it is known that tastes do change and that consumers do choose different combinations of commodities even when prices and incomes remain constant. The idea of a constant utility function is extremely useful in building a practical theory of the behaviour of the consumer, whether or not the utility function exists, is unique or corresponds with reality. The idea of uniform motion of a body subject to no forces in a straight line was most useful in building a practical theory of mechanics. The fact that such a motion never occurs in reality does not stop the idea from being useful. The justification for the introduction of a concept must lie in the results that come from the analysis.

The consumer's level of happiness, U, is taken to be a function of z_1 and is represented as

$$U = U(z_1)$$

† Or assuming that w_{11} has a unique value for any level of x_1 and that the product $w_{11}x_1$ increases as x_1 increases. In subsequent discussion it will be assumed that all w_{ij} are constants.

and we also assume that this function is such that $\delta U/\delta z_1 > 0$ for all levels of z_1. The consumer's objective is to maximise U.

In the case in hand, under these assumptions, U will be maximised when z_1 is a maximum. This will occur when

$$z_1 = \frac{w_{11} y}{p_1}$$

and is where

$$x_1 = \frac{y}{p_1}$$

Thus the consumer's optimum budget is to buy as much water as his income allows at the given price.

2.2.2   *Two commodities*

This case represents the extremely elementary economic problem of the allocation of scarce means between two uses when a single objective is in view. There are two more given quantities, p_2 and w_{12}, and one more variable to be determined, x_2.

The ranges within which x_1 and x_2 must lie are

$$0 \leqslant x_1 \leqslant \frac{y}{p_1}$$

and

$$0 \leqslant x_2 \leqslant \frac{y}{p_2}$$

Let λ be the proportion of y spent on x_1. Then $(1-\lambda)$ is the maximum proportion of y spent on x_2. Hence the range within which z_1 must lie is

$$0 \leqslant z_1 \leqslant y \left[\frac{w_{12}}{p_2} + \lambda \left(\frac{w_{11}}{p_1} - \frac{w_{12}}{p_2} \right) \right]$$

where $0 \leqslant \lambda \leqslant 1$. If $w_{11}/p_1 > w_{12}/p_2$ then the upper limit of z_1 is a maximum when $\lambda = 1$. If $w_{11}/p_1 < w_{12}/p_2$ then the upper limit of z_1 is a maximum when $\lambda = 0$. In the special case when $w_{11}/p_1 = w_{12}/p_2$ the upper limit of z_1 is constant whatever the value of λ. Thus, except for the special case, the maximum level of z_1 can only be obtained by spending income on a single commodity. With a simple utility function, as in the one commodity case, the consumer will want to maximise z_1, since this maximises U.

2.2.3   *Many commodities*

The result from the two commodities case extends very simply to the case where there are many commodities. Except for special cases, the consumer spends all his income on the commodity with the greatest ratio w_{ij}/p_j. In the special case when several commodities tie for the greatest ratio, the consumer's happiness will be maximised however he distributes his income among these commodities.

2.3 THE SATISFACTION OF TWO WANTS

The analysis will now be enlarged by considering the problem of the consumer who has two wants to satisfy. It soon becomes evident that it is necessary to distinguish between cases of joint satisfaction and cases of common satisfaction. First consider the consumer who has only one commodity available to him.

2.3.1 *One commodity*

If this commodity is capable of satisfying both wants, then it may serve these wants in either of two ways: either each unit of the commodity may simultaneously serve both wants, or the consumer has to allocate units of the commodity to the separate wants. If the latter is the case, then, x_{11} and x_{12}, the quantities of x_1 so allocated, will have to be determined. This is the case of common satisfaction. If the former is the case, then no problem of allocation arises. This is joint satisfaction. These cases are considered separately.

(i) *Joint satisfaction.* An example of joint satisfaction is the case of thirst and hunger being jointly served by the commodity milk. Here

$$z_1 = w_{11}x_1$$
and
$$z_2 = w_{21}x_1$$

so that z_1 and z_2 are both at their maximum values when x_1 is a maximum. This is when

$$x_1 = \frac{y}{p_1}$$

The consumer's level of happiness is a function of both z_1 and z_2, and is represented as

$$U = U(z_1, z_2)$$

where U is such a function that its partial derivatives with respect to z_1 and z_2 are positive for all levels of z_1 and z_2. This is the functional representation of the assumption that the consumer always positively desires to satisfy both wants.

In joint satisfaction with only one commodity, the consumer has no choice of the ratio in which he satisfies the wants. The only choice open to him is to choose the scale of satisfaction. With a happiness function such as the above, the consumer's optimum budget is when x_1 is a maximum.

(ii) *Common satisfaction.* An example of common satisfaction is the case of thirst and washing being served by water. Here

$$z_1 = w_{11}x_{11}$$

and

$$z_2 = w_{21}x_{12}$$

Since

$$x_1 = x_{11} + x_{12}$$

x_{11} and x_{12} cannot both be at their maxima simultaneously and hence, with positive values of w_{11} and w_{21}, z_1 and z_2 cannot both be at their maxima simultaneously, as they are in the case of joint satisfaction. In this situation the consumer will need to know something more about the form of the function U than has been assumed so far in order that he may allocate x_1 to the two wants to his maximum advantage.

In subsequent discussion of cases where commodities are capable of satisfying more than one want, it will be assumed that these are cases of joint satisfaction. Commodities requiring allocation can always be regarded as separate commodities with specific uses, despite the fact that the prices and physical characteristics of these commodities are identical. After allocation, the commodity need not be specific and may still provide joint satisfaction. Such cases would probably be rare. In addition it seems certain that no commodity stands in such a relation to a want that it is both a joint and a common satisfier of that want.

2.3.2   *Two commodities*

The simplest case to consider is where commodity 1 is specific to want 1 and commodity 2 is specific to want 2, for example, water serving thirst and bread serving hunger. This rules out joint satisfaction. Then

$$z_1 = w_{11}x_1$$

and

$$z_2 = w_{22}x_2$$

together with

$$y \geqslant p_1x_1 + p_2x_2$$

Hence x_1 and x_2 must lie in the following ranges:

$$0 \leqslant x_1 \leqslant \frac{1}{p_1}(y - p_2x_2)$$

$$0 \leqslant x_2 \leqslant \frac{1}{p_2}(y - p_1x_1)$$

From these inequalities we see that the maximum value of x_1 depends on the value of x_2. Only if $x_2 = 0$ can x_1 (and hence z_1) be a maximum. Similarly for x_2 and z_2. Hence it is not possible to maximise both z_1 and z_2 simultaneously. The manner in which the consumer spends his income will determine various attainable levels of z_1 and z_2. If the consumer has a set of well-ordered preferences between these various attainable combinations, then he can logically determine an optimum budget. Alternatively, if the consumer decides on a unique budget, then he has a set of well ordered preferences between the attainable combinations. If preferences are not well ordered, then there will be several combinations on some particular level of preference (indifference). It is possible in these circumstances that the actual choice would have to be decided by some means outside the preference system, e.g. by tossing a coin.

At this stage, looking back to examine the analysis so far, it is seen that in some very elementary cases the problem of choosing an optimum budget has been formulated and solved with only minimal assumptions regarding the consumer's preferences. However, even in the simplest case of two wants and two commodities, these minimal assumptions are insufficient to lead to a solution. To proceed further with this and more complicated cases some further assumptions are needed about the form of the preference function U. This is done in the next section.

2.4   PREFERENCES BETWEEN WANTS

When the consumer is regarded as having many separate wants, the hypothesis about the form of the consumer's preferences requires stating as an hypothesis about the form of his preferences between wants, rather than between commodities. This has some advantage in that economists may be prepared to make some rather different assumptions about the form of the function in the want space than they would be prepared to make about the form of the function in the commodity space.

The question may be asked whether the function expressing the consumer's preferences between wants is of a similar form to the usual form assumed for the consumer's preferences among commodities. It is probable that, as wants are not commodities, the preference function among wants is very different. In that circumstance, economists may have much to gain by making assumptions about the form of the function in the want space which will have sharper implications than those they are usually prepared to make about the form of the function in the commodity space.

Provided the implications of an hypothesis are not refuted by evidence, their sharpness is a virtue, not a vice.

2.4.1   *Orthodox assumptions*

On orthodox lines a start could be made with a preference hypothesis that the indifference curves between wants are convex to the origin of the want space.† To be in a position to use the calculus, some very

---

† For example, as is done by Hicks (1939) for the preference function between commodities.

specific assumptions about the regularity of these indifference curves are required. These assumptions are also made to ensure the existence of stable optimum budget solutions. Among these regularity assumptions are the assumptions that the utility function, U, and its derivatives of at least the first two orders are continuous, and that all the marginal utilities u_i (the partial derivatives of the utility function) are always positive. The latter assumption is made to ensure that a larger budget is always preferred to a smaller one.† However, to ensure that a larger budget will always be preferred it is sufficient to assume that at every possible consumption point at least one u_i is positive. The *extra* assumptions that *all* u_i are positive are not needed.

Further, it is shown later‡ that when the budget restrictions (a plane in the commodity space) are translated to the want space, an 'efficient budget' is obtained which is downward sloping and concave to the origin. Clearly when the budget restriction is concave to the origin it is no longer necessary to have the indifference curves between wants convex to the origin. All that is required is that the indifference curves shall be less concave than the budget restriction. With a concave budget restriction *and* convex indifference curves, stable budgets are doubly ensured.

A less orthodox alternative would be to start with the preference hypothesis that the consumer has an ordering of all points in the want space, and this ordering is convex.§ However, both these methods fall down on one important point. As assumptions they are not sufficiently precise. Theories *must* be precise enough to be capable of clashing with observational experience. Another way of putting this objection would be to say that these orthodox assumptions are capable of fitting with any behaviour of our consumer – other than inconsistent behaviour. What is needed is a theory which says not only that his behaviour is consistent, but that it follows such and such a precise pattern – an assumption similar to the assumption in mechanics that bodies have a uniform motion in a straight line, or Kepler's assumptions that planets move in ellipses.

Need the calculus be used to find and state the conditions for an optimum budget? In recent years the mathematical tools for the analysis of conditions for maxima have been greatly extended to cover cases where the calculus is not applicable. Thus it is no longer necessary to assume that the utility function has continuous partial derivatives, and it may be preferable to assume that they are not. Some arguments in favour of regarding the utility function between wants as being discontinuous are advanced in the next sections, where the assumptions adopted for the consumer's preferences between wants are set out.

† See especially Wold (1953), pp. 82–3.   ‡ On page 29.
§ For example, as is done by Hicks (1956) for the preference function between commodities.

2.4.2   *Satiation of wants*

That human wants consist of numerous separate wants, each differing in some respects from the others, is accepted as common ground for discussion; that human wants are each individually satiable, is rather less commonly accepted. Marshall accepts both ideas in the beginning of Book III, 'On wants and their satisfaction', of his *Principles*. He observes that 'human wants and desires are countless in number and very various in kind; but they are generally limited and capable of being satisfied',† and 'there is an endless variety of wants, but there is a limit to each separate want'.‡

However, to assert that a level of satiation exists does not imply that it is ever reached. If a want is satiated only when either (a) the price of a commodity capable of satisfying that want has fallen to zero, or (b) with given finite and positive prices of commodities, income is increased to infinity, then the satiation level is reached only when there is no economic problem involved, and no economic analysis is necessary. Hence it seems preferable, and perhaps more logical, to be concerned with satiation levels which are reached when there are still some economic problems to analyse. Thus each separate want is regarded as being satiated at some finite level of income, even though the commodities which can satiate them have positive prices. This does not imply that a consumer ever gets to the stage of complete satiation of all wants, since, as wants are in 'endless variety', no matter how many wants become satiated there will always be other wants yet to be satiated. If, with given prices, some wants are satiated at low levels of income and other wants are not satiated unless income is increased or prices lowered, then the consumer can be regarded as having a system of priorities among his wants.

2.4.3   *Priorities among wants*

The system of priorities that the consumer is regarded as having is extremely simplified. These priorities are assumed to be so ordered that at a given income and prices the consumer will satiate as many wants as possible, going down the order of priority from the most important to the least. And if at these prices his income is increased by a marginal amount, this increase will be devoted to reaching satiation on his marginal want. The wants that have been completely satisfied can be called 'supra-marginal' wants and unsatisfied wants 'sub-marginal' wants.

Notice that it is assumed that the consumer's wants are well-ordered, so that in any particular circumstance he has only one marginal want. The consumer aims at satiating one want at a time. This does not

† Marshall (1890), 8th edn, 1920, p. 86.   ‡ *Ibid*. p. 93.

preclude the possibility of other wants being satiated incidentally to the satiation of the marginal want. This is always likely in cases where commodities provide joint satisfactions. So the sub-marginal wants may include some wants that have been partially or completely satisfied on this account. The priorities among the wants are priorities among the goals at which the consumer aims.

The consumer's first goal is to attain satiation of want 1; his second goal, the satiation of want 2; etc., down the list of priority. However, since the commodity for getting to the first goal may jointly provide some satisfaction for the second want, it is possible that the second goal may be achieved before the first. This does not mean that the second want is prior to the first. If this were so, the consumer would aim at satiating 2 by the best (= cheapest) possible way and this might involve choosing some other commodity – a commodity which may not provide any satisfaction for want 1 at all. If income and prices are such that the consumer can achieve 2 and then go on to achieve 1 through a commodity which achieves 2 incidentally, then, at some point the commodity which was initially bought will no longer be required. At this level of income and prices and with these commodities the final result is the same whichever want is the prior one. It is only at lower levels of real income that the order of priorities will be crucial for choice among the commodities.

In the axiomatic theory of choice there is assumed an ordering of commodity combinations (of points in the commodity space). This ordering is not given any definite structure, apart from the assumption that a position of some goods (say point x) is ordered in at least as preferred a position as less goods (the point y with no element greater than the corresponding element of x and at least one element less than the corresponding element of x).

The assumption of well ordered priorities among wants, together with the necessary satiation levels, what can be called the hierarchy principle, gives to the points in the want space an ordering with a very definite structure. All the indifference curves between wants are straight lines! This may appear to be a very simple assumption – one which is logically less probable. However, comparing two assumptions, the one which is logically less probable is also the one which is more falsifiable, and therefore more useful.

A very similar concept to the hierarchy principle is the concept of lexicographic ordering. This concept has been investigated by Hausner (1954) and Thrall (1954) in regard to behaviour under uncertainty, and also by Debreu (1954) and Georgescu-Roegen (1954). Chipman (1960) has shown that when the axiom of substitution (which expresses the notion that it is always possible to find some quantity of other commodities sufficiently great to compensate for loss of part of a given commodity) fails, utility cannot be represented as a real number but instead can be represented as a lexicographically ordered vector. The ordering of the components of this vector is similar to the ordering of wants in the hierarchy principle.

The assumption of well ordered wants is fairly restrictive, as it does not allow for the consumer to be indifferent between wants nor for the wants to be joint. It may well be that wants at some places in the list of priorities are jointly desired. It is interesting to note that Professor Joan Robinson considers that wants stand in an order of priority but that they overlap so that there are several marginal wants at every level. She says, 'Generally speaking, wants stand in a hierarchy (though with considerable overlap at each level) and an increment in a family's real income is not devoted to buying a little more of everything at the same level, but to stepping down the hierarchy'.† It is indeed probable that wants are in some degree joint or competing. However, the ensuing analysis sticks to the simpler assumption that they are not.

With an ever present goal in view, the consumer will always be looking for higher income, lower prices, and better commodities. Increases in income will always enable a consumer to increase his satisfaction. Reductions in prices, improvements in commodities, and the introduction of new commodities may allow the consumer to increase his satisfaction. But this does not necessarily follow as in the case of an increase in income. The reductions, improvements and introductions may be in commodities that he does not wish to consume. This is running ahead of the argument. A return to the problem of the satisfaction of two wants is necessary, but now armed with assumptions about the nature of priorities among wants.

2.5 CHOICE UNDER PRIORITIES AMONG WANTS

In section 2.3 the consumer's preferences between two wants were represented by the function

$$U = U(z_1, z_2)$$ with positive partial derivatives.

This has to be replaced by a function to represent the assumptions of priorities. This is done by the function

$$U = U_1(z_1) \text{ where } 0 \leqslant z_1 < z_1^* \text{ and } z_2 \geqslant 0,\ \delta U_1/\delta z_1 > 0$$
$$U = U_2(z_2) \text{ where } z_1 \geqslant z_1^* \text{ and } z_2 \geqslant 0,\ \delta U_2/\delta z_2 > 0$$
$$\text{and where } U_2 \geqslant U_1$$

This is a mathematical shorthand for saying that whatever the level of z_2, while z_1 is in the range from zero to less than z_1^* (a certain

† Joan Robinson (1956), p. 354.

constant), happiness is an increasing function of z_1 alone; and when z_1 is at least z_1^*, happiness is an increasing function of the level of z_2 alone. This functional representation is the mathematical expression of the assumptions about preferences between wants discussed in section 2.4 in the case of two wants and where the prior want has a satiation level of z_1^*.

It was not possible to reach solutions in section 2.3, where the consumer had to allocate quantities of the only available commodity (common satisfaction) and in even the simplest case where there were two commodities. These cases can be examined again.

2.5.1   *Two wants*

One commodity: common satisfaction. The consumer is faced with two objective quantities, y and p_1, and, with a system of priorities as above, he solves his allocation problem quite simply by evaluating the ratio z_1^*/w_{11} of two subjective quantities, and comparing it with the ratio y/p_1 of the two objective quantities.

If $\quad \dfrac{y}{p_1} \leqslant \dfrac{z_1^*}{w_{11}}$ then the solution is $x_{11} = \dfrac{y}{p_1} \quad$ and $\quad x_{12} = 0$

If $\quad \dfrac{y}{p_1} > \dfrac{z_1^*}{w_{11}}$ then the solution is $x_{11} = \dfrac{z_1^*}{w_{11}} \quad$ and $\quad x_{12} = \dfrac{y}{p_1} - \dfrac{z_1^*}{w_{11}}$

Two commodities: both specific. Assume that commodity 1 is specific to want 1, and commodity 2 to want 2 so that

$$z_1 = w_{11}x_1$$

and
$$z_2 = w_{22}x_2.$$

The optimum budgets are determined in a similar manner to the previous case. They are

$$x_1 = \frac{y}{p_1} \quad \text{and} \quad x_2 = 0 \qquad \text{if} \quad \frac{y}{p_1} \leqslant \frac{z_1^*}{w_{11}}$$

$$x_1 = \frac{z_1^*}{w_{11}} \quad \text{and} \quad x_2 = \frac{1}{p_2}\left(y - \frac{p_1 z_1^*}{w_{11}}\right) \text{if} \quad \frac{y}{p_1} > \frac{z_1^*}{w_{11}}$$

We shall next consider the more complicated cases of choosing an optimum budget in the two wants and two commodities case; cases in which neither commodity is specific. It will be useful to denote the ratio w_{ij}/p_j by the symbol f_{ij}, which we shall call the 'i-th *efficiency* of the j-th commodity' since it is the number of units of want i obtained from consuming one unit of money's worth of commodity j.

Two commodities: neither specific: common satisfaction

Here $\qquad\qquad z_1 = w_{11}x_{11} + w_{12}x_{21}$

and $\qquad\qquad z_2 = w_{21}x_{12} + w_{22}x_{22}$

Three groups of cases arise according to the relative efficiencies of the two commodities.

(a) One commodity doubly efficient for both wants (i.e. commodity 1 is doubly efficient if $f_{11} > f_{12}$ and $f_{21} > f_{22}$).

In this case, commodity 2 is rejected so that $x_{21} = x_{22} = 0$ and the optimum budget is exactly the same as the one commodity case of common satisfaction.

(b) One commodity efficient for only one want (i.e. if $f_{11} > f_{12}$ and $f_{21} < f_{22}$ then commodity 1 is efficient for the prior want only).

The optimum budgets in this case are:

If $\dfrac{y}{p_1} \leqslant \dfrac{z_1^*}{w_{11}}$ then $x_{11} = \dfrac{y}{p_1}$, $x_{12} = 0$

and $x_{21} = 0$, $x_{22} = 0$

If $\dfrac{y}{p_1} > \dfrac{z_1^*}{w_{11}}$ then $x_{11} = \dfrac{z_1^*}{w_{11}}$, $x_{12} = 0$

and $x_{21} = 0$, $x_{22} = \dfrac{1}{p_2}\left(y - \dfrac{p_1 z_1^*}{w_{11}}\right)$

(c) Special cases of equal efficiencies (i.e. where $f_{11} = f_{12}$ and/or $f_{21} = f_{22}$).

In these cases there may be some indeterminacy in the optimum budget solution, similar to the case where $f_{11} = f_{12}$ on page 18. In general we shall assume that these special cases do not occur and that commodity efficiencies always differ.

Two commodities: neither specific: joint satisfaction

Here $z_1 = w_{11}x_1 + w_{12}x_2$

and $z_2 = w_{21}x_1 + w_{22}x_2$

Here, as with common satisfaction, cases may be grouped according to the relative efficiencies of the two commodities. Neglecting special cases of equal efficiency, this gives two groups.

(a) One commodity doubly efficient for both wants. In this case, regardless of the level of income, the optimum budget is to spend all on the doubly efficient commodity and neglect the other.

(b) One commodity efficient for only one want. Suppose $f_{11} > f_{12}$ and $f_{21} < f_{22}$. The solution depends on the level of income.

If $y \leqslant \dfrac{z_1^*}{f_{11}}$ then $x_1 = \dfrac{y}{p_1}$, $x_2 = 0$

If $\dfrac{z_1^*}{f_{11}} < y < \dfrac{z_1^*}{f_{12}}$ then $x_1 = \dfrac{p_2 z_1^* - w_{12} y}{w_{11} p_2 - w_{12} p_1}$, $x_2 = \dfrac{w_{11} y - p_1 z_1^*}{w_{11} p_2 - w_{12} p_1}$

If $\dfrac{z_1^*}{f_{12}} \leqslant y$ then $x_1 = 0$, $x_2 = \dfrac{y}{p_2}$

This completes the enumeration of the optimum budget solutions for two wants and two commodities.

2.5.2   *Two wants and three commodities*

Here the consumer's technology is represented by the equations

$$\begin{bmatrix} z_1 \\ z_2 \end{bmatrix} = \begin{bmatrix} w_{11} & w_{12} & w_{13} \\ w_{21} & w_{22} & w_{23} \end{bmatrix} \begin{bmatrix} x_1 \\ x_2 \\ x_3 \end{bmatrix}$$

while his budget equation is

$$y = \begin{bmatrix} p_1 & p_2 & p_3 \end{bmatrix} \begin{bmatrix} x_1 \\ x_2 \\ x_3 \end{bmatrix}$$

The output of want satisfaction resulting from spending one unit of income on a single commodity j is shown by the point in the want space Oz_1z_2 with coordinates (f_{1j}, f_{2j}). Then the three points R_1, R_2, R_3, with coordinates (yf_{11}, yf_{21}), (yf_{12}, yf_{22}), (yf_{13}, yf_{23}) represent the output of want satisfactions from spending *all* income on one or other of the three available commodities. These points are shown in figure 2.1.

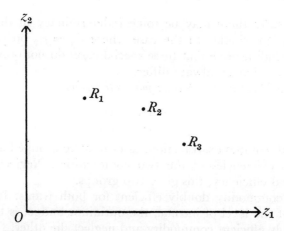

Figure 2.1. Budget points: all income on any one commodity

The commodity efficiencies are assumed to be different so that none of these points coincide, and it is also assumed that no commodity is specific so that the points do not lie on the axes. The ensuing discussion will be materially the same when these assumptions do not hold.

As an alternative to spending all his income on a single commodity, the consumer may spend all his income on any *pair* of commodities. The outputs of want satisfactions arising from all the possible ways of spending his income in this way are shown by the points on the lines joining any pair of the points R_1, R_2, R_3. These lines are shown in figure 2.2.

Similarly expenditure may be spread over all three commodities. The output of want satisfactions from these expenditures is shown by the points inside the triangle $R_1R_2R_3$. This triangle, including its boundaries and extreme points, is the transformation of the budget equation from the commodity space to the want space.

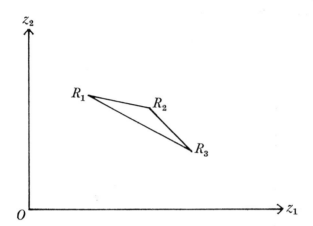

Figure 2.2. Budget points: all income on any two commodities

It is now quite easy to see that in general, when there are more commodities than wants, some commodities or combinations of commodities are inefficient and that at most m ($=$ number of wants) commodities will be required to form an efficient budget. This may be demonstrated for our $m = 2$, $n = 3$ case as follows:

Consider expenditure on commodities one and three only. Both outputs represented by points on the line R_1R_3 can always be simultaneously increased by diverting some expenditure to commodity two as well. This corresponds to a movement from the R_1R_3 border to an internal position of the triangle. All budgets consisting of combinations of commodities one and three are inefficient compared with any budget consisting of a combination of all three commodities.

Similarly both outputs represented by internal points in the triangle can be simultaneously increased on the boundary lines R_1R_2 or R_2R_3 or the point R_2. Hence all budgets consisting of all three commodities are inefficient. This leaves as 'the efficient budgets' those budgets corresponding to the points R_1, R_2, and R_3 and the two segments R_1R_2 and R_2R_3. These efficient points are in figure 2.3.

It is to be noticed that in the want space the efficient budgets are represented by a series of connected segments which are downward sloping and concave to the origin. In want spaces of higher dimensions analogous results hold.

Definitions: An inefficient budget is one where some particular want satisfaction may be increased without decreasing any other want satisfaction. An efficient budget is one where no particular want satisfaction may be increased without decreasing at least one other want satisfaction. We now have to decide which budget among the efficient budgets is the optimum.

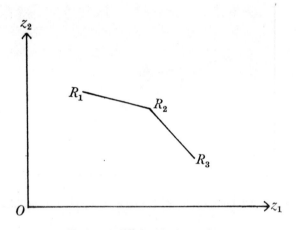

Figure 2.3. Efficient budget points

In the simple two-want case the Oz_1z_2 space is divided into two regions (three if both wants have satiation levels). These are:

(i) $0 \leqslant z_1 < z_1^*$, $z_2 \geqslant 0$ where $\delta U/\delta z_1 > 0$, $\delta U/\delta z_2 = 0$

and (ii) $z_1 \geqslant z_1^*$, $z_2 \geqslant 0$ where $\delta U/\delta z_1 = 0$, $\delta U/\delta z_2 > 0$

These regions are shown in figure 2.4.

Since in each region only one marginal utility at a time is positive, the points of indifference (equal utility) in the space must lie on a line which is perpendicular to the direction of change in utility.

Consider the concave set of downward sloping segments representing the efficient budgets, which lies wholly within a region such as (i). The optimum point among the efficient points will be that point furthest in the direction in which marginal utility is positive, i.e. in the direction of the first want. This lies on the highest attainable indifference line in that region.

When the set of points representing the efficient budgets lies in more than one region, then the optimum point will be

(a) a point in the highest attainable region, say the ith, and
(b) that point furthest in the ith direction.

As the wants are ranked in order of priority, the ith region here is the marginal region and the ith want is the marginal want.

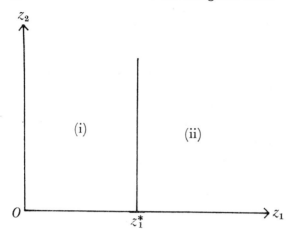

Figure 2.4. Utility regions and utility boundary line

Remembering that an indifference line passes through every point of the want space, we can represent these indifference lines as shown in figure 2.5, where the directions of increase of utility are shown by the arrows, and the levels of utility in region (ii) are higher than in region (i).

It is to be noticed that since the points representing efficient budgets are a set of segments which are downward sloping and concave to the

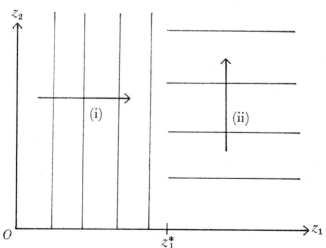

Figure 2.5. Indifference lines

origin, and since the indifference lines are neither concave nor convex to the origin, there will always be a unique optimum point.

2.5.3   *Two wants and many commodities*

Suppose there are n commodities available, so that the consumer's technology is represented by the equations

$$\mathbf{z} = \mathbf{W}\mathbf{x}$$

where $\mathbf{z}$ is a column vector of order 2, $\mathbf{x}$ is a column vector of order n, $\mathbf{W}$ is a $(2 \times n)$ matrix.

The budget equation is

$$y = \mathbf{p}'\mathbf{x}$$

where $\mathbf{p}'$ is a row vector of the n prices.

As in the case of three commodities, the set of points in the want space representing all efficient budgets will consist of at most $n-1$ connected segments representing combinations of pairs of commodities which will be downward sloping and concave to the origin. And as before, the optimum point will be that point in the marginal region furthest in the direction of the marginal want. As before there will be a unique optimum which will consist of a budget containing at most two commodities, however large is n.

2.5.4   *Many wants and many commodities*

Here the difficulty of using diagrams and visual methods of solution is reached and it is necessary to use algebra for cases where m and n are both greater than 3.

The want space $Oz_1z_2z_3...z_m$ is divided into m regions by the priorities among the wants and the saturation levels of these wants.† These regions are:

(i) $0 \leqslant z_1 < z_1^*,\ 0 \leqslant z_2,\ 0 \leqslant z_3,\ ...,\ 0 \leqslant z_m$

(ii) $z_1^* \leqslant z_1,\ 0 \leqslant z_2 < z_2^*,\ 0 \leqslant z_3,\ ...,\ 0 \leqslant z_m$

....

(m) $z_1^* \leqslant z_1,\ z_2^* \leqslant z_2,\ z_3^* \leqslant z_3,\ ...,\ 0 \leqslant z_m$

An alternative view of the way in which the want space is divided is that of regarding each saturation level as dividing the *whole* of the want space into two regions; a region where the want is satiated and a region where it is not. The m boundary planes defining these regions are represented by the m equations

$$\mathbf{z} = \mathbf{z}^*$$

where $\mathbf{z}^*$ is the vector of saturation levels, $z_m^* = \infty$.

† Assuming that the mth want is insatiable.

These boundary planes are specified in the commodity space by the m equations

$$\mathbf{Wx} = \mathbf{z}^*$$

Thus the boundary plane for the ith want cuts the n commodity axes in the points whose coordinates are

$$\left(\frac{z_i^*}{w_{i1}}, 0, ..., 0\right), \left(0, \frac{z_i^*}{w_{i2}}, ..., 0\right), ... \left(0, 0, ..., \frac{z_i^*}{w_{in}}\right)$$

The budget equation in the commodity space cuts these same axes in the points

$$\left(\frac{y}{p_1}, 0, ..., 0\right), \left(0, \frac{y}{p_2}, ..., 0\right), ... \left(0, 0, ..., \frac{y}{p_n}\right)$$

The consumer is able to satiate his ith want if any part of his budget plane lies above the boundary plane for the ith want. This will occur when the budget plane cuts *any* axis further from the origin than the boundary plane, i.e. the ith want *may* be satiated if

$$\frac{y}{p_j} \geqslant \frac{z_i^*}{w_{ij}}$$

for any j. As the consumer has priorities among his wants, he ranks the boundary planes in order of his priorities, and then he satiates his ith want only if he can satiate at the same time all wants prior to the ith.

The consumer *will* satiate his ith want if there exists a point $\bar{\mathbf{x}}$ in the commodity space which satisfies the set of $i+1$ inequalities

$$\mathbf{p}'\bar{\mathbf{x}} \leqslant y$$
$$\mathbf{W}_i\bar{\mathbf{x}} \geqslant \mathbf{z}_i^*$$

where $\mathbf{W}_i$ is the submatrix formed from the first i rows of $\mathbf{W}$ and $\mathbf{z}_i^*$ is the subvector formed from the first i elements of $\mathbf{z}^*$. If an $\bar{\mathbf{x}}$ exists for the $(i-1)$th want but not for the ith, then the ith want is the marginal want. The optimum budget is that budget which maximises the satisfaction of the marginal want.

Procedures for finding whether points such as $\bar{\mathbf{x}}$ exist and for finding optimum points to maximise the appropriate z_i are to be found in the field of mathematics known as linear programming. In the terminology of this field the optimum budget is the solution $\mathbf{x}$, of the linear programme:
Find $\mathbf{x}$ such that

$$z_i = \mathbf{w}_i\mathbf{x} = \max \qquad (\mathbf{w}_i \text{ is the } i\text{th row of } \mathbf{W})$$

subject to the restraints

$$\mathbf{W}_{i-1}\mathbf{x} \geqslant \mathbf{z}_{i-1}^*$$
$$-\mathbf{p}'\mathbf{x} \geqslant -y$$
$$\mathbf{x} \geqslant \mathbf{0}$$

As is well known, every linear programme has a dual. The dual to this programme is

Find **s** such that

$$z_i = [-\mathbf{z}_{i-1}^* \vdots\ y]\mathbf{s} = \min$$

subject to the restraints

$$[-\mathbf{W}_{i-1}' \vdots\ \mathbf{p}]\mathbf{s} \geqslant \mathbf{w}_i$$
$$\mathbf{s} \geqslant \mathbf{0}$$

The variables **s** are imputed (or accounting) prices; s_1 to s_{i-1} are the imputed prices of satisfying the supra-marginal wants 1 to $i-1$; and s_i is the number of units of satisfaction of the marginal want obtained from an extra unit of income. In other words, s_1 to s_{i-1} are the prices of wants 1 to $i-1$ in terms of the marginal want and s_i is the price of money in terms of the marginal want. Thus the marginal utility of money (income) at the optimum budget is $u_i s_i$.

We also know that the linear programme and its dual have equivalent solutions in the sense that the max z_i of one equals the min z_i of the other.

It should be noticed that the linear programme described above is somewhat different from the now classical least-cost diet problem as proposed by Stigler (1945), where the problem is to minimise the money cost of completely satisfying m wants. Here the problem is one of maximising the satisfaction of the marginal want subject to a given income. The similarity of the problems should be apparent, but the latter problem is in a form which is directly comparable to the usual methods of formulating the problem of consumer equilibrium and hence is capable of handling all the usual problems of changes in income and prices. In addition, when formulated in this way, problems of the introduction of new commodities and changes in quality may be dealt with. These are problems of comparative statics, to be discussed in chapter 3.

This completes the main part of the analysis of the choice of an optimum budget in static conditions. Before going on to comparative statics, two of the assumptions made in the course of the analysis are relaxed. Firstly, relaxation of the assumption that commodities are all single-priced perishables allows commodities to have both fixed and variable costs instead of just variable costs. Secondly, relaxation of the assumption that wants are well-ordered allows the consumer to have more than one marginal want at each level of his priorities.

2.6 RELAXED ASSUMPTIONS

2.6.1 *Commodities with fixed and variable costs*

A fixed cost is the price paid for the privilege of having some, rather than none, of the commodity available for the period in question, regardless of the rate of consumption of the commodity. This is a 'possession' price. For a durable the fixed cost is the price of ownership or of possession of the durable for the period. Denote by q_i the fixed cost of commodity i for the period.

The 'use' price is the price paid for consuming one unit of the commodity. These use-prices are the p_i we have been dealing with so far.

If a commodity has both possession and use prices, then the cost per unit of time of using x_i units of it is

$$q_i + p_i x_i$$

the second term being the 'variable cost' and the first the 'fixed cost'. This makes the consumer's problem somewhat more complicated, since he is faced with the possibility of having 'overheads' as well as 'running expenses'. Average and marginal cost are no longer the same for these 'double-priced' commodities.

Assume that there is no problem of determining the exact values of the q_i and that they are simply supplied in a list in the same way as the p_i. Of course one of the difficult problems for the real consumer is to determine the q_i. For commodities such as telephone calls, gas, and electricity sold on two-part tariffs, this is no problem. But for the case of durables, such as cars and refrigerators, which have to be bought outright and hence involve capital, interest and depreciation, the problems are more severe. The assumption that the q_i are given is equivalent to a market where all durables may be rented (the rents, q_i, being given), but cannot be bought outright. In this market perishables and services may be sold on a two-part tariff. Holding of stocks of commodities also involves fixed costs.

Let $\mathbf{j}$ be a column vector of n elements either zero or one. Call this the vector of 'possessions', since $j_i = 0$ is taken to mean that the consumer possesses none of the commodity (i.e. he neither rents nor consumes any of the commodity) and $j_i = 1$ is taken to mean that the consumer does possess or use the commodity. Choice now involves determining not only an optimum $\mathbf{x}$ but also an optimum $\mathbf{j}$.

The budget restriction on the consumer is expressed as

$$y = \mathbf{q'j} + \mathbf{p'x}$$

So long as $q_i + p_i > 0$ it is no longer necessary for $p_i > 0$ nor for $q_i > 0$, though still assuming that they are not negative.

As before, the consumer's technology is

$$\mathbf{z} = \mathbf{W}\mathbf{x}$$

so that no wants are satisfied by the possession of any commodities; want satisfaction comes from use.

The optimum budget of the consumer is the solution of the linear programme:
Find $\mathbf{x}$ and $\mathbf{j}$ such that

$$z_i = \mathbf{W}_i\mathbf{x} = \text{max}$$

subject to the restraints

$$\mathbf{W}_{i-1}\mathbf{x} \geqslant \mathbf{z}^*_{i-1}$$

$$-\mathbf{p}'\mathbf{x} - \mathbf{q}'\mathbf{j} \geqslant -y$$

$$\mathbf{x} \geqslant \mathbf{0}$$

$$\mathbf{j} = 0 \text{ or } 1 \text{ (meaning any } j_j = 0 \text{ or } 1)$$

There is a slight variation on the usual form of linear programme, which would have as its final set of restrictions

$$\mathbf{j} \geqslant \mathbf{0}$$

The manner in which 'double-priced' commodities affect the problem can be seen by considering the alteration in the form of the budget restriction in the commodity use space $Ox_1x_2...x_n$.

Let commodities with $q_i = 0$ be known as 'perishables', and commodities with $q_i > 0$ be known as 'durables'. Consider the budget restriction for just two commodities; commodity 1 a perishable and 2 a durable.

One perishable and one durable. In this situation the feasible budgets are those represented by points within and on the boundaries of the triangle

$$(0, 0), \left(0, \frac{y-q_2}{p_2}\right), \left(\frac{y-q_2}{p_1}, 0\right)$$

and on the line joining

$$\left(\frac{y-q_2}{p_1}, 0\right) \text{ to } \left(\frac{y}{p_1}, 0\right).$$

These points are shown in figure 2.6.

Assuming these commodities satisfy a single want z_1 with no satiation level, then choice of an optimum budget is not simply a matter of choosing the commodity with the greatest efficiency, as in the case of two perishables (see page 18). The durable must be of considerably greater efficiency than the perishable for it to be chosen. In this simple case the solution is:

$$\text{If } f_{11} > \frac{y-q_2}{y} f_{12}, \text{ spend income on perishable}$$

$$\text{If } f_{12} > \frac{y}{y-q_2} f_{11}, \text{ spend income on durable}$$

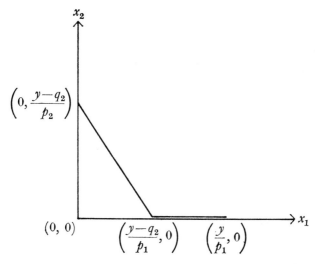

Figure 2.6. Feasible budgets: one perishable and one durable

When a perishable and a durable jointly serve two wants, the perishable will be doubly efficient if both

$$f_{11} y > f_{12}(y-q_2)$$
and
$$f_{21} y > f_{22}(y-q_2)$$

If both of these inequalities are reversed, then the durable will be doubly efficient. For cases when these inequalities do not both run the same way, the relative sizes of y and z_1 will determine whether the optimum budget contains one or the other or both commodities.

Two durables. Consider next the more complicated case of two durables serving two wants, each durable providing joint satisfaction. In the commodity use space Ox_1x_2 the feasible budgets will be represented by a triangle with an extension along each axis. In the want space Oz_1z_2 the feasible budgets will be represented again by a triangle with two extensions. The two diagrams of figure 2.7 show the points representing feasible and efficient budgets in the case when no commodity is doubly efficient.

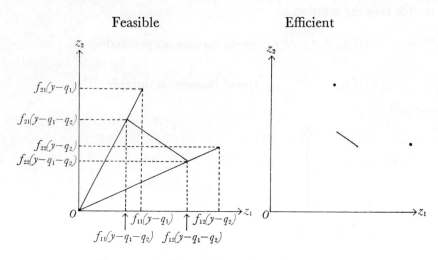

Figure 2.7. Feasible and efficient budgets: two durables

Where certain conditions hold, in particular when the relative efficiencies of the commodities are close together and/or the fixed prices q_1 and q_2 are substantial, no budget containing both commodities will be an efficient one. The exact conditions for this to occur are

$$y < \frac{q_1 f_{21}}{f_{21} - f_{22}} + \frac{q_2 f_{12}}{f_{12} - f_{11}}$$

Since the right-hand side of this inequality is positive, the conditions will be satisfied so long as the possession prices are sufficiently large or the differences in efficiencies are sufficiently small. When the above inequality is satisfied, there will be only two efficient budgets. These are the budgets represented by the extremities of the extensions to the triangle. In this situation, whatever the preference between wants, there is no benefit to be gained from operating both durables.

Many durables. This involves the linear programme as specified on page 36. As can be gathered from the simple cases examined above, the points representing the efficient budgets in the want space are no longer connected. They form a series of disconnected segments (still downward sloping and concave to the origin) *plus* a series of outlying points. The disjointed nature of this representation does not introduce any fundamental feature which would prevent an optimum budget being found. The greater element of discontinuity in this representation of choice among durables is satisfactory in so far that it agrees with the observations of the real consumer that:

(i) while a consumer may choose to buy both of two similar perishables, he buys only one of two similar durables;

(ii) the higher the consumer's income the more likely is he to buy durables rather than perishables; and

(iii) the greater the saturation level for a want the more likely is the consumer to buy a durable rather than a perishable.

So far as choice is concerned, the important distinctions are not whether the commodity is physically durable or not but whether the costs involved in using or consuming it are fixed, variable or both. This formulation leads to some natural associations between commodities, e.g. in running a car, q_i includes registration, insurance and other fixed costs, while p_i includes the price of petrol, oil, and other running costs. Car use is denoted by x_i and car ownership by j_i. In general, as durables get older q_i will decrease while p_i will increase, even though the various w_{ji} may not alter. Here the analysis leads to the consumer with a small income or a low saturation level using the old commodity and the consumer with the large income or a high saturation level using the new commodity. These results follow from differential costs and not from any difference in want satisfying powers between old and new commodities. The fruitfulness of this approach should be apparent.

2.6.2 *Complementary wants*

The essence of the view taken on the nature of preference between wants in section 2.4 is that wants are neither substitutes nor complements. At least the complementary nature is of a rather special kind depending on the assumption that wants are well-ordered. If we relax the assumption of well-orderedness, then the gate seems to be open for admitting substitutability between wants. However, this can be forestalled by assuming that where wants are not well-ordered they are strictly complementary.

Strict complementarity means that in the region where the wants are not well-ordered the locus of complementarity defined by the corners of the indifference surfaces is a continuous function of the z_i concerned. If this function is linear, then we shall say that the wants are 'linearly complementary'; if it is non-linear, then we shall refer to non-linear complementarity. In either case when the point representing an efficient budget lies on the locus of complementarity, that point will be the optimum.

Consider the form of the utility function for two linearly complementary wants. The locus of complementarity is given by the equation

$$z_2 = a_1 z_1$$

where a_1 is a positive constant. The indifference curves will be straight lines parallel to the want axes and will have right-angled kinks at the locus of complementarity. In the region between the z_1 axis and the locus, satisfaction may be increased by increasing z_2, but a change in z_1 does not affect it. Similarly in the region between the z_2 axis and the locus, satisfaction does not change with changes in z_2, but changes directly with changes in z_1. On the locus itself, satisfaction can best be increased if *both* z_1 and z_2 are increased, and if *either* decrease, satisfaction will decrease.

This situation can be represented by the functions

$$U = U_1(z_1)$$

where $z_1 \geqslant 0$ and $z_2 > a_1 z_1$ with $\dfrac{\delta U_1}{\delta z_1} > 0$

$$U = U_2(z_2)$$

where $z_2 \geqslant 0$ and $z_1 > \dfrac{z_2}{a_1}$ with $\dfrac{\delta U_2}{\delta z_2} > 0$

$$U = U_3(z_3)$$

where $z_2 = a_1 z_1 = z_3$ with $\dfrac{\delta U_3}{\delta z_3} > 0$

For the indifference lines to be continuous at the locus of complementarity,

$$U_1(z_1) = U_2(z_2) = U_3(z_3)$$

in the region of this locus. Figure 2.8 shows the shape of the indifference lines for two complementary wants, with no saturation levels.

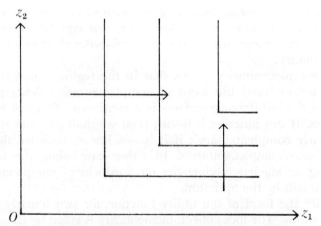

Figure 2.8. Indifference lines: complementary wants
NOTE: The directions of increase in utility are shown by the arrows.

2.7 EXAMPLES

2.7.1 *Two wants and five perishable commodities*

The numerical data are the same as those used by Dorfman, Samuelson and Solow (1958).† The data are hypothetical. The difference in approach is that whereas Dorfman *et al.* find the budget involving the least cost of just satiating both wants, this example is concerned with finding a budget which maximises the satisfaction of the marginal want with a given income. Clearly the problems are different.

The consumer's technology is expressed as the matrix

$$\mathbf{W} = \begin{bmatrix} 1 & 0 & 1 & 1 & 2 \\ 0 & 1 & 0 & 1 & 1 \end{bmatrix}$$

The saturation level of the prior want is $z_1^* = 700$, the price vector for the five commodities is

$$\mathbf{p}' = \begin{bmatrix} 2 & 20 & 3 & 1 & 12 \end{bmatrix}$$

and the consumer's income $y = 5000$.

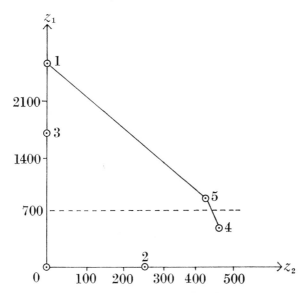

Figure 2.9. Budgets and utility boundary line: want space

Hence the problem is to find $\mathbf{x}$ such that

$$z_2 = \begin{bmatrix} 0 & 1 & 0 & 1 & 1 \end{bmatrix}\mathbf{x} = \text{max subject to}$$
$$\begin{bmatrix} 1 & 0 & 1 & 1 & 2 \end{bmatrix}\mathbf{x} \geqslant 700$$
$$\begin{bmatrix} 2 & 20 & 3 & 11 & 12 \end{bmatrix}\mathbf{x} \leqslant 5000$$
$$\mathbf{x} \geqslant \mathbf{0}$$

† Dorfman, Samuelson, and Solow (1958), p. 13.

Indirect solution: transform the budget restriction to the want space.

In the want space the feasible solutions are represented by the points on and within the five-sided figure formed by joining the exterior points of the points numbered 0 to 5 in figure 2.9, which represent the origin and the budgets where all income is spent on each of the commodities in turn.

Efficient budgets are represented by the line segments joining points 1 and 5 and points 5 and 4. The want space is divided by the boundary line $z_1 = 700$. It can be seen immediately that the point $(700, 430)$ among all those representing efficient budgets is the only one which maximises z_2 while still satiating the prior want.

Since this point lies on the segment joining points 4 and 5 it represents a budget containing commodities 4 and 5 only. The quantities of these commodities in the optimum budget are found from the transformation

$$\begin{bmatrix} x_4 \\ x_5 \end{bmatrix} = \begin{bmatrix} -1 & 2 \\ 1 & -1 \end{bmatrix} \begin{bmatrix} z_1 \\ z_2 \end{bmatrix} \quad \text{with} \quad \begin{bmatrix} z_1 \\ z_2 \end{bmatrix} = \begin{bmatrix} 700 \\ 430 \end{bmatrix}$$

Hence the optimum budget is

$$\mathbf{x}' = \begin{bmatrix} 0 & 0 & 0 & 160 & 270 \end{bmatrix}$$

Direct solution: transform the utility function to the commodity space.

The commodity space has five dimensions, which makes it well nigh impossible to represent graphically. However, since at most two commodities will be required in the solution, it is sufficient to consider the dimensions two at a time. There are ten pairs to consider. The procedure for finding the optimum budget is to find the optimum budget in each partial space, and then select the best of these ten points.

It will be found that the optimum point in the Ox_4x_5 space is the best. The boundary line dividing the want space, when transformed to the Ox_4x_5 space, is the line

$$x_4 + 2x_5 = 700$$

while the budget restriction is the line

$$11x_4 + 12x_5 = 5000$$

These lines intersect at the point $(160, 270)$ and hence all points on the line from this point to the point $(0, 417)$ satiate the prior want (see figure 2.10). The optimum point among these is determined by the slope of the indifference lines in space above the boundary line. This value is -1, which is less negative than the slope of the budget line, $-12/11$, and hence the point $(160, 270)$ is on the highest attainable indifference line. If the indifference curves had slopes which were more negative than the slope of the budget line, say, $-1\frac{1}{2}$, then the point $(0, 417)$ would be the optimum point. This, however, was not the case.

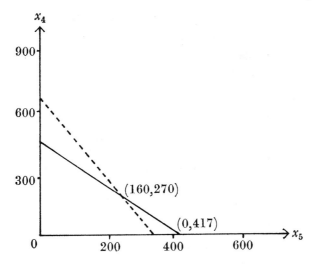

Figure 2.10. Budgets and utility boundary line: partial commodity space

The optimum point in the complete budget space is

$$\mathbf{x}' = [0 \quad 0 \quad 0 \quad 160 \quad 270]$$

As a check we can apply the transformation

$$\mathbf{z} = \mathbf{W}\mathbf{x}$$

to this point. This gives

$$\mathbf{z}' = [700 \quad 430]$$

2.7.2 *Five wants and fifteen perishable commodities*

With this number of wants the graphical method is no longer adequate and the full numerical methods of linear programming are required. In particular, a computer may be suitably employed to choose optimum budgets where there are many wants and many commodities. In the following example and in those in chapter 3, section 3.7, the EDSAC II computer of the Cambridge Mathematical Laboratory was used to solve the linear programmes involved.

The data concern the observed prices and quantities of foods consumed by about 1000 urban working-class households in Great Britain between July and September 1950. The foods have been grouped together into 15 groups and the wants are calories and the four nutrients, protein, calcium, riboflavin and vitamin C. It is of course possible to consider the commodities in greater detail and to consider additional nutrients. However, the data were available in this form in Brown's paper† and the intention is only to provide an illustration.

† Brown (1954), p. 53.

The consumer's technology is the matrix (transposed)

$$
\mathbf{W'} = \begin{bmatrix}
357.6 & 18.681 & 5.994 & 839.100 & 679.3 \\
73.2 & 0.106 & 0.906 & 0.200 & 4.1 \\
72.9 & 4.131 & 0 & 44.000 & 3.9 \\
28.9 & 3.481 & 0 & 35.593 & 11.8 \\
20.7 & 0.515 & 2.000 & 10.021 & 2.1 \\
 & & & & \\
7.9 & 0.607 & 4.987 & 14.639 & 7.6 \\
9.8 & 0.195 & 5.849 & 8.347 & 5.5 \\
71.9 & 2.500 & 0 & 28.180 & 29.8 \\
98.0 & 2.637 & 0 & 28.087 & 31.3 \\
116.1 & 7.070 & 0 & 139.628 & 224.0 \\
 & & & & \\
214.0 & 0.057 & 0 & 0 & 2.7 \\
252.2 & 0.051 & 0 & 0.168 & 0.2 \\
78.2 & 6.219 & 0 & 250.082 & 30.1 \\
108.0 & 0 & 0 & 0 & 0 \\
74.0 & 4.066 & 0 & 70.561 & 3.8
\end{bmatrix}
$$

showing the number of calories, gm of protein, mg of vitamin C, μg of riboflavin, and mg of calcium per oz of the fifteen foods – milk, preserves, other meat, fish, potatoes, vegetables, fruit, bread, cereals, cheese, butter and margarine, fats, eggs, sugar, and carcase meat. (Milk – per pint, and eggs – per egg.) The prices of these foods are – in pence per unit

$$
\mathbf{p} = \begin{bmatrix}
5.116 \\
0.926 \\
1.737 \\
1.317 \\
0.173 \\
 \\
0.397 \\
0.769 \\
0.222 \\
0.895 \\
1.009 \\
 \\
1.047 \\
0.839 \\
3.238 \\
0.317 \\
1.466
\end{bmatrix}
$$

Assume that an individual consumer has saturation levels for each of the five wants and that these wants are arranged in an order of priority. This is specified by the vector

$$\mathbf{z}^* = \begin{bmatrix} 16414 \\ 502 \\ 785 \\ 9893 \\ 6209 \end{bmatrix} \begin{matrix} = \text{calories} \\ \text{protein} \\ \text{vitamin C} \\ \text{riboflavin} \\ \text{calcium} \end{matrix}$$

where the z_i^* are the observed average intakes per head per week of these food factors in the 1950 survey. Of course it is possible to consider other individuals with different saturation levels and different orderings. This will be done in chapter 4. For the moment the concern is with one individual with given tastes.

Finally assume that the individual's income is a given amount. Suppose this were the very modest amount of eight shillings per week, i.e. $y = 96$ pence.

At this level of income it is found that the consumer can satiate his first three wants and can go some of the way towards satiating the fourth. To do this he needs to consume only three commodities, milk, potatoes and bread. The exact solution is

$$\mathbf{x}' = [0.48\ 0\ 0\ 0\ 391.1\ 0\ 0\ 116.7\ 0\ 0\ 0\ 0\ 0\ 0\ 0\ 0]$$

so that the expenditures involved are

$$(\hat{\mathbf{p}}\mathbf{x})' = [2.5\ 0\ 0\ 0\ 67.6\ 0\ 0\ 25.9\ 0\ 0\ 0\ 0\ 0\ 0\ 0\ 0]$$

Also, the income required to satiate all five wants can be found. This turns out to be just short of nine shillings, and the optimum budget contains still just the three foods, milk, potatoes and bread. The solution is

$$\mathbf{x}' = [3.91\ 0\ 0\ 0\ 380.8\ 0\ 0\ 99.2\ 0\ 0\ 0\ 0\ 0\ 0\ 0\ 0]$$

Thus if this consumer had an income of 9s. or more we should have to specify his preference function for further wants in his hierarchy beyond the initial five.

2.7.3 *Two wants and 32 durable commodities*

The data for this example concern 32 saloon cars available on the United Kingdom market in October 1958. The prices of possession per annum and of use per 1000 miles for these cars together with the consumer's technology have been estimated from the data published in *The Economist*.† The fixed price has been taken as the sum of

---

† *The Economist* **189** (1958), 'Motors in the lead', supplement to issue of 25 October 1958, p. 14.

registration ($£12.5$), garaging ($£13$), insurance (from $£22.1$ to $£42.25$ according to capacity of engine and value) and 10% of the new price including purchase tax. The price per 1000 miles of use has been taken as $£3$ plus the cost of petrol at 57d. per gallon. These price estimates should be sufficiently accurate to make the example approximate the true relative costs of these cars.

The prices of possession **q** and the prices of use **p** (in $£$ per annum and $£$ per 1000 miles) together with the consumer's technology **W** are

$$
\mathbf{q} = \begin{bmatrix} 159.50 \\ 153.25 \\ 176.00 \\ 147.35 \\ 139.00 \\ 141.85 \\ 174.40 \\ 127.45 \\ 133.95 \\ 132.35 \\ 113.15 \\ 115.70 \\ 121.50 \\ 105.65 \\ 113.60 \\ 193.93 \\ 177.35 \\ 210.20 \\ 161.60 \\ 158.50 \\ 165.75 \\ 139.75 \\ 141.85 \\ 171.70 \\ 124.00 \\ 111.50 \\ 94.00 \\ 124.75 \\ 114.05 \\ 113.05 \\ 107.70 \\ 127.25 \end{bmatrix} \quad
\mathbf{p} = \begin{bmatrix} 12.17 \\ 11.33 \\ 12.42 \\ 11.33 \\ 13.75 \\ 11.80 \\ 10.59 \\ 10.66 \\ 10.24 \\ 10.47 \\ 10.01 \\ 10.18 \\ 8.91 \\ 8.72 \\ 9.25 \\ 12.03 \\ 13.28 \\ 9.82 \\ 12.31 \\ 10.89 \\ 11.33 \\ 10.24 \\ 11.11 \\ 9.65 \\ 10.40 \\ 8.16 \\ 10.09 \\ 8.14 \\ 7.98 \\ 8.31 \\ 7.78 \\ 10.71 \end{bmatrix} \quad
\mathbf{W}' = [\mathbf{w}_1' \mathbf{w}_2'] = \begin{bmatrix} 1 & .02390 \\ 1 & .02254 \\ 1 & .02272 \\ 1 & .02578 \\ 1 & .02522 \\ 1 & .02688 \\ 1 & .02472 \\ 1 & .02688 \\ 1 & .02496 \\ 1 & .02600 \\ 1 & .02968 \\ 1 & .02828 \\ 1 & .02848 \\ 1 & .02782 \\ 1 & .02762 \\ 1 & .02482 \\ 1 & .02334 \\ 1 & .02312 \\ 1 & .02332 \\ 1 & .02286 \\ 1 & .02112 \\ 1 & .02342 \\ 1 & .02436 \\ 1 & .02356 \\ 1 & .02666 \\ 1 & .03008 \\ 1 & .03344 \\ 1 & .03012 \\ 1 & .03220 \\ 1 & .03430 \\ 1 & .04238 \\ 1 & .02932 \end{bmatrix}
$$

where the coefficients $\mathbf{w}_2'$ are the driving times in hours per mile estimated as the reciprocals of half the maximum speed in miles per hour.

Suppose now a consumer has a given income to spend on car transport, $y = £200$, and requires first to obtain 10,000 miles of car transport per annum and second to minimise the driving time involved in these 10,000 miles. The linear programme to be solved is:

$$z_2 = \mathbf{w}_2\mathbf{x} = \min$$

subject to

$$\mathbf{w}_1\mathbf{x} \geqslant 10{,}000$$

$$-\mathbf{p}'\mathbf{x}-\mathbf{q}'\mathbf{j} \geqslant -200$$

$$\mathbf{x} \geqslant \mathbf{0}$$

$$\mathbf{j} = 0 \text{ or } 1$$

The prior want of 10,000 miles of transport can be obtained with this income from cars 14, 27, 29, 30, and 31. Of these, car 14 minimises the driving time at 278.2 hours, and the consumer will only need to spend £192.85 of the £200 available.

It is possible to go on to consider additional wants satisfied by cars and to select an optimum budget using the method of integer programming. However, since many of the measurable qualities of the transport service provided by cars can be expressed as coefficients relating to the car, rather than in terms of coefficients relating to miles travelled, it is not necessary to make use of the techniques involved in integer programming.

3. INDIVIDUAL BEHAVIOUR (2):
THE COMPARATIVE STATICS OF CHOICE

'So, new commodities which prove technically superior or satisfy important psychological wants are ready to march forward to success.'

A. F. Burns (1934), p. 127

This chapter examines the effect on the optimum budget chosen by the consumer of various changes in the conditions of that choice. The method used is the method of comparative statics where the effect of a given change in conditions is found by comparing two equilibrium positions. No account is taken of the manner of movement between these two equilibria, though any number of equilibria can be considered and hence curves can be obtained relating changes in variables to smooth changes in conditions.

Changes in tastes are dealt with first; then changes in technology; and finally changes in prices and income.

3.1 CHANGES IN TASTES

For the type of consumer postulated, changes in tastes are limited to changes in the priority ordering among wants and in the saturation levels of these wants. Changes in the consumer's estimates of the want satisfying powers of commodities will be considered as changes in technology.

If the consumer's tastes change to any marked extent, then the vector z^* representing the saturation levels of his wants and their priority ordering will be very different and we would expect a great change in the optimum budget. However, if the taste change is merely a matter of a change in the priority ordering with no change in saturation levels, then there may be little or no change in the optimum budget. In particular, if the change in ordering occurs merely among the supramarginal wants or the sub-marginal wants, there will be no change since the same want will be marginal and no want changes its category.

What factors will lead to changes in the priority ordering of wants or in the saturation levels? Regarding the 'individual consumer' as a family, these changes occur as the family composition alters and a person enters or leaves the family unit. They also occur as people grow older. Obviously as the individual consumer gets older his activities and capacities alter; the priorities and saturation levels of his wants, and thus of the family unit, alter accordingly.

Consider a family consisting of a man and wife and with saturation levels z_1^*. Consider this same family after the addition of a child. Suppose the family retains the same priority ordering among wants but that the saturation levels z_2^* in the second situation are greater than z_1^* on account of the child.

Let $z_2^* = \hat{h}z_1^*$. Then $\mathbf{h}$ is the vector of specific coefficients for the family consisting of a couple and child in terms of a family consisting of a couple only. Suppose the family is able to choose in both situations an optimum budget which just satiates the first n wants, and that the same n commodities are included in both budgets. Then, letting z_1^* and z_2^* refer to these n wants and $\mathbf{x}_1$ and $\mathbf{x}_2$ to these n commodities, we have

$$z_1^* = \mathbf{W}_1\mathbf{x}_1$$

and

$$z_2^* = \mathbf{W}_1\mathbf{x}_2$$

also assuming the same $n \times n$ technology matrix $\mathbf{W}_1$.

So that

$$\mathbf{W}_1\mathbf{x}_2 = \hat{\mathbf{h}}\mathbf{W}_1\mathbf{x}_1$$

and hence

$$\mathbf{x}_2 = \mathbf{W}_1^{-1}\hat{\mathbf{h}}\mathbf{W}_1\mathbf{x}_1$$

Now in the special case where $\mathbf{W}_1$ is a diagonal matrix, we obtain

$$\mathbf{x}_2 = \hat{\mathbf{h}}\mathbf{x}_1$$

And similarly in the special case where $\mathbf{h}$ is a scalar, $\hat{\mathbf{h}} = h\mathbf{I}$,

$$\mathbf{x}_2 = h\mathbf{x}_1$$

But in general the technology coefficients do not disappear from the transformation between $\mathbf{x}_2$ and $\mathbf{x}_1$.†

From this discussion it can be seen that the problems in estimating equivalent adult scales from budget studies are fairly complex since, unless the commodities are so defined as to make the commodities specific satisfiers of wants (rather than joint satisfiers), the technology matrix will not be diagonal and the two sets of commodities, such as $\mathbf{x}_2$ and $\mathbf{x}_1$ above, will not be related in a simple manner as in $\mathbf{x}_2 = \hat{\mathbf{h}}\mathbf{x}_1$. In so far as the data are arranged so that $\mathbf{W}$ is diagonal and $\mathbf{h}$ is scalar, then simple estimation of equivalent adult scales will be successful.

---

† For example, when $n = 2$,
$$\mathbf{x}_2 = \frac{1}{|\mathbf{W}_1|}\begin{bmatrix} w_{11}w_{22}h_1 - w_{12}w_{21}h_2 & w_{22}w_{12}(h_1 - h_2) \\ w_{11}w_{21}(h_2 - h_1) & w_{11}w_{22}h_2 - w_{12}w_{21}h_1 \end{bmatrix}\mathbf{x}_1$$

3.2 CHANGES IN TECHNOLOGY: QUALITY

A change in the consumer's technology means a change in the matrix **W** of the want satisfying powers of commodities. When a new commodity becomes available to the consumer, this means the appearance of an extra column in **W**. Changes of this type will be considered in the next section. For simplicity, first consider a change in the quality of one or more existing commodities which is represented by a change in one or more of the elements w_{ij} of the matrix **W** for an existing set of commodities.

3.2.1 *Single quality changes*

By this is meant a change in one element only of **W**. Suppose w_{ij} increases. Then for any given level of consumption of commodity j the quantity of satisfaction of the ith want is increased. The slope of the vector for commodity j in the want space in respect of the ith want is decreased, so that the commodity vector moves nearer to the ith want axis.

We also find that the length of the vector (from the want-space origin) also changes. The coordinates of the extreme point of the vector are

$$y\mathbf{f}_j = \frac{1}{p_j} y\mathbf{w}_j$$

The length r of this vector is given by

$$r^2 = y^2 \mathbf{f}_j' \mathbf{f}_j = \frac{y^2}{p_j^2} \mathbf{w}_j' \mathbf{w}_j$$

So that when w_{ij} increases and all other qualities of the commodity remain constant, the change in r^2 is

$$\Delta(r^2) = y^2 \Delta(f_{ij}^2) = \frac{y^2}{p_j^2} (\Delta(w_{ij}^2))$$

which is positive.

Thus the extreme point of the jth commodity vector is pushed further away from the origin and in the direction of the ith axis. If this point represents an efficient budget, then it will remain efficient; if it does not, it may become efficient. In either of these events, the position of the budget restraint in the want space will be altered, and hence the optimum budget may alter. A sufficient condition for a change in the optimum budget is that the set of points representing efficient budgets should change completely in the marginal region.† By a complete change in these points, we mean that there are no points in common in the two sets. However, this is not a necessary condition.

† The highest attainable region. See page 31 above.

These remarks may be illustrated by considering the jth commodity vector in the Oz_1z_2 want space, as in figure 3.1. Let the extreme point of this vector be initially P_0 with coordinates $y(w_{1j}/p_j), y(w_{2j}/p_j)$.

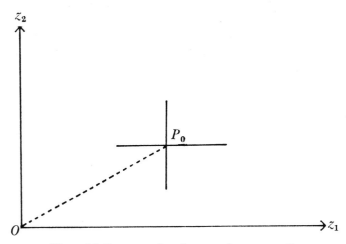

Figure 3.1. Extreme point of a vector for a commodity

Then changes in w_{1j} alone move P_0 along the line through P_0 parallel to the Oz_1 axis. Similarly changes in w_{2j} alone move P_0 along the line parallel to the Oz_2 axis.

Since increases in w_{1j} or in w_{2j} result in movements of P_0 which increase the amount of satisfaction of one want without decreasing the satisfaction of the other, if P_0 initially represents an efficient budget, increases in w_{1j} or w_{2j} must leave P_0 still representing an efficient budget. On the other hand, if P_0 is initially inefficient, as in figure 3.2, a sufficiently large increase in either w_{1j} or w_{2j} will lead to P_0 becoming

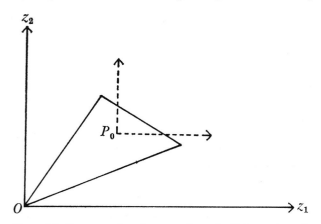

Figure 3.2. Extreme point of a vector for an inefficient commodity

efficient and hence the possibility of the jth commodity being included in the optimum budget which is selected from among efficient budgets. If the increase in quality is sufficiently large, then the position of the points representing efficient budgets will change, as for example, if w_{1j} increases so that P_0 moves to P_2, the set of points representing efficient budgets changes from the line P_1P_3 to the connected segments P_1P_2, P_2P_3 (see figure 3.3). This is not a *complete* change in efficient sets

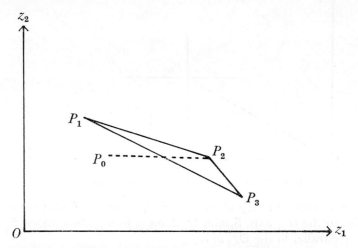

Figure 3.3. Quality change leading to a commodity becoming efficient

since points P_1 and P_3 are common to both. Hence if either P_1 or P_3 were optimum initially, and with both sets in the marginal region, the optimum budget will not alter.

3.2.2   *Multiple quality changes*

By this is meant changes in more than one element of **W**. Suppose the quality changes are confined to one commodity, the jth, then changes occur only in the jth column $\mathbf{w}_j$ of **W**. Then only the jth commodity vector in the want space is affected.

Suppose all elements of $\mathbf{w}_j$ change by the same proportion, say by a factor λ. Then the direction of the jth commodity vector in the want space is unchanged, but the length of the vector is changed by the factor λ. This change will in general lead to a change in the set of points representing efficient budgets, and hence to the possibility of a change in the optimum budget as in the case of a single quality change.

When the elements of $\mathbf{w}_j$ change, but not proportionately, then the direction of the jth commodity vector will certainly change, but its length will remain constant if $\mathbf{w}_j'\mathbf{w}_j$ remains constant. In general both length and direction will change and we can expect as a result a change in the sets of points representing efficient budgets and hence the possibility of a change in the optimum budget.

Suppose a consumer with given income, prices and available commodities at time t chooses an optimum budget $\mathbf{x}_t$. Then in terms of wants this consumer's standard of living is

$$\mathbf{z}_t = \mathbf{W}_t\mathbf{x}_t$$

Suppose some elements of $\mathbf{W}_t$, not necessarily confined to the same column, change so that at the new period θ, the consumer's technology is represented by $\mathbf{W}_\theta$. What is the optimum budget which gives him the same standard of living? Let this budget be $\mathbf{x}_\theta$. Then it is such that

$$\mathbf{W}_\theta\mathbf{x}_\theta = \mathbf{z}_t$$
$$= \mathbf{W}_t\mathbf{x}_t$$

so that $\qquad\qquad \mathbf{x}_\theta = \mathbf{W}_\theta^{-1}\mathbf{W}_t\mathbf{x}_t$

The number of positive elements in $\mathbf{x}_t$ is at most equal to the number of marginal and supra-marginal wants. Let this number be i. Then he is at most concerned with the $i \times i$ square sub-matrix of $\mathbf{W}_t$ consisting of elements in the columns and rows corresponding to these i wants and at most i commodities. Similarly in $\mathbf{W}_\theta$ he is at most concerned with the $i \times i$ square sub-matrix formed from elements from the same rows and at most i columns, but not necessarily corresponding to the same commodities. Suppose, however, that in fact i commodities are required in $\mathbf{x}_t$ and that the *same* i commodities are required in $\mathbf{x}_\theta$. Then leaving $\mathbf{W}_t$ and $\mathbf{W}_\theta$ to denote $i \times i$ square matrices with which he is concerned, $\mathbf{W}_\theta^{-1}$ can be found and hence so can the $i \times i$ matrix

$$\mathbf{Q}_{\theta t} = \mathbf{W}_\theta^{-1}\mathbf{W}_t$$

Thus the optimum budget resulting from the change in quality of commodities can be expressed as a transformation of the previous optimum budget. Notice that both $\mathbf{x}_\theta$ and $\mathbf{x}_t$ are observables, so that in principle the elements of $\mathbf{Q}_{\theta t}$ are estimable.

3.2.3 *Substitution and income effects of quality changes*

In the orthodox theory of consumer behaviour, the effects of a price change can be divided into income effects and substitution effects. Any *quality* change can also be considered as producing both income effects and substitution effects. The consumer can be compensated for the effect of a price change by a change in his income so that he just reaches the same indifference curve as before. With a quality change, changes in income or in prices, or both, may be made to compensate the consumer in a similar way.

Thus real income can be kept constant by changes in money income and/or in prices. The whole discussion about income and substitution effects in positive economics was really† concerned with finding out whether, when considering price changes, it is better to consider money income constant or real income constant.

3.3   Changes in technology: new commodities

When a new commodity becomes available to the consumer, he now has a new technology and this is represented by the insertion of an additional column in **W**. The elements of this column are ordered in the order of priority of his wants and if the commodity does not provide any satisfaction of a particular want, then the element has a value of zero. As we have assumed the consumer knows the want satisfying powers of all commodities, we assume he knows the values for all elements of the new column of **W** and that he does not have to take time to find these out. Notice that none of the other elements of **W** changes because of the insertion of the new column.

3.3.1   *One new commodity*

In the want space there is now an additional vector, representing this new commodity. If the vector lies *within* the vectors of the other commodities, then there will be no alteration in the set of points representing efficient budgets; and even if the vector lies outside the existing set of vectors it will only alter the set of efficient points if its extreme point lies beyond the set or the lines from the extreme points of the set perpendicular to the want axes. Thus let $P_1P_2P_3$ and P_4 represent possible extreme points of the new vector in the want space with an already existing set of efficient points represented by the continuous line segments $Q_1Q_2Q_3$ (see figure 3.4). Thus if the extreme point lies at P_1 or at P_4 the set of efficient points will alter, but if at P_2 or at P_3 the set will not.

The first condition for a change in the optimum budget is that the set of efficient points in the want space must change. Whether this is met or not depends on both the length and the direction of the new vector. The introduction of an extra commodity does not of itself result in a change in the optimum budget. The values of its want satisfying powers and its price must be suitable.

Another feature of this situation is the following: suppose the new commodity is such that it meets the first condition (that is that the set of efficient points changes), then if there is any change at all in the optimum budget, the new commodity must be included in the new budget. When shown a menu, a consumer chooses celery soup and

---

† This in so far as practical applications are concerned, neglecting the welfare aspects of comparisons between individuals.

roast beef. He is then told that he could also have tomato soup (not on the printed menu). If he changes his order to celery soup and lamb, he is not acting consistently according to unchanged preferences. To act consistently, he must include tomato soup in his new order or stick to the old.

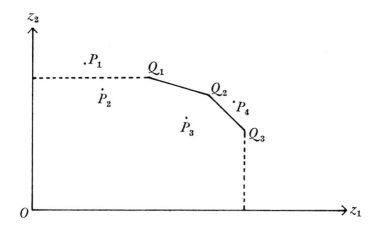

Figure 3.4. Possible extreme points of a vector for a new commodity

3.3.2   *Substitution and income effects of a new commodity*

As with the quality changes considered in section 3.2, both price and income changes can be considered to bring the consumer back to the same level of satisfaction as before the new commodity was introduced.

3.3.3   *Efficiency and redundancy*

Consider the introduction of a new commodity, 3, which is represented in the Oz_1z_2 want space by the vector OP_3. Vectors OP_1 and OP_2 represent existing commodities. The saturation level of the first want is z_1^* (see figure 3.5).

Then the new commodity is efficient but redundant, since it leads to a change in the set of efficient budgets but not to a change in the optimum budget. Here commodity 3 is the most efficient for satisfying want 1, but consumption of commodity 2 alone will carry the consumer to higher satisfaction levels and some combinations of 1 and 2 even higher.

Statements about efficiency and redundancy may be contrasted as follows:

'Inefficient commodities are redundant.'

'Efficiency does not depend on income level whereas redundancy does.' In the example above, at some lower levels of income, say at about two thirds or less of that shown in the diagram, commodity 3 would be doubly efficient and hence the only commodity bought.

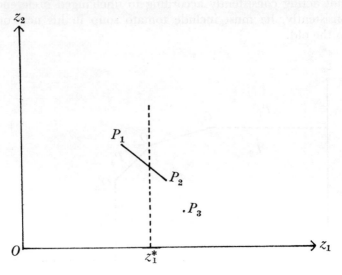

Figure 3.5. An efficient but redundant new commodity

3.4   CHANGES IN INCOME

Consider the effect of a change in income on the optimum position chosen by the consumer with prices, technology and tastes remaining unchanged throughout.

3.4.1   *Engel paths and curves*

A complete specification of *the Engel path* for the consumer can be obtained by finding the solutions to the linear programmes for the infinite number of possible values that y may take from 0 to ∞.† The income variation can of course be limited to some finite range and the Engel path determined between these two income limits.

For any given set of prices, technology and tastes, the Engel path lies in the $(m+n+1)$-dimensional space consisting of the m want axes, the n commodity axes, and the income axis, and consists of the locus of the solution points to the linear programme of choice as income varies over the range. The complete Engel path can be regarded as consisting of two partial paths; the Engel path in the *want* and income space $(m+1$ dimensions) and the Engel path in the *commodity* and income space $(n+1$ dimensions). Disregarding all dimensions except one want

† See Appendix (p. 69) for a note on the problems involved in solving the large number of linear programmes that results from changing one of the parameters, such as y, through a range of values.

and income gives us a two-dimensional want-Engel *curve* and similarly disregarding all dimensions except one commodity and income gives us a two-dimensional commodity-Engel curve. Thus there will be m want-Engel curves and n commodity-Engel curves for any given price, technology and taste situation. The consumer's actual position on these curves of course depends on his income, but the positions of the curves do not.

3.4.2 *Inclusion of additional commodities in the budget*

In general the individual's Engel curves for commodities are kinked. As each want becomes saturated, the consumer's objective changes to the satisfaction of the next want in his hierarchy of wants, and in general this means the inclusion of an additional commodity in his budget. In consequence the Engel curves for the commodities already in the budget change their slopes; usually a reduction in slope occurs. The combined slopes of the Engel curves of the commodities already in the budget must decline to allow the commodity to enter at all. This decline occurs whether the introduced commodity is a substitute or not.

The argument that substitutes are dominant in the system is not supported by the necessary decline in the Engel curves on the inclusion of an additional commodity.† For example, if the consumer's technology matrix $\mathbf{W}$ is diagonal so that there is only one commodity suitable for each consumer want, and if these wants stand in order of priority, then the slope of the Engel curve for each commodity will decline to zero on the inclusion of the next commodity as income is increased and one marginal want is substituted for another. Here no commodity is substitutable for another in satisfying a particular want. Commodities already in the budget are in some sense complementary to the introduced commodity in enabling the consumer to continue to satisfy his supra-marginal wants while he attends to his marginal want.

If the consumer's technology matrix has non-zero off-diagonal elements, then the inclusion of another commodity in the optimum budget as income is increased can lead to a decline beyond zero in the slopes of the Engel curves for some commodities. The relationship of the newly-included commodity to these commodities is one of substitution. In general we may say that all commodities with positive elements in the ith row of $\mathbf{W}$ are potential substitutes between each other for the ith want.

3.4.3 *Use and possession Engel curves for durables*

For commodities that have fixed costs, there is a set of *possession*-Engel curves which take the form of step functions between the values zero

† Prais and Houthakker (1955) argue that this necessary decline means that 'substitutes must be more important in the total than the complements', p. 16.

and one, with the steps occurring at various levels of income. The *use*-Engel curves for the commodity relate the rate of use of the commodity to income, as in the usual commodity-Engel curves considered previously in this section.

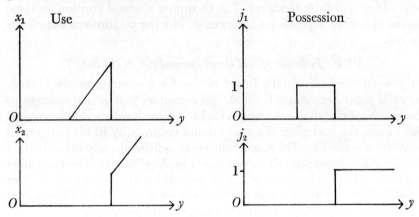

Figure 3.6. Use and possession curves: no overlap

Suppose a consumer has available to him two commodities which have fixed costs and which serve two wants. Suppose there is a saturation level to the prior want so that when income reaches a certain level he switches from one commodity to the other. Then the use- and

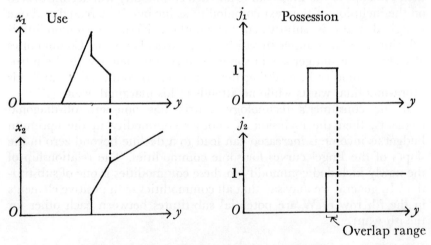

Figure 3.7. Use and possession curves: with overlap

possession-Engel curves for these two commodities will be shaped as shown in figure 3.6. This example assumes that there is no overlap range of income where both commodities are possessed. The Engel curves for use and possession in such a case would be as in figure 3.7.

3.5 CHANGES IN PRICES

An important difference between the usual theory of consumer behaviour and the theory set out in this work is that no longer does everything depend on everything else. This aspect is particularly important in respect to price changes. The demand for or consumption of a particular commodity by an individual consumer does not depend on the prices of all commodities. In general, at a given level of income and with a given set of prices, some commodities will not be bought by our individual consumer. The prices of the commodities not included in his budget can alter, perhaps by a large amount, without affecting in the slightest the quantities of commodities included in the optimum budget. Again, if commodities are specific to wants, an alteration in the price of the commodity satisfying the marginal want cannot alter the quantities of *other* commodities already in the budget.

Although this lack of connection is not entirely excluded from the usual theory of individual consumer behaviour, it is regarded as being of minor importance. On the other hand, the view taken here is that, at the level of the individual consumer, there is an important lack of connection for many commodities between changes in their prices and the quantities consumed. It is through the grouping of individuals of heterogeneous tastes, incomes and technologies that connections are established between changes in prices and consumption levels. It should also be noted that changes in prices do not have symmetric effects on demand, since positive changes and negative changes from an initial situation will in general have effects of different magnitude on demand.

3.5.1 *Demand paths for simple price changes*

A simple price change means a change in the price of a single commodity available to a consumer who has a given money income when the prices of all other commodities remain constant. The tastes and technology of the consumer are also regarded as being fixed.

If all the possible values from ∞ to zero that this price may take are considered, and the solutions to the linear programmes for all these prices are found, then a complete specification of the *demand path* for this commodity price is obtained. As in the case of income changes, the price variation could be limited to some finite range and the demand path determined for this range.

The complete demand path for this commodity price will be specified in the space of $m+n+1$ dimensions, consisting of the m want axes, the n commodity axes, and the price of the commodity axis. It consists of the locus of the solution points to the linear programmes as price varies over the range. The complete demand path can be regarded as consisting of two partial paths: the demand path in the want and price space, and the demand path in the commodity and price space. Disregarding all dimensions except one want and the price gives a two-dimensional demand *curve* for a want, and similarly disregarding all dimensions except one commodity and one price gives a two-dimensional demand *curve* for a commodity. The curve for the commodity whose price is changing is the *direct*-demand curve, while curves for other commodities are *cross*-demand curves.

3.5.2   *Substitution and income effects of a simple price change*

These effects can be illustrated as in figure 3.8 by considering an example with two wants and three commodities, each capable of providing satisfaction of both wants jointly. The efficient budget segments in the want space are represented by the lines joining $P_1 P_2$ and $P_2 P_3$ in the diagram. The initial optimum point is A. Suppose now

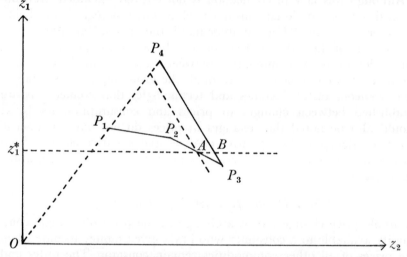

Figure 3.8. Efficient budgets: change in a price

P_1 moves to P_4 as a result of a reduction in the price of commodity 1, other prices and money income staying fixed. Then P_2 and P_3 will remain fixed and if p_1 falls sufficiently the new efficient budget will be the single line segment $P_4 P_3$ as shown in the diagram. The new optimum point is B where the highest indifference line is reached.

If at the new price money income is reduced, so that a new optimum point α is reached which is on the same indifference curve as the original optimum point A, then the full effect of the price change (the movement from A to B) can be divided into two parts – the income effect (the movement from α to B) and the substitution effect (the movement from A to α).

Now in the system of priorities among wants, α will be at A, so that the substitution effects on the amounts of want satisfaction z_1 and z_2 are zero. But the substitution effects on the commodities are considerable, since A represents a budget containing commodities 2 and 3 whereas α represents a budget containing commodities 1 and 3. Hence the substitution effects are: x_2 becomes zero, x_1 rises from zero to a positive quantity, and x_3 may remain constant, increase or decrease. The income effects on the wants are zero on z_1 and positive on z_2. The income effect on x_1 is negative and on x_3 is positive.

This example has been concerned with the case of a fall in the price of a commodity which is not already in the budget. If the fall in price is sufficient it will be included, but considerable changes in its price can occur without this happening.

3.5.4 *Perfect substitutes and perfect complements*

'Perfect substitutes tend to have constant price-ratios, perfect complements constant quantity-ratios.'[†] The reasons behind this generalisation of Hicks can be seen if the two wants and two commodities case is examined.

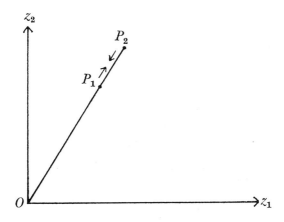

Figure 3.9. Perfect substitutes

(a) *Perfect substitutes.* If two commodities are perfect substitutes, then they provide satisfaction of wants in the same proportions, even though say physically different. In the want space the vectors for these two commodities will have the same slopes. Now if the prices of the two are adjusted, the lengths of these two vectors can be made equal. The points P_1 and P_2 in figure 3.9 can be made to coincide. With the price ratio kept at this level, the consumers will be indifferent between the two commodities. Both will tend to be bought, though the exact

† Hicks (1956), p. 165, n. 1.

quantities of each will tend to fluctuate according to the chance factors influencing choice in this indifferent situation. If the price ratios get out of step, one commodity will clearly be more efficient than the other and the inefficient one will not be bought. Hence competition among the sellers will keep the prices in step.

(b) *Perfect complements*. Suppose there is a situation where two specific commodities are available to meet a consumer's first two wants, with commodity 1 specific to want 1 and commodity 2 to want 2. Suppose also that the consumer's income is always more than sufficient for the satiation of both wants, and that none of the commodities which he purchases to satisfy other wants gives any satisfaction of wants 1 and 2. Then in this situation the order of priority between the wants is immaterial and the wants will be perfect complements. Whatever the prices of the commodities, the wants will be exactly satiated, the consumer always spending enough to just reach the point A in figure 3.10. The commodities also are perfect complements.

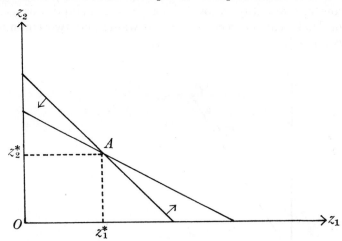

Figure 3.10. Perfect complements

Since $\begin{bmatrix} z_1^* \\ z_2^* \end{bmatrix} = \begin{bmatrix} w_{11} & \cdot \\ \cdot & w_{22} \end{bmatrix} \begin{bmatrix} x_1 \\ x_2 \end{bmatrix}$

$$x_1 = \frac{z_1^*}{w_{11}} \text{ and } x_2 = \frac{z_2^*}{w_{22}}$$

so that whatever the prices of the commodities, the quantities bought will be constant.

3.6 COMPARATIVE STATICS IN LINEAR PROGRAMMING

Following on from the discussion of Samuelson (1946), Beckmann (1956) and Bailey (1956) the various types of changes in the data considered in this chapter can be summarised in terms of mathematics and some results stated which hold in the case when the changes concern all groups of variables – tastes, technology, income and prices.

The linear programming problem of the consumer is to find a budget which maximises the satisfaction of the marginal want subject to the restrictions that the supra-marginal wants are satiated and expenditure does not exceed income.

In symbols this is:

Find $\mathbf{x}$ such that $\quad\quad z_i = \mathbf{w}_i\mathbf{x} = \max$

subject to
$$\begin{bmatrix} -\mathbf{W}_{i-1} \\ \mathbf{p}' \end{bmatrix} \mathbf{x} \leqslant \begin{bmatrix} -\mathbf{z}^*_{i-1} \\ y \end{bmatrix}$$
$$\mathbf{x} \geqslant 0$$

With a slight change of terminology, this can be written:

Find $\mathbf{x}$ such that $\quad\quad \mathbf{b}'\mathbf{x} = \max$

subject to $\quad\quad\quad\quad \mathbf{Ax} \leqslant \mathbf{c}$
$$\mathbf{x} \geqslant 0$$

Now for any arbitrary changes in the parameters $\mathbf{A}$, $\mathbf{b}$ and $\mathbf{c}$ to $\mathbf{A}+\Delta\mathbf{A}$, $\mathbf{b}+\Delta\mathbf{b}$ and $\mathbf{c}+\Delta\mathbf{c}$, Bailey (1956) has shown that the directions of change in the levels of consumption $\mathbf{x}$ and in the efficiency prices $\mathbf{s}$ can be determined.

For every commodity n

(1) $(\Delta b_n - \sum_m \Delta s_m . a_{mn} - \sum_m s_m . \Delta a_{mn})\Delta x_n \geqslant 0$

and for every capacity m

(2) $\Delta s_m(\Delta c_m - \sum_n \Delta x_n . a_{mn} - \sum_n x_n . \Delta a_{mn}) \leqslant 0$

Hence by summation

(3) $\Delta\mathbf{b}'\Delta\mathbf{x} - \Delta\mathbf{s}'\mathbf{A}\Delta\mathbf{x} - \mathbf{s}'\Delta\mathbf{A}\Delta\mathbf{x} \geqslant 0$

and

(4) $\Delta\mathbf{s}'\Delta\mathbf{c} - \Delta\mathbf{s}'\mathbf{A}\Delta\mathbf{x} - \Delta\mathbf{s}'\Delta\mathbf{A}\mathbf{x} \leqslant 0$

Subtracting (4) from (3)

(5)† $(\Delta\mathbf{b}' - \mathbf{s}'\Delta\mathbf{A})\Delta\mathbf{x} - \Delta\mathbf{s}'(\Delta\mathbf{c} - \Delta\mathbf{A}\mathbf{x}) \geqslant 0$

Similarly by re-arranging the terms of (3) and (4)

(6) $\Delta\mathbf{b}'\Delta\mathbf{x} + \Delta\mathbf{s}'\Delta\mathbf{A}\mathbf{x} - \mathbf{s}'\Delta\mathbf{A}\Delta\mathbf{x} \geqslant \Delta\mathbf{s}'\mathbf{A}\Delta\mathbf{x} + \Delta\mathbf{s}'\Delta\mathbf{A}\mathbf{x}$

(7) $\Delta\mathbf{s}'\mathbf{A}\Delta\mathbf{x} + \Delta\mathbf{s}'\Delta\mathbf{A}\mathbf{x} \geqslant \Delta\mathbf{s}'\Delta\mathbf{c}$

† This is Beckmann's result (9) in Beckmann (1956), p. 233.

With these inequalities some of the special cases which occur when the changes are confined to a group of the parameters of the choice situation (for example changes in prices) can be considered.

These special cases may be summarised as follows:

(1) *Changes in tastes:* change in the supra-marginal want saturation levels z_{i-1}^*:

$$0 \geqslant \Delta s' \left[\frac{-W_{i-1}}{p'} \right] \Delta x \geqslant \Delta s' \Delta z_{i-1}^*$$

(2) *Change in technology:*

   (a) Change in marginal want qualities only

$$\Delta w_i . \Delta x \geqslant \Delta s' \left[\frac{-W_{i-1}}{p'} \right] \Delta x \geqslant 0$$

   (b) Change in supra-marginal want qualities only

$$s' \Delta W_{i-1} \Delta x \geqslant \Delta s' \left[\frac{-W_{i-1}}{p'} \right] \Delta x \geqslant \Delta s' \Delta W_{i-1} x$$

(3) *Change in income*

$$0 \geqslant \Delta s' \left[\frac{-W_{i-1}}{p'} \right] \Delta x \geqslant \Delta s_i \Delta y$$

(4) *Change in commodity prices*

$$-s_i \Delta p' \Delta x \geqslant \Delta s' \left[\frac{-W_{i-1}}{p'} \right] \Delta x \geqslant -\Delta s_i \Delta p' x$$

Further special cases follow from considering a change in just one coefficient, such as a change in one price p_j.

(5) *Change in a single price p_j*

In this case:

$$\Delta s_i \Delta p_j x_j \geqslant s_i \Delta p_j \Delta x_j$$

If $x_j = 0$, then if Δp_j is positive, since s_i is positive, $\Delta x_j \leqslant 0$. $\therefore x_j = 0$. Putting this in words, an increase in the price of a commodity not included in the budget cannot result in its being included. If $x_j = 0$, and Δp_j is negative, then $\Delta x_j \geqslant 0$. In words, a decrease in the price of a commodity not included in the budget may result in its being included. If $x_j > 0$ and if Δp_j is negative, then $\Delta x_j / x_j \geqslant \Delta s_i / s_i$, so for $\Delta x_j = 0$ then $\Delta s_i \leqslant 0$. That is to say, a decrease in the price of a commodity in the budget without any increase in its quantity tends to decrease the marginal price of money. If $x_j > 0$ and if Δp_j is positive, then $\Delta x_j / x_j \leqslant \Delta s_i / s_i$, so for $\Delta x_j = 0$, $\Delta s_i \geqslant 0$. That is to say an increase in the price of a commodity in the budget without any increase in its quantity tends to increase the marginal price of money.

Results similar to the single price change can be obtained for changes in a marginal want quality Δw_{ij}, a supra-marginal want quality Δw_{kj} or a change in a supra-marginal want saturation level Δz_k^*.

(6) *Change in a single marginal want quality w_{ij}*
Then

$$\Delta w_{ij} \Delta x_j \geqslant 0$$

so that Δw_{ij} and Δx_j cannot be of different sign.

(7) *Change in a single supra-marginal want quality w_{kj}*

$$s_k \Delta w_{kj} \Delta x_j \geqslant \Delta s_k \Delta w_{kj} x_j$$

Thus if $\Delta w_{kj} > 0$, then

$$s_k \Delta x_j \geqslant \Delta s_k x_j$$

so if $x_j = 0$,

$$\Delta x_j \geqslant 0$$

and since $s_k > 0$, if $x_j > 0$,

$$\frac{\Delta x_j}{x_j} \geqslant \frac{\Delta s_k}{s_k} \geqslant 0$$

Again if $\Delta w_{kj} < 0$, then

$$s_k \Delta x_j \leqslant \Delta s_k x_j$$

so if $x_j = 0$, $\Delta x_j \leqslant 0$ and since $s_k > 0$, if $x_j > 0$,

$$\frac{\Delta x_j}{x_j} \leqslant \frac{\Delta s_k}{s_k} \leqslant 0$$

(8) *Change in a single supra-marginal want saturation level z_k^**

$$0 \geqslant \Delta s_k \Delta z_k^*$$

so that an increase in z_k^* means that the price of want k in terms of the marginal want i decreases, or, putting it the other way, the price of the marginal want i in terms of the supra-marginal want k, increases.

3.7 EXAMPLES

3.7.1 *Engel curves*

In the example given on pages 43–5 illustrating the choice of an optimum budget, the consumer's wants (their saturation levels and priority) were specified by the vector

$$\mathbf{z}^* = \begin{bmatrix} 16414 \\ 502 \\ 785 \\ 9893 \\ 6209 \end{bmatrix}$$

With the consumer's commodity technology matrix as specified on page 44 and with a set of given prices, the optimum budget for the consumer was found when he had an income of 96 pence per week. Following on from this the optimum budgets for this consumer can be determined for all levels of income up to the point where all five wants are satiated. This will provide the Engel curves for the commodities available to this consumer.

Solving these programmes reveals that over the range of income from zero up to 107.91 pence per week (where all five wants are satiated) this consumer includes only sugar, bread, potatoes, and milk in his budget, and at no point does he include more than three of these. The consumer starts at incomes above zero with sugar and reaches his first objective, sufficient calories, at an income of 48.178 pence, after

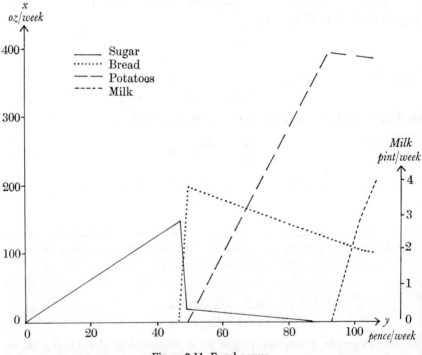

Figure 3.11. Engel curves

which he introduces bread so as to move to his second objective which he reaches at income 50.379. After this he introduces potatoes so as to advance towards the third objective. At an income of 87.294 pence sugar disappears from his budget, and the third objective is reached at income 94.530. At this point milk is introduced into the budget and the fourth objective is reached at income 107.91. With this budget the fifth objective is already obtained and a slight surplus of calcium remains in the diet.

The Engel curves for sugar, bread, potatoes and milk for this consumer are shown in figure 3.11.

3.7.2 *Demand curves*

Consider the situation when the consumer of the previous example is at the subsistence level of income, so that he can just satiate his first two wants, calories and protein, by buying sugar and bread.

The relevant data are

$$
\begin{array}{cc}
& \text{Sugar} \quad \text{Bread} \\
\mathbf{W} = & \begin{bmatrix} 108.0 & 71.9 \\ — & 2.5 \end{bmatrix} \quad \begin{array}{l} \text{calories/oz} \\ \text{protein gm/oz} \end{array}
\end{array}
$$

$$\mathbf{p}' = [0.317 \quad 0.222] \quad \text{pence/oz}$$

$$z_1^* = 16414 \quad \text{calories/week}, \quad y = 50.38 \text{ pence/week}$$

$$z_2^* = \quad 502 \quad \text{protein gms/week}.$$

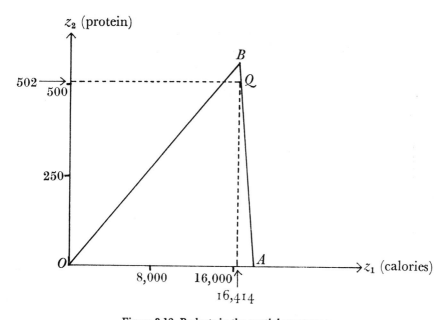

Figure 3.12. Budgets in the partial want space

Consider what happens to the optimum budget when the prices of these two commodities change, and with the added assumption that no other commodities are available.

In the want space the initial situation is shown in figure 3.12.

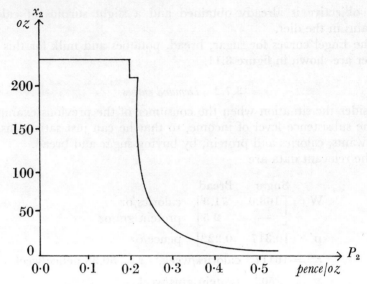

Figure 3.13. Uncompensated demand curve: bread

As the price of bread increases, the point B moves directly towards the origin and the optimum point Q moves along the line $z_1 = 16414$, so that for bread prices in the range $0.222 < p_2 < \infty$

$$x_2 = \frac{237.802}{108p_2 - 22.7923}$$

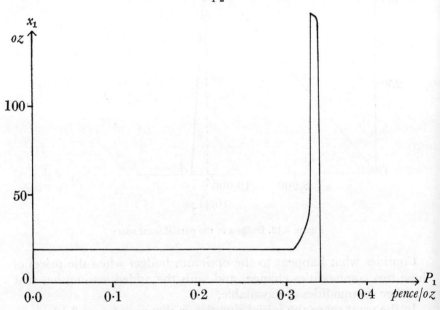

Figure 3.14. Uncompensated demand curve: sugar

If savings are allowed to occur, then when p_2 decreases below 0.222 the optimum point will remain at $Q(16414, 502)$ and x_2 will remain constant at 200.84 until the price $p_2 = 0.21104$ is reached, when the optimum point jumps to the point $(16414, 570.723)$ with x_2 jumping to 228.3 and sugar disappearing from the diet. Thus the uncompensated demand curve for bread is as in figure 3.13.

Similarly by keeping income and the price of bread constant, the demand curve for sugar is as in figure 3.14.

These demand curves are the uncompensated curves; however the compensated demand curves are more interesting. For this consumer if price changes are compensated for by altering income, so as to keep him on the same indifference curve as his initial equilibrium (or as near to that as possible, erring in his favour when this is not exactly possible), the compensated demand curves are as in figure 3.15.

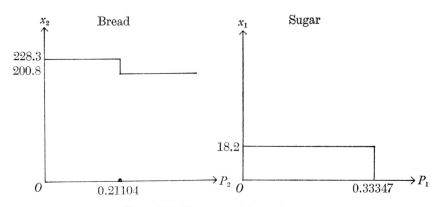

Figure 3.15. Compensated demand curves

APPENDIX TO CHAPTER 3

Engel curves from solving a series of linear programmes

It is possible to find the minimum cost, y, of obtaining a subsistence level of nutrient intakes from a given set of commodities obtainable at fixed prices.

This takes the form of solving a linear programme of the form

$$y = \mathbf{p}'\mathbf{x} = \min$$

subject to

$$\mathbf{W}\mathbf{x} \geqslant \mathbf{z}^*$$

$$\mathbf{x} \geqslant \mathbf{0}$$

where $\mathbf{p}$ is the vector of prices for the n commodities

$\mathbf{x}$ is the (unknown) vector of quantities of the n commodities

$\mathbf{z}^*$ is the vector of minimum levels of intake of m nutrients and $\mathbf{W}$ is the $(m \times n)$ matrix of nutrient densities of the commodities. The classic example of this method is Stigler (1945).

Suppose the nutrients are ranked in order of priority so that in the preceding example, when the consumer is given an income just less than the minimum cost of satiating the m nutrient intakes, he chooses to satiate $m-1$ of them, and almost satiate the mth, which has the least priority. Similarly for further reductions of income.

Now given the order of priority among the nutrients (wants) it is possible to determine the minimum costs of satiating the most prior want, the minimum cost of satiating the first two prior wants, etc., by solving the set of linear programmes

(i) $\qquad\qquad y = \mathbf{p}'\mathbf{x} = \min$

subject to $\qquad\qquad \mathbf{w}_1\mathbf{x} \geqslant z_1^*$

$\qquad\qquad\qquad\quad \mathbf{x} \geqslant \mathbf{0}$

where z_1^* is the satiation level of intake for the most prior nutrient

(ii) $\qquad\qquad y = \mathbf{p}'\mathbf{x} = \min$

subject to $\qquad\qquad \mathbf{w}_1\mathbf{x} \geqslant z_1^*$

$\qquad\qquad\qquad \mathbf{w}_2\mathbf{x} \geqslant z_2^*$

$\qquad\qquad\qquad\quad \mathbf{x} \geqslant \mathbf{0}$

where z_2^* is the satiation level of intake of the second most prior nutrient

(iii) $\qquad\qquad y = \mathbf{p}'\mathbf{x} = \min$

subject to $\qquad\qquad \mathbf{w}_1\mathbf{x} \geqslant z_1^*$

$\qquad\qquad\qquad \mathbf{w}_2\mathbf{x} \geqslant z_2^*$

$\qquad\qquad\qquad \mathbf{w}_3\mathbf{x} \geqslant z_3^*$

$\qquad\qquad\qquad\quad \mathbf{x} \geqslant \mathbf{0} \qquad$ etc.

This gives vector solutions

$$\mathbf{x}^{(1)}, \mathbf{x}^{(2)}, \mathbf{x}^{(3)}, \text{ etc.}$$

and corresponding income (least cost) levels

$$y^{(1)}, y^{(2)}, y^{(3)}, \text{ etc.}$$

These vector solutions, together with the corresponding income levels, describe points on the Engel (income variation) path in the commodity space.

Points on the Engel path for any income level y^* intermediate to the levels $y^{(i)}$, $y^{(j)}$ can be obtained by finding the solutions to the linear programmes of the form

(iv)

$$z_j = \mathbf{w}_j \mathbf{x} = \max$$

subject to

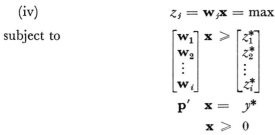

$$\begin{bmatrix} \mathbf{w}_1 \\ \mathbf{w}_2 \\ \vdots \\ \mathbf{w}_i \end{bmatrix} \mathbf{x} \geqslant \begin{bmatrix} z_1^* \\ z_2^* \\ \vdots \\ z_i^* \end{bmatrix}$$

$$\mathbf{p}' \ \mathbf{x} = y^*$$

$$\mathbf{x} \geqslant 0$$

and where $j = i+1$.

From the complete Engel path the Engel curve for a single commodity can be obtained.

A practical problem involved in the application of the method is that, to obtain a description of the Engel path for 'intermediate' levels, the calculation of a large number of programmes of type (iv) may be required. However, if there are no 'substitution' points where the basket of commodities changes between the income levels of $y^{(i)}$ and $y^{(j)}$, then the Engel path will be the straight line joining the two solution vectors $\mathbf{x}^{(i)}$ and $\mathbf{x}^{(j)}$. In these cases programmes of type (iv) will not need to be calculated.

Where some 'substitution' points occur between the income levels $y^{(i)}$ and $y^{(j)}$, then the Engel path will be the series of straight lines joining the solution vectors for the income levels $y^{(i)}$ and $y^{(j)}$ through the substitution points in the order of increasing income level. For example, suppose there exists one substitution point $\mathbf{x}^{(k)}$ between the solution vectors $\mathbf{x}^{(i)}$ and $\mathbf{x}^{(j)}$ where $y^{(i)} \ y^{(k)} \ y^{(j)}$, then the Engel path is the straight line joining $\mathbf{x}^{(i)}$ to $\mathbf{x}^{(k)}$ and the straight line joining $\mathbf{x}^{(k)}$ to $\mathbf{x}^{(j)}$.

There may be more than one substitution point between any adjoining solution points. The methods by which *all* substitution points between $\mathbf{x}^{(i)}$ and $\mathbf{x}^{(j)}$ can be found are known as *parametric programming*.[†] The Engel path and curves are completely described by the set of all solution points and substitution points.

† See for example Dantzig (1963), p. 245.

4. GROUP BEHAVIOUR

'But economics is not, in the end, much interested in the behaviour of single individuals. Its concern is with the behaviour of groups.'

J. R. Hicks (1939), 2nd edn 1946, p. 34

Economists are interested in individual behaviour only in so far as a study of it throws some light on the economic behaviour of the group. Moreover, most available observations are of the behaviour of the group, rather than the behaviour of the individual.

Chapters 2 and 3 outlined a theory of the behaviour of the individual consuming unit. This theory shows the individual as acting in a very discontinuous manner, perhaps startlingly so for those used to the smooth curves in which this behaviour is usually pictured. The purpose of the present chapter is to demonstrate that, although individuals may act in a very discontinuous manner, the behaviour of the group is of a smooth nature. The kinks of individual behaviour are ironed out in the process of aggregation.

To form a macro-behaviour model for a group of economic units, it will be necessary to make some assumptions about the distribution between the units of the various factors which determine the micro-behaviour. In the present case, this means making assumptions about the distribution among consumers of tastes, technology, price and income. This chapter will show that differences between consumers in regard to these factors lead to smooth group behaviour, and that the exact form of the distribution of these differences may be immaterial to the result.

To begin with, the possible manner in which the factors determining individual behaviour are distributed among the individual consuming units will be examined. This will be followed by a discussion of the way in which the group behaves in response to the introduction of a new commodity, the form of the budget study Engel curves and the form of the demand curves relating consumption to price changes. Finally there is an example drawn from linear programming which demonstrates how the extremely discontinuous individual Engel curves for 10 consumers are smoothed out in the aggregate.

4.1   THE DISTRIBUTION OF TASTES, TECHNOLOGIES, PRICES AND INCOME

The distribution assumptions made in this section are the assumptions that seem natural *a priori*. In the following sections, the implications of these assumptions for the behaviour of groups of consumers are considered. However, in developing these implications there are some departures from the *a priori* assumptions made now.

4.1.1   *Independence*

During any period, the aggregate quantity consumed is the sum of quantities consumed by the individuals. By assuming that the aggregate behaviour relation is the aggregate of the individual behaviour relations, the assumption is made that individual behaviour relations are independent of each other. This assumption does not necessarily correspond with reality.

Pigou (1913) sets out to enquire under what circumstances the assumption of the additivity of individual demand curves 'adequately conforms to the facts, and, when it does not so conform, what alternative assumption ought to be substituted for it'. Similarly Morgenstern (1948) holds that in some cases the market demand curve is not the lateral summation of the individual demand curves. For Duesenberry (1949) the interdependence of individual consumer behaviour relations forms the basis of his reformulation of the theory of consumer saving.

While not completely relaxing the assumption of independence between consumers' tastes, technologies, and incomes, it will be shown in section 4.2 how changes in consumers' technologies may occur when a new commodity is introduced into the market.

4.1.2   *Tastes*

It has often been assumed that individual tastes are identical, as in Marschak (1939) and de Wolff (1941), or alternatively that the micro-behaviour theory refers to a 'representative' individual. In the first case, aggregation of individuals of different tastes does not arise, although it does in regard to individuals of different incomes. With the 'representative' individual, aggregation is unnecessary for both tastes and incomes, since he is regarded as having a representative income.

The idea that tastes are distributed among individuals according to some particular distribution can be found in Allen and Bowley (1935), Malmquist (1948), Tobin (1952) and Farrell (1954).

The distributions of the want-saturation levels z^* among consumers can be assumed to be normal distributions with mean values $\bar{z}^*$ and variances σ_z^2. This assumption is equivalent to assuming that the want-saturation levels are determined by many *additive* factors with random deviations. Alternatively it could be assumed that the want-saturation levels are determined by many *multiplicative* factors with random deviations. This alternative assumption would mean that the $\mathbf{z}^*$ were log-normally distributed. A factor in favour of the latter assumption is that the $\mathbf{z}^*$ are essentially non-negative variates.

Some assumption must also be made about the way in which consumers rank their wants in priority. It could of course be assumed that the priority orderings are identical for all consumers. However, a more realistic assumption would be that they are not identical and that if the ranking orders given to a particular want by all consumers were obtained they would reveal a unimodal distribution of ranks. Roy (1943) suggests such a method of classification of commodities according to their mean ranking. Pyatt (1964) examines priority rankings of consumers' demand for household durables.

4.1.3   *Technology*

The elements of the consumers' technology matrix may also be assumed to be either normally or log-normally distributed. Again, since the elements of $\mathbf{W}$ for each individual are essentially non-negative, there is some merit in regarding these distributions as log-normal too.

Referring back to section 5 of chapter 2, on page 33 the discussion was concerned with the coordinates of the points where the 'boundary plane' for the ith want cuts the n commodity axes. It was found that the ith want may be satisfied if

$$\frac{y}{p_j} \geqslant \frac{z_i^*}{w_{ij}} \qquad \text{for any } i.$$

The ratios z_i^*/w_{ij} are important in the theory. Now if z_i^* and w_{ij} are both sets of independently distributed log-normal variates, then the ratios z_i^*/w_{ij} are also log-normally distributed.†

In the particular case where all individual $\mathbf{W}$ are diagonal matrices, the elements of $\mathbf{W}^{-1}\mathbf{z}^*$ for an individual are the satiation levels for *commodities* for that individual. If these levels are denoted by $\mathbf{x}^*$, then the elements of $\mathbf{x}^*$ will be log-normally distributed if the want-satiation levels (tastes) and the want-densities (technology coefficients) are log-normally distributed.

4.1.4   *Prices*

It will be assumed that these are identical for every consumer. In general, whether this assumption corresponds with reality or not depends on how large a group of consumers is being considered – on the size

† For this convenient result see Aitchison and Brown (1957), p. 11.

of the market being considered, and on the conditions of competition, price-discrimination, etc. in that market. The simplifying assumption made here is that there is only one price at which a particular commodity is offered for sale.

4.1.5 *Incomes*

There have been many investigations of the distribution of incomes. It is commonly accepted that it is a unimodal skewed distribution with a tail extending far into the higher incomes. This suggests that it would be appropriate to assume that incomes are distributed among consumers according to the log-normal distribution.

In summary then, the *a priori* assumptions made about the distributions among consumers of the variables affecting their behaviour are that prices are identical for all consumers and that tastes, technical coefficients and incomes are log-normally distributed. In the next section the theory of group behaviour will be built up, based in part on these distribution assumptions. It is realised, of course, that empirical observation and testing may lead, at any stage, to the modification or abandonment of the assumptions. On the other hand provided tastes, technologies and incomes are assumed to have *some* variance between consumers, the *exact* form of the distribution may be immaterial.

4.2 DIFFUSION CURVES FOR NEW COMMODITIES

Throughout this section it is assumed that individuals' priority ordering of wants and the size of their want saturation levels are constant through time.

4.2.1 *Static situation*

By a 'static situation' is meant a situation where prices of commodities and the incomes and technology coefficients of consumers also are constant, but where a new commodity is made available to the market at some instant of time.

Initially it should be supposed that, at the instant of time, t_0, when a new commodity, j, becomes available, the elements of the columns $\mathbf{w}_j$ of the consumers' technology matrices will be zero for all consumers. In this case there would be no reason for any consumer to include the commodity in his optimum budget, so that aggregate consumption of the commodity would be nil.

However, it seems likely that some (perhaps only a few) consumers might have some advance knowledge of the new commodity, having experienced it in another country, or read about it in some advertising literature. In this case, for these consumers, some of the elements of $\mathbf{w}_j$ would be positive. Suppose further, for simplification, that the new commodity provides satisfaction for only one want, the kth, so that $\overline{w}_{kj} > 0$, $\sigma^2_{kj} > 0$ and for $i \neq k$, $\overline{w}_{ij} = \sigma^2_{ij} = 0$.

Consider next the linear programmes for consumers:

$$z_i = \mathbf{w}_i \mathbf{x} = \max$$

$$\begin{bmatrix} -\mathbf{W}_{i-1} \\ \mathbf{p}' \end{bmatrix} \mathbf{x} \leqslant \begin{bmatrix} -\mathbf{z}^*_{i-1} \\ y \end{bmatrix}$$

$$\mathbf{x} \geqslant \mathbf{0}.$$

Consumers with $i < k$ will not alter their optimum budgets, even if $w_{kj} > 0$, since the new commodity provides satisfaction for a sub-marginal want, and hence w_{kj} does not appear in the specification of their programme, though it does of course appear in $\mathbf{W}$. Consumers with $i = k$ (i.e. where the new commodity satisfies the marginal want) will now change their optimum budget to include some of the new commodity if the set of efficient points in the want space changes the facet on which the optimum point lies. This change occurs if there exist certain relationships between the elements of $\mathbf{W}$, $\mathbf{z}^*$ and $\mathbf{p}$.† Similarly, consumers with $i > k$ (i.e. where the new commodity satisfies a supra-marginal want) will also change their optimum budgets to include some of the new commodity if similar conditions hold.

Thus in an essentially static situation in which a few consumers have some advance information of the want-satisfying powers of the new commodity, there will be an immediate adjustment to the new commodity. It will be included in the budgets of those consumers for which the commodity satisfies marginal or supra-marginal wants and for which conditions are suitable.

For all individuals the rate of consumption, x_j, of the new commodity will be zero up to the time of its introduction, t_0. After t_0, for some individuals (type a consumers) x_j will be positive but for the remainder (type b consumers) x_j will continue to be zero (see figure 4.1). Hence in this static situation the aggregate diffusion curve for the new commodity will be a step function with a height equal to the sum of the consumptions of type a consumers (not necessarily identical amounts).

4.2.2   *Changes in the static situation*

Now if the consumers increase their evaluations of the want-satisfying powers of the new commodity, there will be a change in the static situation and a further diffusion of the new commodity can be expected. A greater proportion of consumers will buy the commodity and perhaps those already buying will buy more.

† *See* chapter 3, section 3.6, for linear programming results.

What is it that will lead consumers to increase their evaluations of the want satisfying powers of a new commodity? Just as it was supposed that the initial buyers had some knowledge of the new commodity – and it is indeed essential that they obtain this knowledge – then it can be supposed that other consumers are likely to obtain a knowledge

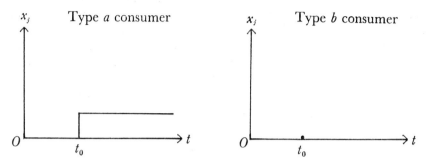

Figure 4.1. Consumption paths: two types of consumers

of the characteristics of the new commodity. This diffusion or spread of knowledge through the body of consumers will be governed by the amount of advertising and display of the new commodity, by whether the commodity is by its nature one that will be easily noticed by others when it is consumed, etc. The spread of knowledge will also no doubt depend on how important an opportunity the new commodity presents for economising or achieving a hitherto unattainable direction of consumption. Knowledge about important new commodities may spread more quickly than knowledge of the unimportant.

Such a diffusion of knowledge will lead to an evaluation of the want satisfying powers of the new commodity – a filling in of the blanks in the consumer's technology matrix for this commodity. This spread of knowledge through the body of consumers can be regarded as being similar to the diffusion of a gas or the spread of an epidemic disease.

To describe systematically this diffusion process, and to attempt some measurement of it, a function to explicitly describe the process is needed. A function that readily comes to mind is the epidemic curve used for the description of the spread of infectious diseases such as measles. This curve has as its core the idea of a constant infection rate.

4.2.4 *Deterministic diffusion process*

The spread of consumption of the new commodity through the population of consumers is due to the successive re-adjustment, as knowledge is obtained, of elements of the column $\mathbf{w}_j$ of the consumers' technology matrices so that the mean values of the distributions of the elements of $\mathbf{w}_j$ are increasing through time. This is to be expected with a new commodity for which initially the great majority of consumers do not know anything of its want-satisfying powers.† As some consumers start to consume the new commodity, this consumption is observed by other consumers so that, as time goes on, more and more consumers obtain some knowledge of the want-satisfying powers of the new commodity.‡ This process leads to further increases in the number of consumers of the commodity and so continues until stability is reached, if other conditions remain unchanged.

If the main cause of the diffusion in consumption of a new commodity among consumers is due to the successive re-evaluation of the want-satisfying powers of the commodity, then we may consider a simple model of this behaviour in terms of a constant infection rate β so that the absolute number of new buyers per unit of time is

$$\frac{dn_a}{dt} = \beta n_a n_b$$

$$= N\beta n_a - \beta n_a^2,$$

where n_a = number of buyers

n_b = number of non-buyers

and N = total number of consumers

$$= n_a + n_b$$

The solution of this differential equation gives us the logistic equation

$$n_a = \frac{N}{1 + be^{-N\beta t + c}}$$

usually taken with $c = 0$. Hence at $t = 0$ the initial number of type a consumers is $N/(1+b)$. Expressed as a percentage, the initial number of consumers buying is

$$p_0 = \frac{100}{1+b}$$

Hence the coefficient

$$b = \frac{100 - p_0}{p_0}$$

This initial number of buyers starts to infect the remaining population so that the proportion of buyers in the population increases, exhibiting the sigmoid-shaped growth curve of the logistic.§

† Hence they put these powers at zero values for purposes of planning an optimum budget.
‡ Hence putting these powers at above zero values.
§ The behaviour model just described is known as the deterministic epidemic model, *see* for example Bailey (1950).

Put in terms of the rates at which consumers shift from being type b to being type a, we can regard the growth as having four stages:

(i) a stage when a few initial consumers shift

(ii) a stage when an increasing number shift, the rate of shifting moving up to a maximum

(iii) a stage when the rate of shifting declines

(iv) stability when practically no more shifts occur

Stage (iv) is reached since all (or all potential) consumers of the commodity have become consumers of it.

4.2.5 Logistic and Gompertz curves

If we examine the pattern of diffusion in consumption of new products that is revealed in the statistical series for the United Kingdom presented subsequently in chapter 7, we see that the pattern of diffusion through time has a sigmoid shape.

Studies such as Derksen and Rombouts (1937) and Dernberg (1957) have used the logistic curve to describe the general shape of the diffusion of demand through time. This curve has the general sigmoid shape of a cumulative normal distribution.

The 1937 study suggested that the equation

$$P = \frac{100}{1 + e^{-\beta t}}$$

where P is percentage ownership and t is time – 'the well-known form of a saturation curve'† – could be used to describe the diffusion in consumption, whereas the 1957 study used the equation

$$P = \frac{100}{1 + e^{-(a + \sum_{i} b_i x_i)}}$$

where P is percentage of the population owning the commodity and x_i is the i-th of a set of n independent variables (not including time explicitly).

Similar sigmoid characteristics are described well by the Gompertz curve

$$P = 100 a^{b^t}$$

where P is the percentage of the population owning the commodity and t is time (a and b constants). Croxton and Cowden (1939) fit this curve to the growth in the United States of total consumption of rayon, a new commodity. Prescott (1922) concludes that Gompertz curve trends are common to many industries and puts the period of growth into four stages: (1) a period of experimentation, (2) a period of growth

† Derksen and Rombouts (1937), p. 296.

7

'into the social fabric', (3) a period during which the rate of growth is retarded as saturation point is reached, and (4) a period of stability.

Both the logistic and the Gompertz curves come from the family of curves defined by the first-order differential equation of the form

$$\frac{dy}{dt} = g(t)F\left(\frac{y}{k}\right)y$$

where $g(t)$ is some function of time and $F(y/k)$ is a function which is zero when $y = k$.

Putting

$$F(y/k) = y/k - 1$$

we get the logistic

$$\frac{dy}{dt} = g(t)\frac{(y-k)}{k}y$$

and putting

$$F(y/k) = \log(y/k)$$

we obtain the Gompertz

$$\frac{dy}{dt} = g(t)\log(y/k)y$$

In fitting these curves $g(t)$ is usually taken as a constant. The main practical difference between the logistic and Gompertz forms is that the first differences of the former form a symmetric distribution round the period of fastest growth while the first differences of the latter form a skewed distribution, with a tail extending to the right along the time axis.

It is suggested that the observed strong growth in consumption of new commodities probably occurs through their diffusion in this manner. From the limited knowledge of the growth patterns of new commodities, it would appear that it is this upward revision of the consumers' estimates of the commodities' want-satisfying powers that is the major determinant of the growth. However, of course, prices of the new commodity may also undergo a relative fall on account of improved techniques of production and also it is probable that real incomes will be rising. Both these changes should act in the same direction of stimulating growth, nevertheless the suggestion here is that these factors are incidental, the main stimulus being the revision of the consumers' estimates of the quality of the commodity.

The interdependence of consumers' estimates of these qualities is probably of great importance in effecting these revisions. Duesenberry gives an example of the diffusion of consumption of a new product which is either bought as one unit or not bought at all, and where preferences for the new product depend on its rate of sale in the period just passed.†

Can it be said that one of the important effects of new products is that they give a 'ratchet effect' to the consumption function? In so far as the new product just replaces old products, say by doing the same job more cheaply, then there is no ratchet effect. But if the new products mean that the consumer is able to satisfy wants he was unable to satisfy before, i.e. unable to satisfy even with an increased income, then there is a ratchet effect. A ratchet effect implies a pushing up of the consumption function so that although the instantaneous consumption function, with any given range of commodities, shows that savings become a higher proportion of income as income is increased, when new products are introduced, the consumption function for the now enlarged range of commodities still shows the same shape as before but at a higher level. The mean real income will probably have increased meanwhile so that at the mean income, the proportion saved is approximately the same both before and after the range of commodities has been enlarged.

4.3 BUDGET STUDY ENGEL CURVES

In the analysis of family budgets, much attention has been paid to the mathematical form of the Engel curves for commodities. For example, Prais and Houthakker (1955) consider five forms of Engel curves‡

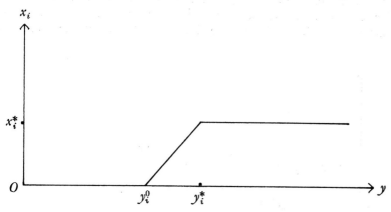

Figure 4.2. Individual Engel curve for a commodity

and in relation to the 1937–9 United Kingdom budget studies of expenditure on broad groups of commodities they conclude that it is best to fit the semi-log for foods and the double log for non-foods.

† Duesenberry (1949), pp. 104–10.

‡ The double log: $\log x = a + b \log y$; the log inverse: $\log x = a - by^{-1}$; the semi-log: $x = a + b \log y$; the linear $x = a + by$; and the hyperbola: $x = a - by^{-1}$.

The form that budget study Engel curves would take under the assumptions of the present theory will therefore be investigated.

In the very simplified case of non-overlapping wants and specific commodities, the commodity saturation levels for an individual consumer are $\mathbf{x}^* = \mathbf{W}^{-1}\mathbf{z}^*$. For any given set of prices, the threshold and saturation levels of income corresponding to the commodity saturation levels can be specified. For example, the threshold level of income for commodity 2 equals the saturation level of income for commodity 1, which in turn equals $p_1 x_1^*$. These threshold and saturation levels of income specify where the 'kinks' occur in the individual's Engel curve for a commodity. In general, for the individual consumer, the Engel curve for the ith commodity is as in figure 4.2, where x_i^* is the commodity saturation level and y_i^0 and y_i^* are the threshold and saturation levels of income respectively.

For consumers with non-overlapping wants and specific commodities, the slope of the Engel curve between y_i^0 and y_i^* is $1/p_i$ and hence under the assumption made about prices in section 1 of this chapter, this slope is the same for all consumers. However the y_i^0 and y_i^* will not be identical for all consumers, since the x_i^* have been assumed to be log-normally distributed so that y_i^0 and y_i^* will be distributed as the weighted sum of $i-1$ and i log-normally distributed variates. This is rather awkward, since aggregates of log-normal variates are more easily handled as products than as sums. If however the x_i^* are normally distributed, then the y_i^0 and y_i^* will also be normally distributed.

For any commodity, let us examine the joint distribution of consumers on the $Oy_i^0 y_i^*$ plane. The line $y^0 = y^*$ divides the consumers

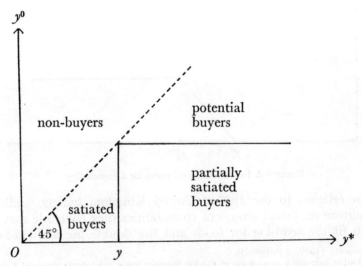

Figure 4.3. Threshold and saturation incomes: types of buyers

naturally into two groups: buyers and potential buyers (where $y_0 < y^*$) and non-buyers (where $y_0 \geqslant y^*$). In addition, for any actual level of income y, the group of buyers and potential buyers is further divided into three groups – satiated buyers (where $y \geqslant y^*$), partially satiated buyers (where $y^0 < y < y^*$) and potential buyers (where $y \leqslant y^0$). These regions on the Oy^0y^* plane are shown in figure 4.3.

The quantity x_r bought by the rth consumer is given by the equations

$$
\left.
\begin{aligned}
x_r &= 0 & \text{where } y \leqslant y_r^0 \\
x_r &= \frac{1}{p}(y - y_r^0) & \text{where } y_r^0 < y < y_r^* \\
x_r &= \frac{1}{p}(y_r^* - y_r^0) & \text{where } y_r^* \leqslant y
\end{aligned}
\right\} \text{ for } y_r^* > y_r^0
$$

$$
x_r = 0 \qquad \text{whatever } y \qquad \text{for } y_r^* \leqslant y_r^0
$$

These equations are used in the ensuing sections to derive the budget-study Engel curve for a commodity on two alternative assumptions about the bivariate distribution of threshold and saturation levels of income.

4.3.1 *A bivariate rectangular distribution of threshold and saturation incomes*
With the further assumption that consumers are not distributed uniformly over the whole Oy^0y^* plane but are concentrated in some part of it, the aggregate budget study Engel curve may be found.

A simple hypothesis is that they are distributed uniformly over the

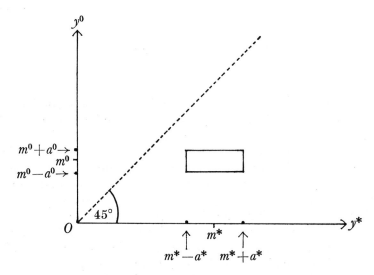

Figure 4.4. Uniform distribution of threshold and saturation incomes

area $m^0 \pm a^0$, $m^* \pm a^*$, and that $m^0 + a^0 = m^* - a^*$ so that no consumers are non-buyers (see figure 4.4).

At any level of income y let $f_1, f_2, f_3 f_4$ be the proportions of consumers who are non-buyers, potential buyers, partially satiated buyers, and satiated buyers, and let x_1, x_2, x_3, x_4 be the mean quantities bought by the consumers in these groups. Then $\sum_{i=1}^{4} f_i x_i$ is the aggregate quantity bought, x, and the overall average quantity $\bar{x}$ is $x/\sum_{i=1}^{4} f_i = x$, since $\sum_{=1}^{4} f_i = 1$.

A table showing the frequencies and mean quantities for various levels of income can be constructed. As x_1 and x_2 are always zero, we need only consider f_3, f_4, x_3, x_4.

Income	Proportion of consumers		Mean quantity bought		
y	f_3	f_4	x_3	x_4	x
$y < m^0 - a^0$	0	0	0	0	0
$m^0 - a^0 < y < m^0 + a^0$	$\dfrac{y - m^0 + a^0}{2a^0}$	0	$\dfrac{y - m^0 + a^0}{2p}$	0	$\dfrac{(y - m^0 + a^0)^2}{4a^0 p}$
$m^0 + a^0 < y < m^* - a^*$	1	0	$\dfrac{y - m^0}{p}$	0	$\dfrac{y - m^0}{p}$
$m^* - a^* < y < m^* a^*$	$\dfrac{m^* + a^* - y}{2a^*}$	$\dfrac{y - m^* + a^*}{2a^0}$	$\dfrac{y - m^0}{p}$	$\dfrac{y - m^* - 2m^0 - a^*}{2p}$	$\dfrac{m^* - m^0}{p} -$ $\dfrac{(y - (m^* + a^*))^2}{4a^* p}$
$m^* + a^* < y$	0	1	$\cdots$	$\dfrac{m^* - m^0}{p}$	$\dfrac{m^* - m^0}{p}$

Thus the Engel curve for all consumers is a combination of linear and parabolic functions, which form an S-shaped curve (see figure 4.5). Over the range of income from $m^0 - a^0$ to $m^0 + a^0$ consumption is increasing at an increasing rate since (a) the proportion of consumers buying a positive quantity is increasing at a constant rate and (b) the mean quantity bought by those who buy is increasing at a constant rate.

Over the range of income $m^* - a^*$ to $m^* + a^*$ consumption is increasing at a decreasing rate since (a) although the proportion of satiated consumers and the mean quantity consumed by these are both increasing at a constant rate, (b) the proportion of partially satiated consumers is decreasing and the aggregate quantity bought by this group eventually (for $y > \frac{1}{2}\{m^* + a^* + m^0\}$) decreases.

When there are non-buyers, some modification of the equations describing the aggregate budget-study Engel curves will be necessary.

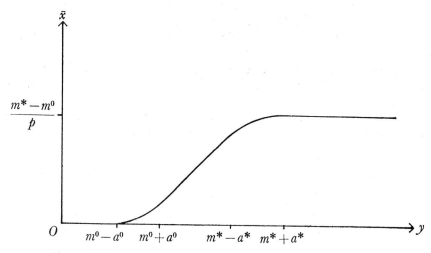

Figure 4.5. Aggregate Engel curve derived from a uniform distribution

4.3.2   *A bivariate normal distribution of threshold and saturation incomes*

Suppose that consumers are distributed over the Oy^0y^* plane in a bivariate normal distribution with means m^0, m^*, standard deviations σ_0, σ_1 and correlation coefficient ρ. Suppose further that $\rho = 0$ so that initial and saturation incomes are independent, and that the mean

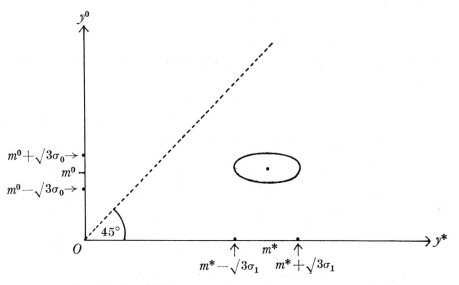

Figure 4.6. Normal distribution of threshold and saturation incomes

point (m^0, m^*) is sufficiently far away from the line $y^0 = y^*$ for the proportion of non-buyers to be insignificant.

The ellipse of concentration for the distribution can be represented as in figure 4.6, and will be a circle when $\sigma_0 = \sigma_1$.

As with the previous example of a uniform distribution for any level of actual income, y, the distribution will be divided into three classes of consumers, and a table showing the proportion of consumers in each class and mean quantities bought by each class can be calculated.

Let $y = m^0 + r\sigma_0$ and $\bar{}_3 = m^0 - \bar{r}_3\sigma_0$ then for various values of r, we can calculate the lower tail of the Engel curve as:

r	f_3	$\bar{r}_3$	$r - \bar{r}_3$	$\dfrac{px}{\sigma_0} = f_3(r - \bar{r}_3)$
-3.0	0.0013499	-3.2831321	0.2831321	0.0003822
-2.0	0.0227501	-2.3732200	0.3732200	0.0084908
-1.0	0.1586553	-1.5251347	0.5251347	0.0833154
-0.5	0.3085375	-1.1410778	0.6410778	0.1977965
0	0.5000000	-0.7978846	0.7978846	0.3989423
0.5	0.6914625	-0.5091604	1.0091604	0.6977966
1.0	0.8413447	-0.2876000	1.2876000	1.0833154
2.0	0.9772499	-0.0552479	2.0552479	2.0084908
3.0	0.9986501	-0.0044379	3.0044379	3.0003822

Notes: f_3 from tables of areas under standard normal curve.

$\bar{r}_3$ from tables of means of truncated standard normal distribution.

Similarly with $\quad y = m^* + r\sigma_1$

$$\bar{y}_4 = m^* + \bar{r}_4\sigma_1$$

and $\qquad m^0 = m^* - h\sigma_1$

we can calculate the upper tail of the Engel curve for various values of r as follows:

r	f_3	f_4	$\bar{r}_4$	$\dfrac{px - h}{\sigma_1} = rf_3 + f_4\bar{r}_4$
-3.0	0.9986501	0.0013499	-3.2831321	-3.0003822
-2.0	0.9772499	0.0227501	-2.3732200	-2.0084908
-1.0	0.8413447	0.1586553	-1.5251347	-1.0833154
-0.5	0.6914625	0.3085375	-1.1410778	-0.6977966
0.0	0.5000000	0.5000000	-0.7978846	-0.3989423
0.5	0.3085375	0.6914625	-0.5091604	-0.1977965
1.0	0.1586553	0.8413447	-0.2876000	-0.0833154
2.0	0.0227501	0.9772499	-0.0552479	-0.0084908
3.0	0.0013499	0.9986501	-0.0044379	-0.0003822

Notes: f_3 and f_4 from tables of areas under standard normal curve.

$\bar{r}_4$ from tables of means of truncated standard normal distribution.

4.3.3   *Comparison of Engel curves derived from uniform and normal distributions of threshold and saturation incomes*

We can compare the Engel curves for two groups of consumers – one with a uniform distribution of tastes and the other with a normal distribution of tastes. Suppose the means and standard errors of the

	Consumption x	
Income y	Uniform	Normal
3.0	0	0.0085
4.0	0	0.0833
4.5	0.0625	0.1978
5.0	0.2500	0.3989
5.5	0.5625	0.6978
6.0	1.0000	1.0833
7.0	2.0000	2.0085
8.0	3.0000	2.9915
9.0	4.0000	3.9167
9.5	4.4375	4.3921
10.0	4.7500	4.6011
10.5	4.9375	4.8022
11.0	5.0000	4.9167
12.0	5.0000	4.9915

(In units with $\sigma_1 = 1$.)

threshold income are identical for each group and that similarly the means and standard errors of the saturation incomes are identical. We

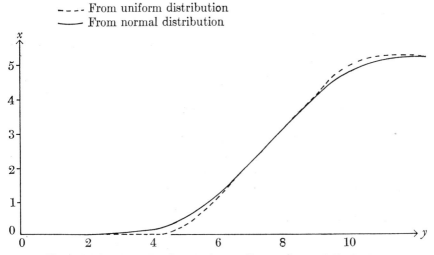

Figure 4.7. Aggregate Engel curves from uniform and normal distributions

shall also assume that the standard errors, σ_0 and σ_1, are equal and that the difference between the mean saturation income and the mean threshold income equals $5\sigma_1$. Also assuming that $p = 1$ and that $m^0 = 5\sigma_1$ say, we can calculate (from the equations in the table on page 84 and the tables on page 86 the Engel curves for both groups of consumers.

It will be noticed from the table and figure 4.7 that the resultant curves are very nearly the same. This suggests that the form of the distribution does not alter the shape of the aggregate curves very much.

4.4 DEMAND CURVES

Various hypotheses have been made about the mathematical form of the aggregate demand function relating aggregate consumption of a commodity to its price. For example Marshall mentions† the form $xp^a = b$ with a constant elasticity a, and Allen shows‡ eight function types as examples of suitable demand laws. A demand curve with a point of inflexion and which cuts the quantity axis sharply has been suggested by Farrell (1954). Subsequently Brown has found demand curves for butter and margarine with sigmoid characteristics.§

We propose to examine the form of the demand curves for groups of consumers with different incomes, different saturation levels and different technologies, to see whether, under the assumptions of the present theory, the aggregate demand curve cuts off sharply at either the price or the quantity axis.

4.4.1 *Different incomes*

Consider a group of consumers with the same tastes (priorities and saturation levels of wants) and the same technologies (technical co-efficients) but with different incomes. To make the situation extremely simple, consider the case where there are just two wants, of which the first has a saturation level z_1^*, and just two commodities, each capable of jointly satisfying both wants, but commodity 1 is more specific to want 1 than commodity 2, and hence 2 is more specific to want 2 than 1.

In the want space A is the extreme point of the vector representing commodity 1 and B is the extreme point for the vector representing commodity 2. Thus A is the point with coordinates $w_{11}y/p_1$, $w_{21}y/p_1$ and B is the point $w_{12}y/p_2$, $w_{22}y/p_2$. Consider the situation as p_2 varies with p_1 and y fixed. Here A will remain fixed but B will move along the line joining it to the origin.

† Marshall (1890), 8th edn 1920, Mathematical Appendix, p. 840.
‡ Allen (1938), p. 114.   § Brown (1959), p. 9.

(a) Consider those consumers with income levels such that $A < z_1^*$, as shown in figure 4.8.

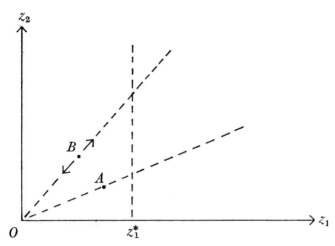

Figure 4.8. Want space: price changes with income less than saturation

Then as long as the z_1 coordinate of B is less than the z_1 coordinate of A (i.e. $w_{12}y/p_2 < w_{11}y/p_1$), A is the chosen budget point. When $w_{12}y/p_2 > w_{11}y/p_1$ then B is the chosen budget point. Hence the uncompensated demand curve for x_2 is of the form of a truncated hyperbola, as shown in figure 4.9.

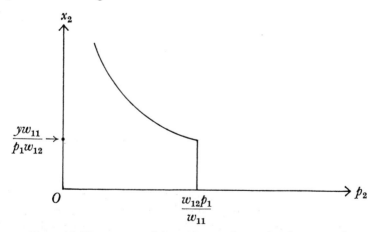

Figure 4.9. Uncompensated demand curve: income less than saturation

The 'opening' price at which x_2 is bought is $p_2 = w_{12}p_1/w_{11}$, and the quantity bought at this price is yw_{11}/p_1w_{12}. Hence for these consumers the opening price is independent of income but the opening quantity is not, so that for different income levels the demand curves will be in different positions corresponding to figure 4.10, curves further from the origin corresponding to higher income levels.

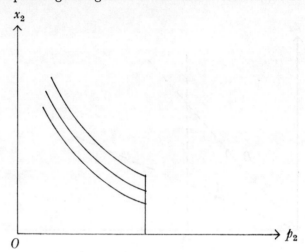

Figure 4.10. Uncompensated demand curves: different income levels

(b) Next consider those consumers with income levels such that $A > z_1^*$ (see figure 4.11).

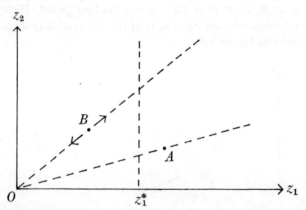

Figure 4.11. Want space: price changes with income greater than saturation

In this situation, the opening price at which some of commodity 2 will be bought is where the z_2 coordinate of B is greater than the z_2 coordinate of A (i.e. where $w_{22}y/p_2 > w_{21}y/p_1$). Hence this opening price is $p_2 = w_{22}p_1/w_{21}$, which is independent of the income level. Now as p_2 is decreased below its opening price, x_2 will increase according to the relation

$$x_2 = \frac{w_{11}y - p_1 z_1^*}{p_2 w_{11} - p_1 w_{12}}$$

so long as the z_1 coordinate of B is less than z_1^*. Beyond this point, where $p_2 = w_{12}y/z_1^*$, the relationship between x_2 and p_2 becomes $x_2 = y/p_2$.

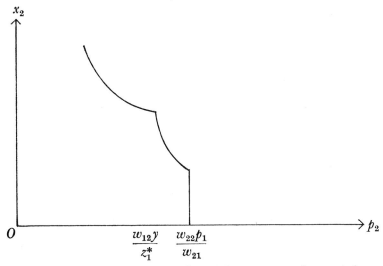

Figure 4.12. Uncompensated demand curve: income greater than saturation

Thus for these consumers the uncompensated demand curve will have the form shown in figure 4.12. However, the second discontinuity, where $p_2 = w_{12}y/z_1^*$, does depend on income, so that for those consumers with incomes $y > p_1 w_{22} z_* / w_{12} w_{21}$, there will be only one

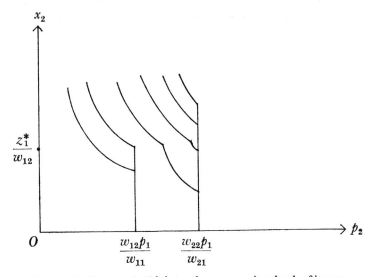

Figure 4.13. Uncompensated demand curves: various levels of income

discontinuity point at $p_2 = w_{22}p_1/w_{21}$, with consumption switching immediately from commodity 1 to commodity 2 without any intermediate stage of consuming both.

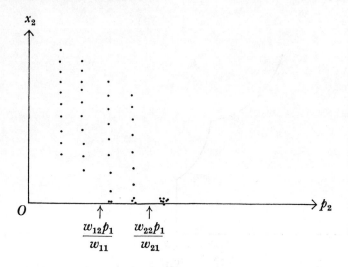

Figure 4.14. Uncompensated distribution of ten consumers: five price levels

(c) Now considering all consumer's together, the pattern of their individual demand curves will be as shown in figure 4.13. At any particular price the distribution of consumers over various levels of consumption will be determined by the distribution of incomes. The distribution of 10 consumers with different incomes, at five different levels of prices, might be expected to be somewhat as in figure 4.14.

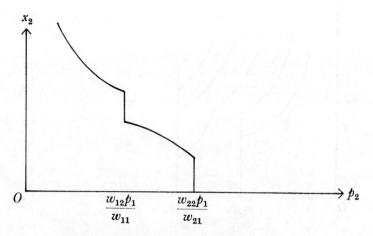

Figure 4.15. Aggregate demand curve: uncompensated

With these distributions, the aggregate uncompensated demand curve for these consumers would have a shape something like the curve in figure 4.15, regardless of whether the income distribution was log-normal or not.

The compensated demand curves for these consumers with different incomes but with the same tastes and technologies can also be considered. To do this needs consideration of a method of compensation which involves compensating the consumer for changes in p_2 by adjustments to y_0, his original income, that will put him in a situation where he is as well off as he could be if commodity 2 were not available at all. This involves adjustments in the incomes of the consumers to return them to the indifference line through the point A $(w_{11}y_0/p_1, w_{22}y_0/p_1)$, which is the extreme point of the vector in the want space representing commodity 1.

(a) Again consider those consumers where incomes, y_0, are such that

$$y_0 < \frac{z_1^* p_1}{w_{11}}$$

Now when $p_2 = w_{12}p_1/w_{11}$, A and B are on the same indifference line. At this level of price either $x_1 = y_0/p_1$ or $x_2 = w_{11}y_0/w_{12}p_1$. Suppose consumers are compensated for changes in the price of commodity 2 by adjustments of income to return them to the indifference line passing through A. Then at prices $p_2 > w_{12}p_1/w_{11}$ no compensation is necessary and consumption of commodity 2 is zero, while at prices below this point, income reductions will be necessary to bring the optimum point back to the indifference line of the original situation. This means that $x_2 = w_{11}y_0/w_{12}p_1$, where $y_0 =$ original income level. Hence the compensated demand curves for these consumers will be of the form given in figure 4.16.

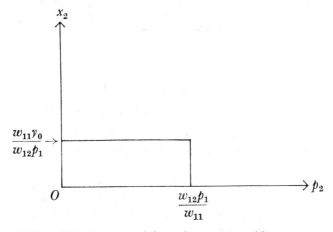

Figure 4.16. Compensated demand curve: group (a) consumers

(b) Next consider those consumers whose incomes y_0 are such that

$$\frac{p_1 w_{22} z_1^*}{w_{12} w_{21}} > y_0 > \frac{z_1^* p_1}{w_{11}}$$

Then A lies somewhere along the section (b) of the line $z_2 = (w_{21}/w_{11}) z_1$, through the origin of the want space (see figure 4.17).

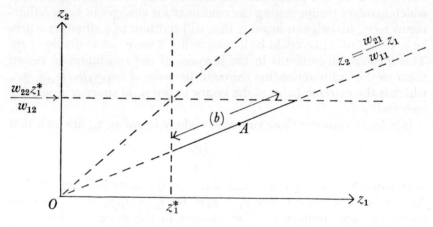

Figure 4.17. Want space: group (b) consumers

Now consider keeping the consumer on the indifference line passing through A (parallel to the Oz_1 axis), by adjusting income to allow for changes in p_2.

(i) When $p_2 > w_{22} p_1 / w_{21}$ no income compensation is needed and x_2 is zero.

(ii) When $w_{22} p_1 / w_{21} > p_2 > w_{12} p_1 / w_{11}$ cutting income can always compensate to bring the consumer back to the point $(z_1^*, w_{21} y_0 / p_1)$ on the indifference curve passing through A.

Here

$$x_2 = \frac{w_{21}(w_{11} y_0 - p_1 z_1^*)}{p_1(w_{11} w_{22} - w_{21} w_{12})}$$

= a constant whatever the value of p_2 within these limits.

(iii) But for $p_2 < w_{12} p_1 / w_{11}$ no amount of income cutting can bring the consumer exactly back to the indifference curve passing through A. Cuts in income will reduce his utility level but still leave him better off than originally, until B reaches the point $(z_1^*, w_{22} z_1^* / w_{12})$, where any further income reductions make the consumer much worse off than originally. Therefore consider reducing income to this point but no further. Here $x_2 = z_1^* / w_{12}$ = a constant for any value of

$p_2 < w_{12}p_1/w_{11}$. Thus the compensated demand curves for this group of consumers will be of the form given in figure 4.18.

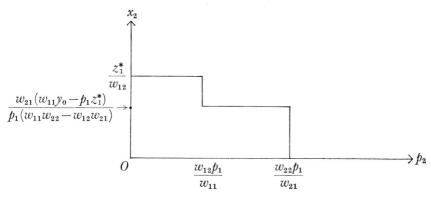

Figure 4.18. Compensated demand curve: group (b) consumers

(c) There is a possible third group of consumers whose incomes, y_0, are greater than $p_1w_{22}z_1^*/w_{12}w_{21}$. The point A for a consumer in this group will be on the section of the line $z_2 = (w_{21}/w_{11})z_1$ further from the origin than the section marked (b) in figure 4.17.

For these consumers no income compensation will be necessary while $p_2 > w_{22}p_1/w_{21}$ and $x_2 = 0$. Exact income compensation will always be possible for $p_2 < w_{22}p_1/w_{21}$, the optimum point being brought back to the point

$$\left(\frac{w_{12}w_{21}y_0}{w_{22}p_1}, \frac{w_{21}y_0}{p_1} \right)$$

where $x_2 = y_0w_{21}/p_1w_{22}$.

The compensated demand curves for the consumers with the highest

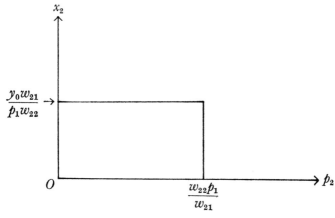

Figure 4.19. Compensated demand curve: group (c) consumers

incomes will therefore be of the form given in figure 4.19. Considering all consumers together, the pattern of their compensated demand curves when put onto the same diagram is as in figure 4.20. Considering

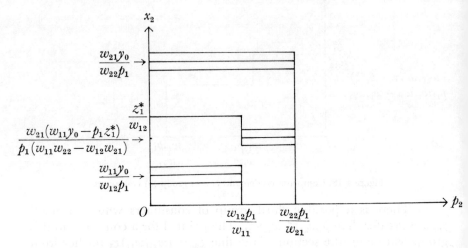

Figure 4.20. Compensated demand curves: all levels of income

the actual distribution of say, ten consumers with various incomes, at five different levels of price they will be distributed somewhat as in figure 4.21. The aggregate compensated demand curve for this group of consumers would form a double step-function, with steps at the prices indicated in figure 4.22. The actual heights of the steps will depend on the actual distribution of income.

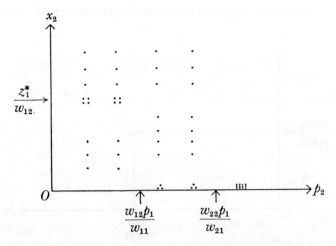

Figure 4.21. Compensated distribution of ten consumers: five price levels

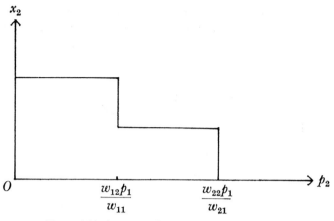

Figure 4.22. Aggregate demand curve: compensated

4.4.2 *Different saturation levels*

The situation can be examined from the aspect of different saturation levels, rather than from the aspect of different income levels. Consider two consumers, consumer 1 having a higher saturation level for the first of two wants. There are two commodities, the technologies being the same for both consumers, and $w_{11}/w_{21} > w_{12}/w_{22}$. Income is the same for both and will remain constant along with p_1, while changes in p_2 are studied. Let z_{11}^* and z_{12}^* represent the saturation levels for the prior want for the two consumers.

Case 1 (see figure 4.23). Income is such that A is below both z_{11}^* and z_{12}^*, i.e.

$$\frac{w_{11}y}{p_1} < z_{12}^* < z_{11}^*$$

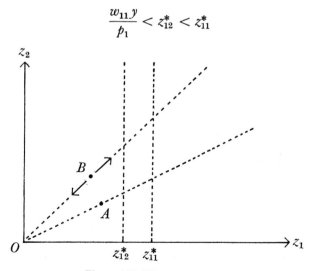

Figure 4.23. Want space: case 1

In this situation both consumers will consume identical amounts at all levels of p_2, their uncompensated demand curve being a truncated hyperbola with an 'opening' price at $p_2 = w_{12}p_1/w_{11}$.

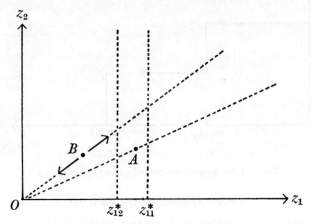

Figure 4.24. Want space: case 2

Case 2 (see figure 4.24). Income is such that A lies between z_{11}^* and z_{12}^*, i.e.

$$z_{12}^* < \frac{w_{11}y}{p_1} < z_{11}^*$$

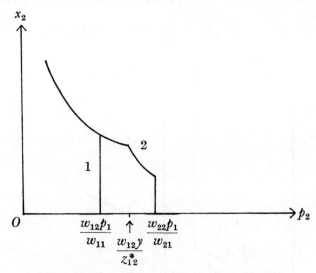

Figure 4.25. Individual demand curves: cases 1 and 2

This results in the consumers having common demand curves for p_2 *outside* the range

$$\frac{w_{12}p_1}{w_{11}} < p_2 < \frac{w_{22}p_1}{w_{21}}$$

but within this range only consumer 2's consumption of commodity 2 is positive. The two demand curves are shown in figure 4.25.

Case 3 (see figure 4.26.) Income is such that A lies above both z_{11}^* and z_{12}^*, i.e.

$$z_{12}^* < z_{11}^* < \frac{w_{11}y}{p_1}$$

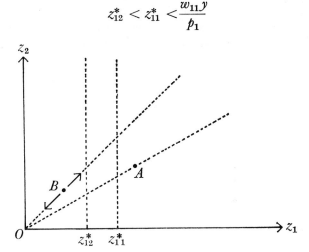

Figure 4.26. Want space: case 3

So long as $p_2 > w_{22}p_1/w_{21}$, neither will buy any of commodity 2, but at this opening price, consumer 2 will buy more than consumer 1 of commodity 2, and as p_2 declines further, consumer 2, with the lower saturation level, will increase his consumption of commodity 2 at a

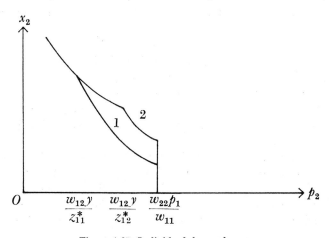

Figure 4.27. Individual demand curves

faster rate† than consumer 1, until price has declined to $p_2 = w_{12}y/z^*_{12}$. At this point consumer 2 will not be buying commodity 1, whereas the other will still be buying both. As price declines further, x_{21} (consumption of commodity 2 by consumer 1) will increase at a faster rate than x_{22} until at price $p_2 = w_{12}y/w_{11}$, $x_{22} = x_{21}$. The relative shapes of their demand curves are as in figure 4.27.

Considering a group of consumers with different income levels and different saturation levels again the aggregate uncompensated demand curve would be expected to have a general shape similar to the curve in figure 4.15 above, i.e. downward sloping with two steps at the prices

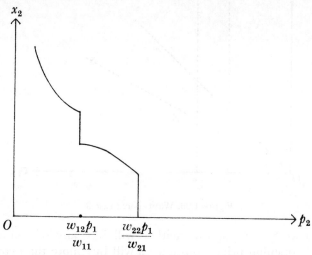

Figure 4.28. Aggregate demand curve: uncompensated

indicated (see figure 4.28). The distribution of saturation levels will determine the shape of the aggregate curve between the two step-prices.

4.4.3 *Different technologies*

Consider next two consumers with identical saturation levels and incomes, facing two wants and two commodities as before, but for which the technology matrices are not quite identical; three coefficients are equal but $w_{12(1)} < w_{12(2)}$. That is to say, consumer 1 rates the ability of commodity 2 to satisfy the first want somewhat lower than does consumer 2.

In the want space, A, the point $(w_{11}y/p_1, w_{21}y/p_1)$ will be identical for both consumers, but the points B_1 $(w_{12(1)}y/p_2, w_{22}y/p_2)$ and B_2 $(w_{12(2)}y/p_2, w_{22}y/p_2)$ differ in their z_1 coordinates (see figure 4.29).

Consider the case where $y < p_1z^*_1/w_{11}$. Then as p_2 declines, the opening price at which consumer 2 switches to commodity 2 will be

† But with the same elasticity.

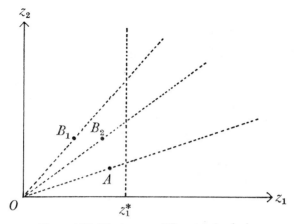

Figure 4.29. Want space: different technologies

$p_2 = w_{12(2)}p_1/w_{11}$ (for consumer 2) which is greater than the opening price $p_2 = w_{12(1)}p_1/w_{11}$ for consumer 1. The uncompensated demand curves will be as in figure 4.30.

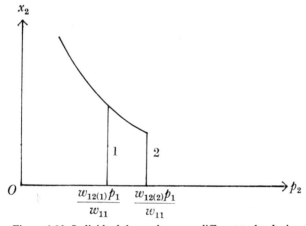

Figure 4.30. Individual demand curves: different technologies

As in the cases of different saturation levels and different incomes, the various curves resulting from various combinations of different technologies and different incomes could be considered. However, enough has been shown to indicate that the double steps of the aggregate uncompensated demand curves (in figures 4.15 and 4.27 above) and of the compensated curve (in figure 4.22 above) would tend to smooth out if consumers had different technical coefficients. The shape of the aggregate demand curve is still rather inexact, and whether or not it cuts off sharply at either the price or the quantity axis would seem difficult to decide on the basis of the factors considered here.

4.5 Examples: aggregate Engel curves

Consider 10 consumers, faced with the range of 15 commodities listed
on page 44 above, which satisfy the five needs, calories, protein,
vitamin C, riboflavin and calcium. Suppose that the technology
matrix of the want satisfying powers of these commodities is identical
for each consumer and is as specified in the matrix on page 44. Further
suppose that the saturation levels for the wants are identical for each
consumer *but* the consumers have different tastes in that they rank the
order of priority of the five wants differently.

There are 120 possible different ways of ranking five wants. Suppose
the rankings of our 10 consumers are as follows:

					Consumer					
Rank	1	2	3	4	5	6	7	8	9	10
1	c	p	v	r	m	m	p	c	r	v
2	p	v	m	c	r	p	r	m	v	c
3	v	m	r	p	c	c	m	v	p	r
4	r	c	p	m	v	r	v	p	c	m
5	m	r	c	v	p	v	c	r	m	p

(where: c = calories, p = protein, v = vitamin C, r = riboflavin, m = calcium.)

With an income of 107.91 pence per week and the prices of the
commodities as given on page 44, these consumers will all be able to
satiate their five wants and will all have identical budgets consisting
of 99 oz of bread, 381 oz of potatoes, and 4 pints of milk (to nearest oz
or pint). However, at incomes less than these, each consumer will
tend to have a different optimum budget than his fellows since the
different priority orderings will affect the choices made. The Engel
curves for each consumer can be found in the same way that we found
the Engel curves for consumer 1 on pages 65–7. These individual
curves show similar kinks and bends. However, on aggregation we
find that the aggregate Engel curves are more regular in shape, the
individual kinks tending to smooth out, even with a sample of only
10 consumers.

The Engel curves for individuals are summarised in the tables
shown in the appendix to this chapter. The aggregate average Engel
curves for the six commodities which appear at any stage in the
optimum budgets and the distribution of expenditure at the various
income levels are shown in figure 4.31 in the appendix.

4.6 Summary

In the previous sections of this chapter the implications of aggregating over individual consumers to obtain a pattern of aggregate behaviour were considered. In aggregating over all consumers at various points of time through the period of the introduction of a new commodity and beyond, reasons were advanced why the diffusion curve might be expected to take a particular form. Similarly, when aggregating over all consumers at a particular level of income per head, it was found that under certain assumptions about the distribution of tastes and technology, S-shaped budget-study Engel curves were obtained. However, when aggregating over all consumers under price changes, it was found that the expected aggregate pattern of behaviour was not as clearly defined as in the other cases.

The importance of aggregation is in smoothing out the discontinuous individual relations to produce aggregate behaviour relations which exhibit more gradual changes, and which may be described by a relatively simple mathematical equation (or equations).

APPENDIX TO CHAPTER 4

Summary of the solutions of linear programmes for ten consumers and individual and aggregate Engel curves for: milk, potatoes, vegetables, bread, cheese, and sugar

The incomes at which each of the 10 different consumers given in the example in chapter 4, section 4.5, reach various stages of satiating their wants are given in the following section. The optimum budgets corresponding to these incomes are indicated by the consumption figures marked with asterisks in the succeeding tables. All consumers start from an initial zero income and arrive at their fifth objective, sufficient of all five wants, when their incomes reach 107.9 pence per head per week.

Consumer 1

Income
46.178	1st objective reached: sufficient calories.
50.379	2nd objective reached: sufficient calories and protein.
87.294	Sugar disappears from optimum budget.
94.530	3rd objective reached: sufficient calories, protein and vitamin C.
107.91	4th objective reached: sufficient calories, protein, vitamin C, and riboflavin.

Consumer 2

Income

44.6   1st objective reached: sufficient protein.

94.5   2nd objective reached: sufficient protein and vitamin C.

98.6   Potatoes disappear from optimum budget.

99.0   3rd objective reached: sufficient protein, vitamin C and calcium.

99.5   Vegetables disappear from optimum budget.

100.7   4th objective reached: sufficient protein, vitamin C, calcium and calories.

106.5   Cheese disappears from optimum budget.

Consumer 3

Income

62.5   1st objective reached: sufficient vitamin C.

85.1   2nd objective reached: sufficient vitamin C and calcium.

92.2   Vegetables disappear from optimum budget.

102.6   3rd objective reached: sufficient vitamin C, calcium and riboflavin.

105.9   Cheese disappears from optimum budget.

107.4   4th objective reached: sufficient vitamin C, calcium, riboflavin and protein.

Consumer 4

Income

60.3   1st objective reached: sufficient riboflavin.

70.5   2nd objective reached: sufficient riboflavin and calories.

70.5   3rd objective reached: sufficient riboflavin, calories and protein

70.5   4th objective reached: sufficient riboflavin, calories, protein and calcium.

Consumer 5

Income

28.0   1st objective reached: sufficient calcium.

46.8   Cheese disappears from optimum budget.

60.3   2nd objective reached: sufficient calcium and riboflavin.

70.5   3rd objective reached: sufficient calcium, riboflavin and calories.

107.9   4th objective reached: sufficient calcium, riboflavin, calories and vitamin C.

Consumer 6
Income
28.0 1st objective reached: sufficient calcium.
45.2 2nd objective reached: sufficient calcium and protein.
46.3 Cheese disappears from optimum budget.
50.5 3rd objective reached: sufficient calcium, protein and calories.
50.7 Sugar disappears from optimum budget.
70.5 4th objective reached: sufficient calcium, protein, calories and riboflavin.

Consumer 7
Income
44.6 1st objective reached: sufficient protein.
67.9 2nd objective reached: sufficient protein and riboflavin.
67.9 3rd objective reached: sufficient protein, riboflavin and calcium.
107.4 4th objective reached: sufficient protein, riboflavin, calcium and vitamin C.

Consumer 8
Income
48.2 1st objective reached: sufficient calories.
50.5 2nd objective reached: sufficient calories and calcium.
60.7 Sugar disappears from optimum budget.
100.7 3rd objective reached: sufficient calories, calcium and vitamin C.
100.7 4th objective reached: sufficient calories, calcium, vitamin C and protein.
106.5 Cheese disappears from optimum budget.

Consumer 9
Income
60.3 1st objective reached: sufficient riboflavin.
101.8 2nd objective reached: sufficient riboflavin and vitamin C.
107.4 3rd objective reached: sufficient riboflavin, vitamin C and protein.
107.9 4th objective reached: sufficient riboflavin, vitamin C, protein and calories.

Consumer 10
Income
62.5 1st objective reached: sufficient vitamin C.
67.9 Vegetables disappear from optimum budget.
92.2 2nd objective reached: sufficient vitamin C and calories.
93.5 Sugar disappears from optimum budget.

107.9   3rd objective reached: sufficient vitamin C, calories and ribo-flavin.

107.9   4th objective reached: sufficient vitamin C, calories, riboflavin and calcium.

Tables 4.1 *to* 4.5

Figures marked with an asterisk in these tables are the consumption levels at the crucial points where objectives are reached or where commodities disappear from the optimum budget. The remaining figures are linear interpolations between adjacent crucial points.

The details for commodity 1 (milk) are extremely imprecise since the machine results were printed out to the nearest pint, although calculated to several decimals. For this reason the expenditure on milk in the first table has only been taken to the nearest penny.

TABLE 4.1.   *Consumption levels at critical income points: milk (commodity* 1)
(Price = 5.116d/pt)

Income d/h/w	Consumption in pint/h/w for consumer										Mean	
	1	2	3	4	5	6	7	8	9	10	pint	pence
0.0	—	—	—	—	—	—	—	—	—	—	—	—
28.0	—	—	—	6	—*	—*	—	—	6	—	1.2	6
44.6	—	—*	—	9	8	—	—*	—	9	—	2.6	13
45.2	—	—	—	9	9	—*	—	—	9	—	2.7	14
46.3	—	—	—	9	9	—*	1	—	9	—	2.8	14
46.8	—	—	—	9	9*	—	1	—	9	—	2.8	14
48.2	—*	—	—	9	9	—	2	—*	9	—	2.9	15
50.4	—*	—	—	10	10	—	2	—	10	—	3.2	16
50.5	—	—	—	10	10	—*	2	—*	10	—	3.2	16
50.7	—	—	—	10	10	—*	2	—	10	—	3.2	16
60.3	—	—	—	12*	12*	2	5	—	12*	—	4.3	22
60.7	—	—	—	12	12	2	5	—	12	—	4.2	22
62.5	—	—	—*	11	11	2	5	—	12	—*	4.1	21
67.9	—	—	—	7	7	4	7*	—	11	—*	3.6	18
70.5	—	—	—	5*	5*	5*	7	—	11	—	3.3	17
85.1	—	—	—*	5	5	5	5	—	8	—	2.8	14
87.3	—*	—	—	5	5	5	5	—	8	—	2.8	14
92.2	—	—	—*	4	4	4	5	—	8	—*	2.5	13
93.5	—	—	1	4	4	4	5	—	8	—*	2.6	13
94.5	—*	—*	2	4	4	4	5	—	8	—	2.7	14
98.6	1	—*	4	4	4	4	5	—	8	1	3.1	16
99.0	1	—*	5	4	4	4	5	—	8	1	3.2	16
99.5	2	—*	5	4	4	4	5	—	7	2	3.3	17
99.7	2	—	5	4	4	4	5	—	7	2	3.3	17
100.7	2	—*	6	4	4	4	5	—*	7	2	3.4	17
101.8	3	1	6	4	4	4	4	1	7*	2	3.6	18
102.6	3	1	7*	4	4	4	4	1	7	3	3.8	19
105.9	4	4	5*	4	4	4	4	4	5	3	4.1	21
106.5	4	4*	5	4	4	4	4	4*	4	4	4.1	21
107.4	4	4	4*	4	4	4	4*	4	4*	4	4.0	20
107.9	4	4	4	4	4	4	4	4	4	4	4.0	20

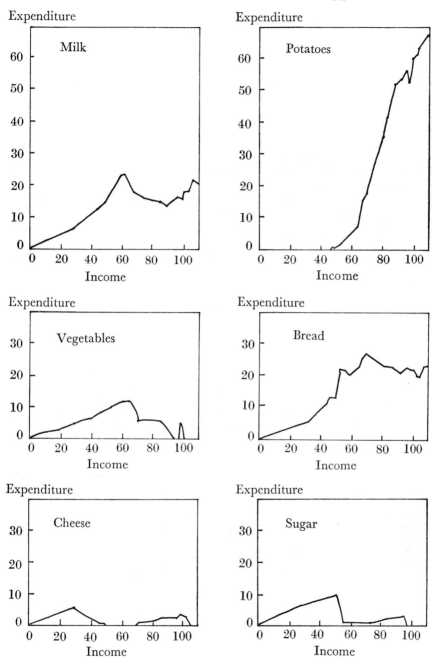

Figure 4.31. Aggregate Engel curves: ten consumers

NOTE: The data for these charts are in the tables of this appendix (first and last columns of each table).

TABLE 4.2. *Consumption levels at critical income points: potatoes (commodity 5)*

(Price = 0.173d/oz)

Income d/h/w	1	2	3	4	5	6	7	8	9	10	Mean oz	Mean pence
				Consumption in oz/h/w for consumer								
0.0	—	—	—	—	—	—	—	—	—	—	—	0.00
28.0	—	—	—	—	—*	—*	—	—	—	—	—	0.00
44.6	—	—*	—	—	—	—	—*	—	—	—	—	0.00
45.2	—	5	—	—	—	—*	—	—	—	—	0.5	0.08
46.3	—	13	—	—	—	—*	—	—	—	—	1.3	0.22
46.8	—	17	—	—*	—	—	—	—	—	—	1.7	0.29
48.2	—*	29	—	—	—	—	—	—*	—	—	2.9	0.50
50.4	—*	46	—	—	—	—	—	—	—	—	4.6	0.80
50.5	1	46	—	—	—	—*	—	—*	—	—	4.7	0.81
50.7	3	48	—	—	—	—*	—	1	—	—	5.2	0.90
60.3	90	124	—	—*	—*	—	—	88	—*	—	30.2	5.22
60.7	94	127	—	—	—	—	—	92*	4	—	31.7	5.48
62.5	110	141	—*	—	—	—	—	106	20	—*	37.7	6.52
67.9	159	184	—	—	—	—	—*	146	68	393*	95.0	16.44
70.5	183	204	—	—*	—*	—*	25	166	91	393	106.2	18.37
85.1	316	319	—*	149	149	149	165	276	221	393	213.7	36.97
87.3	336*	336	122	171	171	171	187	292	241	393	242.0	41.87
92.2	375	275	393*	221	221	221	234	329	284	393*	304.6	52.70
93.5	385	385	390	234	234	234	246	339	296	393*	313.6	54.25
94.5	393*	393*	388	244	244	244	256	346	305	392	320.5	55.45
98.6	388	—*	380	286	286	286	295	377	341	389	302.8	52.38
99.0	388	—*	379	290	290	290	299	380	345	388	304.9	52.75
99.5	387	393*	378	295	295	295	304	384	349	388	346.8	60.00
99.7	387	393	378	297	297	306	365	351	351	388	347.9	60.19
100.7	386	393*	376	308	308	308	316	393*	360	387	353.5	61.16
101.8	385	391	374	319	319	319	326	391	370*	386	358.0	61.93
102.6	385	389	372*	327	327	327	334	389	369	385	360.4	62.35
105.9	382	383	377*	361	361	361	366	383	363	383	372.0	64.36
106.5	382	382	378	367	367	367	371	382	382	382	376.0	65.05
107.4	381	381	380*	376	376	376	380*	381	380*	381	379.2	65.60
107.9	381*	381*	381	381	381	381	381	381	381	381	381.0	65.91

TABLE 4.3.   *Consumption levels at critical income points: bread (commodity 8)*

(Price = 0.222d/oz)

Income	Consumption in oz/h/w for consumer										Mean	
d/h/w	1	2	3	4	5	6	7	8	9	10	oz	pence
0.0	—	—	—	—	—	—	—	—	—	—	0	0.00
28.0	—	126	—	—	—*	—*	126	—	—	—	25.2	5.59
44.6	—	201	—	—	—	189	201*	—	—	—	59.1	13.12
45.2	—	200	—	—	—	196*	200	—	—	—	59.6	13.23
46.3	—	198	—	—	—	208*	197	—	—	—	60.3	13.39
46.8	—	196	—	—	—*	208	196	—	—	—	60.0	13.32
48.2	—*	195	—	—	—	208	193	—*	—	—	59.6	13.23
50.4	201*	192	—	—	—	208	188	201	—	—	99.0	21.98
50.5	201	191	—	—	—	208*	188	208*	—	—	99.6	22.11
50.7	200	191	—	—	—	228*	188	208	—	—	101.5	22.53
60.3	182	176	—	—*	—*	216	167	202	—*	—	94.3	20.93
60.7	182	175	—	8	8	216	166	202*	—	—	95.7	21.25
62.5	178	172	—*	44	44	214	162	197	—	—*	101.1	22.44
67.9	168	163	—	152	152	207	150*	183	—	—*	117.5	26.09
70.5	163	159	—	204*	204*	204*	146	176	—	—	125.6	27.88
85.1	136	135	—*	163	163	163	124	158	—	—	104.2	23.13
87.3	132*	132	—	157	157	157	121	132	—	—	98.8	21.93
92.2	124	124	—*	143	143	143	114	119	—	—*	91.0	20.20
93.5	122	122	—	139	139	139	112	116	—	115*	100.4	22.29
94.5	120*	120*	—	137	137	137	110	113	—	114	98.8	21.93
98.6	111	163*	—	125	125	125	104	103	—	109	96.5	21.42
99.0	110	159*	—	124	124	124	104	101	—	109	95.5	21.20
99.5	108	83	—	123	123	123	103	100	—	108	87.1	19.34
99.7	108	85	—	122	122	122	103	100	—	108	87.0	19.31
100.7	107	97*	—	119	119	119	101	97*	—	107	86.6	19.23
101.8	106	98	—	116	116	116	99	98	—*	106	85.5	18.98
102.6	105	98	—*	114	114	114	98	98	13	105	85.9	19.07
105.9	101	101	67*	105	105	105	93	101	67	101	94.6	21.00
106.5	101	101*	77	103	103	103	92	101*	76	101	95.8	21.27
107.4	100	100	91*	99	99	99	91*	100	91*	100	97.0	21.53
107.9	99*	99*	99	99	99	99	99	99	99	99	99.0	21.98

TABLE 4.4. *Consumption levels at critical income points : cheese (commodity 10)*
(Price = 1.009d/oz)

Income d/h/w	Consumption in oz/h/w for consumer										Mean	
	1	2	3	4	5	6	7	8	9	10	oz	pence
0.0	—	—	—	—	—	—	—	—	—	—	—	0.00
28.0	—	—	—	—	28*	28*	—	—	—	—	5.6	5.65
44.6	—	—	—	—	3	3	—	—	—	—	0.6	0.61
45.2	—	—	—	—	2	2*	—	—	—	—	0.4	0.40
46.3	—	—	—	—	1	—*	—	—	—	—	0.1	0.10
46.8	—	—	—	—	—*	—	—	—	—	—	—	—
48.2	—	—	—	—	—	—	—	—	—	—	—	—
50.4	—	—	—	—	—	—	—	—	—	—	—	—
50.5	—	—	—	—	—	—	—	—	—	—	—	—
50.7	—	—	—	—	—	—	—	—	—	—	—	—
60.3	—	—	—	—	—	—	—	—	—	—	—	—
60.7	—	—	—	—	—	—	—	—*	—	—	—	—
62.5	—	—	—*	—	—	—	—	—	—	—	—	—
67.9	—	—	5	—	—	—	—	2	—	—	0.7	0.71
70.5	—	—	8	—	—	—	—	3	—	—	1.1	1.11
85.1	—	—	22*	—	—	—	—	7	—	—	2.9	2.93
87.3	—	—	23	—	—	—	—	7	—	—	3.0	3.03
92.2	—	—	24*	—	—	—	—	9	—	—	3.3	3.33
93.5	—	—	21	—	—	—	—	9	—	—	3.0	3.03
94.5	—	—	20	—	—	—	—	9	—	—	2.9	2.93
98.6	—	—*	12	—	—	—	—	10	—	—	2.2	2.22
99.0	—	1*	11	—	—	—	—	11	—	—	2.3	2.32
99.5	—	13*	10	—	—	—	—	11	—	—	3.4	3.43
99.7	—	13	10	—	—	—	—	11	—	—	3.4	3.43
100.7	—	11*	8	—	—	—	—	11*	—	—	3.0	3.03
101.8	—	9	6	—	—	—	—	9	—	—	2.4	2.42
102.6	—	7	4*	—	—	—	—	7	—	—	1.8	1.82
105.9	—	1	—*	—	—	—	—	1	—	—	0.2	0.20
106.5	—	—*	—	—	—	—	—	—*	—	—	—	—
107.4	—	—	—	—	—	—	—	—	—	—	—	—
107.9	—	—	—	—	—	—	—	—	—	—	—	—

TABLE 4.5. *Consumption levels at critical income points: vegetables (commodity 6) and sugar (commodity 14)*

	Vegetables (Price = 0.397d/oz)					Sugar (Price = 0.317d/oz)					
	Consumption in oz/h/w by consumer			Mean		Consumption in oz/h/w by consumer				Mean	
Income d/h/w	2	3	10	oz	pence	1	6	8	10	oz	pence
0.0	—	—	—	—	0.00	—	—	—	—	—	0.00
28.0	—	70	71	14.1	5.60	139	—	139	—	17.8	5.64
44.6	—	112	112	22.4	8.89	141	—	142	—	28.3	8.97
45.2	—	114	113	22.7	9.01	143	—	144	—	28.7	9.10
46.3	—	117	116	23.3	9.25	147	—*	147	—	29.4	9.32
46.8	—	118	117	23.5	9.33	148	2	148	—	29.8	9.45
48.2	—	121	121	24.2	9.61	152*	6	152*	—	31.0	9.83
50.4	—	126	127	25.3	10.04	18*	13	19	—	5.0	1.59
50.5	—	127	127	25.4	10.08	18	13*	13*	—	4.4	1.39
50.7	—	127	128	25.5	10.12	18	—*	13	—	3.1	0.98
60.3	—	152	151	30.3	12.03	13	—	1	—	1.4	0.44
60.7	—	153	152	30.5	12.11	13	—	—	—	1.3	0.41
62.5	—	157*	157*	31.4	12.47	12	—	—	—	1.2	0.38
67.9	—	157	—*	15.7	6.23	9	—	—	—*	0.9	0.29
70.5	—	157	—	15.7	6.23	8	—	—	8	1.6	0.51
85.1	—	157*	—	15.7	6.23	1	—	—	55	5.6	1.78
87.3	—	108	—	10.8	4.29	—*	—	—	61	6.1	1.93
92.2	—	—	—	—	—	—	—	—	77*	7.7	2.44
93.5	—	—	—	—	—	—	—	—	—	—	—
94.5	—*	—	—	—	—						—
98.6	157*	—	—	15.7	6.23						—
99.0	157*	—	—	15.7	6.23						—
99.5	—*	—	—	—	—						—
99.7					—						—
100.7					—						—
101.8					—						—
102.6					—						—
105.9					—						—
106.5					—						—
107.4					—						—
107.9					—						—

5. APPLICATIONS OF THE THEORY

'It is a complete mistake to regard the economist, whatever his degree of "purity", as concerned merely with pure deduction. It is quite true that much of his work is in the nature of elaborate processes of inference. But it is quite untrue to suppose that it is only, or indeed mainly, thus. The concern of the economist is the interpretation of reality.'

L. Robbins (1932), 2nd edn, 1935, p. 105

In the theory of individual and group behaviour developed in this study, priority has been given to the influence of new commodities and quality changes, rather than to the influence of changes in prices and incomes. The inability of the current theory to handle the introduction of new commodities and changes in the qualities of commodities led to the formulation of a theory which distinguishes between the consumer's separate wants.

In the course of the development of the theory, some of its implications for the measurement of consumer behaviour have been suggested. In this chapter, an attempt will be made to show how the concept of separate wants can be used in analysis.

First, the theory will be applied to a situation where a quality of an existing commodity is varied. Secondly, the introduction of a sequence of related new commodities will be analysed. Finally, some comments will be made on the temporal relationships between consumption levels.

5.1 ANALYSIS OF A QUALITY CHANGE

Consider the variation in the alcoholic strength of beer.† Suppose consumers may choose between two commodities, spirits and beer (with levels of consumption denoted by x_1 and x_2 respectively) and that spirits has a constant alcoholic strength w_{11} and satisfies no other want than the want for alcohol. Beer has a variable alcoholic strength w_{12} and consumption of beer also enables the satisfaction of a second want, the want for company with one's fellows, since beer is mostly drunk in a public house.

† The first explicit demand analysis of the effects of variation in the quality of a commodity appears to be Stone's analysis of the effect on consumption of changes in the alcoholic strength of beer. See chapter 6, section 6.4, below.

Then $\begin{bmatrix} z_1 \\ z_2 \end{bmatrix} = \begin{bmatrix} w_{11} & w_{12} \\ . & w_{22} \end{bmatrix} \begin{bmatrix} x_1 \\ x_2 \end{bmatrix}$

In the want space, the equilibrium position of a consumer who consumes both spirits and beer can be represented by the point A in figure 5.1.

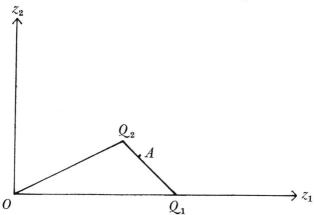

Figure 5.1. Want space: consumer of both beer and spirits

The effect of an increase in the alcoholic strength of beer, w_{12}, will be to move the point Q_2 in the direction parallel to the Oz_1 axis.† This will affect various consumers in different ways. Each consumer will be considered separately.

5.1.1   *Constant real income*

Consider income-compensating the consumer to bring him back to the original standard of living at the equilibrium point A. Denoting by subscript θ the new period, and by subscript t the original, the following relationships exist between the two optimum budgets:

$$x_{1\theta} = x_{1t} + \frac{1}{w_{11}} (w_{12t} - w_{12\theta}) x_{2t}$$

$$x_{2\theta} = x_{2t}$$

Hence when the strength of beer increases, the consumption of beer is *constant* but the consumption of spirits declines, the consumer being income-compensated to the same standard of living.

Now assume consumers to have constant money income, and consider the effect of an increase in the strength of beer on all the possible types of consumers.

5.1.2   *Constant money income*

Consumers fall into five possible types, a to e, according to the order in which they rank their desire for alcohol and for company and then

† See p. 51.

according to whether these wants are supra-marginal, marginal or sub-marginal. The accompanying table shows these five types of consumers.

Consumer type	Wants		
	Supra-marginal	Marginal	Sub-marginal
a	Alcohol	Company	—
b	Company	Alcohol	—
c	—	Alcohol	Company
d	—	Company	Alcohol
e	Alcohol and company	—	—

The changes in the optimum budgets for these consumers can now be examined.

Type a. When w_{12} increases, Q_2 moves as before, and the new equilibrium is at point B (in figure 5.2) on the line $z_1 = z_1^*$ through A, thus increasing the amount of satisfaction of the second want while maintaining alcohol consumption at a steady rate.

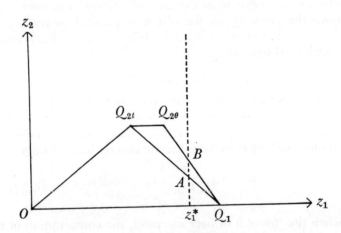

Figure 5.2. Want space: increase in beer strength

The commodity consumption levels at period t can be expressed† as:

$$x_{1t} = \frac{p_2 z_1^* - w_{12} y}{w_{11} p_2 - w_{12t} p_1}$$

and

$$x_{2t} = \frac{w_{11} y - p_1 z_1^*}{w_{11} p_2 - w_{12t} p_1}$$

† See section 2.5.1, p. 27.

Differentiating x_{1t} and x_{2t} with respect to w_{12t} and remembering that $p_1 z_1^* < w_{11} y$, we find

$$\frac{\partial x_1}{\partial w_{12}} < 0 \quad \text{and} \quad \frac{\partial x_2}{\partial w_{12}} > 0$$

Hence for consumers of type a, beer consumption increases and spirits consumption decreases when the strength of beer is increased.

Type b. When w_{12} increases, this consumer moves to a new equilibrium point on the line $z_2 = z_2^*$ through his initial equilibrium point A. Alcohol consumption increases while the satisfaction of the need for company stays constant. Since in this situation the consumer must consume a constant quantity of beer in order to maintain a constant level of satisfaction of the need for company, there is also no change in the consumption level of spirits.

Type c. This consumer does not include beer in his optimum budget until its efficiency in satisfying his alcoholic wants becomes greater than the efficiency of spirits. Hence if w_{12} increased beyond the value $p_2 w_{11}/p_1$ he would switch completely from spirits to beer. Further increases in alcoholic strength of beer may enable him to satiate fully his want for alcohol, but would not alter his optimum budget (now entirely devoted to beer).

Type d. This consumer is already devoting his entire expenditure to beer and increases in its alcoholic strength do not alter this budget.

Type e. Increases in w_{12} initially mean a saving of income for this consumer. He does his own income compensation so as not to over-satiate his wants for alcohol and company. Consumption of beer stays constant but spirits consumption declines, until it disappears from his optimum budget. If w_{12} increases beyond this point, the consumer will continue to consume the same quantity of beer, allowing the want for alcohol to be over-satiated, unless the model is changed to include a third commodity, such as lemon squash, which satisfies the want for company but not for alcohol. This change would bring in a set of new circumstances which will not be considered.

In summary, when the alcoholic strength of beer increases, consumers of types b, d and e will not alter their consumption of beer. Consumers of type a will immediately increase their beer consumption until the point where $w_{12} y = p_2 z_1^*$, after which no further increase in w_{12} will cause any change. Type c consumers do not switch from spirits to beer until w_{12} increases sufficiently to make $f_{12} > f_{11}$. Hence the total effect on consumption will depend on the proportions of consumers in the various types a to e, and in particular on the proportions in situations a and c.

5.1.3   *Interpretation of a positive strength elasticity*

Stone (1954) finds a significant positive partial regression of beer consumption on its alcoholic strength. On the basis of the foregoing analysis this positive reaction can be interpreted as follows:

(i) The partial regression on real income did not adequately adjust for changes in the standard of living, hence the assumption of constant real income did not apply.

(ii) Some consumers had satiated their wants for alcohol but not the other wants that consumption of beer satisfies, such as company in a public house.

(iii) In addition, it seems that if beer reached the point where it was of equal alcoholic efficiency with spirits, strength changes would cause the switching to and fro from spirits to beer of those consumers for whom alcohol was a marginal want and ranked prior to the desire for company.

In so far as increasing income will tend to increase the proportion of consumers of type *a* then an increase of income will tend to reduce the strength of the aggregate reaction of beer consumption to changes in strength. This reaction will also be reduced if there is an increase in the proportion of consumers ranking company prior to alcohol in their hierarchy of wants.

5.2   ANALYSIS OF A SEQUENCE OF RELATED NEW COMMODITIES

Different methods of heating, lighting and providing power in the home have been used over the years. Today consumers have a wide choice among methods of satisfying the wants for heat, light and power. A century ago this choice was very restricted.

Suppose initially that heat was provided by firewood, light by candles, and power by servants. Neglecting the use of kerosene and fuel oil, a hypothesis can be formulated regarding the sequence in which new sources of heat, light and power were introduced into the home.

This hypothesis is:

(i) Coal is introduced as a means of heating;
(ii) Gas is introduced as a means of lighting;
(iii) Gas is introduced as a means of heating;
(iv) Electricity is introduced as a means of lighting;
(v) Electricity is introduced as a means of heating;
(vi) Electricity is introduced as a means of power.

On the assumption that this is the correct sequence in which these related commodities were introduced, what behaviour hypotheses should the demand analyst test? And how? What parameters can he hope to estimate from the data on consumption, prices, etc. over this period? To see in a little more detail what is involved, break into this sequence at stage (iii), when gas is introduced as a means of heating.

Gas introduced for heating. Assume that coal has completely replaced firewood as a heat source, and that gas has completely replaced candles as a light source. Servants and power requirements will be disregarded.

The quantity of gas used for heating will be expected to increase, and conversely the quantity of coal consumed will be expected to decline. These changes in the commodity consumption rates would be paralleled by changes in the *average* consumer's estimates of the want-satisfying powers of the commodities. In terms of the disaggregated matrix **W** in the equations

$$\begin{matrix} \text{heat} \\ \text{light} \end{matrix} \begin{bmatrix} z_1 \\ z_2 \end{bmatrix} = \begin{bmatrix} w_{11} & w_{12} & . \\ . & . & w_{22} \end{bmatrix} \begin{bmatrix} x_{11} \\ x_{21} \\ x_{22} \end{bmatrix} \begin{matrix} \text{coal} \\ \text{gas, heat} \\ \text{gas, light} \end{matrix}$$

the average estimate of w_{12} would be expected to increase, w_{11} to remain constant (or perhaps decline) and w_{22} to remain constant.

In general, individual consumers will select either coal or gas, but rarely both, to provide heat and so the population of consumers can be divided into two types – *type a:* coal and gas users, and *type b:* gas users.

For type a, $w_{11}:w_{12} > p_1:p_2$ and for type b this inequality is reversed. Assuming prices p_1 and p_2 and income y constant, if the proportion of consumers of type b increases, this is because $f_{11} < f_{12}$ for a greater proportion of consumers. This means that the average ratio $w_{12}:w_{11}$ for the total of all consumers increases, on the assumption that these ratios for type a and type b consumers are constants.

Suppose at period t the proportion of type b consumers is b_t (and hence the proportion of type a consumers is $1-n_t$) and that for all consumers demand for heat and light are always completely satiated at the levels z_1^* and z_2^*. Then the relationships shown below exist:

Consumer	Coal	Gas, heat	Gas, light
Type a	$x_{11a}^* = \dfrac{z_1^*}{w_{11a}}$	—	$x_{22a}^* = \dfrac{z_2^*}{w_{22}}$
Type b	—	$x_{21b}^* = \dfrac{z_1^*}{w_{12b}}$	$x_{22b}^* = \dfrac{z_2^*}{w_{22}}$
Total	$X_{11t} = (1-n_.)x_{11a}^*$	$X_{21t} = n_t x_{21b}^*$	$X_{22t} = x_{22}^*$

Hence the changes in total coal consumption and in total gas consumption are related to the changes in n_t as follows:

$$\Delta X_{1t} = -x^*_{11a}\Delta n_t$$

and
$$\Delta X_{2t} = x^*_{21b}\Delta n_t$$

If the number of gas-only consumers (type b) can be expected to increase through time according to the operation of a constant infection rate r, then during period t,

$$\Delta n_t = r(1-n_t)n_t$$

This is the equation from which the logistic equation of section 5.1.4 above is derived, except that this time it has been expressed as a first-order difference equation instead of a first-order differential equation.

TABLE 5.1.   *Values of* n_{t+1} *for* *different values of* r *and* n_t

(Logistic)

n_t	r					
	0.1	0.3	0.5	0.7	0.9	1.1
0.1	0.109	0.127	0.145	0.163	0.181	0.199
0.2	0.216	0.248	0.280	0.312	0.344	0.376
0.3	0.321	0.363	0.405	0.447	0.489	0.531
0.4	0.424	0.472	0.520	0.568	0.616	0.664
0.5	0.525	0.575	0.625	0.675	0.725	0.775
0.6	0.624	0.672	0.720	0.768	0.816	0.864
0.7	0.721	0.763	0.805	0.847	0.889	0.931
0.8	0.816	0.848	0.880	0.912	0.944	0.976
0.9	0.909	0.927	0.945	0.963	0.981	0.999
k	23	8	5	4	3	3

Table 5.1 shows values of n_{t+1} for different values of r and n_t and figure 5.3 shows the relations between n_{t+1} and n_t for three values of r. The figures in row k of the table are the number of periods it takes for the value of n_t to rise from 0.10 to at least 0.50. Thus in the analysis of the introduction of gas heating, if the proportion of gas-only consumers took eight years to rise from 10 per cent to just over 50 per cent, it could be said that this was equivalent to an infection rate of 0.3 per annum.

Thus the changes in consumption of coal and gas can be summarised in terms of parameters such as r or k which are connected with the speed at which consumers are shifting between types a and b, together with the parameters x^*_{11a} and x^*_{21b} of mean consumption levels of coal and gas for heating.

Provided the market does not move out of stage (iii) to stage (iv) too quickly, there should be some chance of estimating these parameters from the data. However, if stages (iv), (v) and (vi) come following

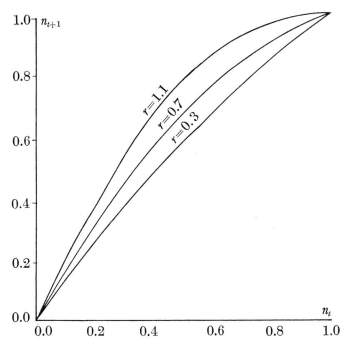

Figure 5.3. The lag sequence for the proportion of consumers: three values of a constant infection rate

each other in fairly quick succession, it will be extremely difficult to separate the stages so as to estimate the parameters associated with the introduction of each new commodity.

5.3   TEMPORAL RELATIONSHIPS BETWEEN CONSUMPTION LEVELS

The elements q_{ij} of the matrix $\mathbf{Q}_{\theta t} = \mathbf{W}_\theta^{-1}\mathbf{W}_t$ are coefficients connecting the optimum budgets $\mathbf{x}_\theta$ and $\mathbf{x}_t$ when the qualities of commodities change from $\mathbf{W}_t$ in period t to $\mathbf{W}_\theta$ in period θ.† In this situation $\mathbf{x}_\theta$ and $\mathbf{x}_t$ give the consumer the same standard of living.

In the special case where all commodities are specific, $\mathbf{W}_\theta$ and $\mathbf{W}_t$ are diagonal matrices, and so also is $\mathbf{Q}_{\theta t}$ with elements

$$q_{ii} = \frac{w_{tii}}{w_{\theta ii}}$$

$$q_{ij} = 0, \ i \neq j$$

† See chapter 3, section 3.2.2, for the derivation of $\mathbf{Q}_{\theta t}$.

Hence if the want satisfying power of commodity i changes by a factor h from period t to period θ, then $q_{ii} = 1/h$, and the quantity consumed of commodity i changes by the factor $1/h$.†

Hence in this special case, the level of consumption of a commodity in period θ is a function of the level of consumption of the commodity in period t. Provided the commodities are specific and the standard of living remains constant,‡ then q_{ii} can be estimated as the ratio of the two levels of consumption, $x_{\theta i}/x_{ti}$.

Let x_t be the level of consumption in period t of commodity i and x_{t-1} its level of consumption in period $t-1$, so that q_{ii} refers to the ratio w_{t-1}/w_t for commodity i. If there is no change in the want satisfying power, then the expected value of q_{ii} is 1. If it has increased, the expected value of $q_{ii} < 1$ and conversely, if decreased, $q_{ii} > 1$.

These expectations appear to conflict with our analysis of the introduction of a new commodity. In that case, an upward revision of the want-satisfying powers, originally put at zero by most consumers, led to consumption increases; hence in the present situation it might be supposed that $q_{ii} > 1$. This conflict is resolved when it is remembered that strictly $\mathbf{Q}_{\theta t}$ can only apply when the *same* commodities are required in $\mathbf{x}_\theta$ as in $\mathbf{x}_t$, and hence is inappropriate as a transformation between two different sets of commodities. In the case of the new commodity, as in the previous section on the introduction of gas for heating, while the average estimate of the heat satisfying power of gas could be expected to increase, the relationship between consumption and lagged consumption depended on the form of the relationship between the current proportion and the lagged proportion of gas-only consumers. It was suggested that this takes the form

$$n_{t+1} = (1+r)n_t - rn_t^2$$

Hence, apart from the question of origin and units, gas consumption takes the same form

$$x_{t+1} = (1+r)x_t - rx_t^2$$

However, it can be seen from figure 5.3 above that if the parameter r is fairly small, or if we are considering only a small portion of the full diffusion period, the function relating x_{t+1} and x_t can be approximated by the linear relationship

$$x_{t+1} = a + bx_t$$

† For example, if the want-satisfying power doubles, the quantity consumed falls to one half.
‡ Or if we can arrange things so that commodities are classified into specific groups and allow for changes in living standards.

5.4 CONCLUSIONS

In conclusion, the main qualitative results of Part I are as follows:

(i) Smoothness of the group behaviour of consumers arises out of the differences between individual consumers – differences between individual saturation levels, priority orderings and technologies for the Engel curves that are observed in budget studies – and these differences plus income differences for the diffusion curves and demand curves that are observed from time series.

(ii) Changes in technical coefficients (i.e. changes in individual consumers' estimates of commodities' want-satisfying powers, whether reflecting physical changes in the commodities or the spread of knowledge) cause changes in the efficiencies of commodities; this leads to a significant change in the commodities included in the optimum budget for the individual. Unless these changes occur simultaneously for all consumers, and it is unlikely that they will, this leads to smooth growth or decline in aggregate consumption levels.

(iii) Some consumers may be infinitesimal calculators; rather more, we expect, are linear programmers.

The infinitesimal calculators make smooth and continuous adjustments to their optimum budgets, keeping the ratios of marginal utilities to prices equal for all commodities, but make discontinuous changes to their utility functions and budgets when their tastes change in response to the arrival of a new commodity or to a change in the quality of a commodity. The linear programmers keep their supra-marginal wants satisfied as far as possible, but are willing to make large and discontinuous changes to their optimum budgets to effect this. Their fundamental preference patterns are unaffected by changes in the number or quality of commodities, but their expenditure patterns change in accordance with revisions of the relative want-satisfying powers of commodities.

These two ways of formulating the model of individual behaviour lead to much the same group behaviour in respect of income and price changes considered *ceteris paribus*. But the second approach offers a more suitable theoretical framework for considering behaviour responses to innovations and quality changes.

PART II

NEW COMMODITIES AND THE
MEASUREMENT OF CONSUMER BEHAVIOUR

6. THE SITUATION IN DEMAND ANALYSIS

'Demand analysis should not be conceived as confined to the estimation of the influence of income and prices, but should seek to draw upon as complete an understanding as possible of the whole complex of factors influencing consumption.'

Report of the informal consultation of experts on demand analysis, Geneva, June 1957. FAO/ECE Agric., p. 5

The current situation in the analysis of demand is that most analysts do not view commodities as being new or outmoded but as being 'established'. Demand analysts who take the 'established' view of commodities find that, in many cases, influences other than prices and income are responsible for a major part of the variation in consumption through time. Perhaps these influences are largely accounted for by the introduction of new commodities or by the alteration of commodity qualities.

While the effects of new commodities have been referred to by several economists, only a handful of explicit studies of new commodities or of quality changes have been made. This may be due primarily to a lack of knowledge of the extent and importance of these events. A few commodities such as cars and television are well known as new commodities, but it is not generally realised that new commodities and new forms of commodities have been numerous and widespread.

6.1 EMPIRICAL DIFFICULTIES

The difficulties in empirical demand analysis of sorting out price, income and other causes of change in demand have been recognised in most studies. For budget studies, much attention has been given to the problem of sorting out the effects of differences in income from known differences in family composition in terms of the numbers of individuals of different ages and sex.

Some attention has also been given in budget studies to the influence of quality, as measured by prices. For time series analysis, attempts have been made to separate income and price effects and this has been done fairly successfully by using income reactions derived from budget studies, so that the time series do not have the double task of determining both the income and the price reactions. However, this method of combining budget studies with time series is not always used, mainly because adequate data from a budget study are lacking, but perhaps also on account of misgivings as to whether the budget study gives a true estimate of the aggregate income reaction of the consumers.

However, whatever the method used for determining the income reaction, a difficulty remains in using the time-series data. This is the possibility, or rather certainty, that other causes besides income changes and price changes have been at work. The usual method of isolating possible other causes has been to insert in the estimating equation extra variables such as time or discontinuity with the hope that the estimation technique will separate out the influences of these other unspecified variables. When this method is used in demand analysis it is sometimes found that these other influences have rather more importance than was expected.

For example, Farrell (1952), commenting on Prest's analyses for the demand for consumer goods in the United Kingdom for the period 1870–1938 says: 'Thus in every case, the economic variables† were quite unimportant in determining demand, as compared with the "social variables" – the time trends, and the discontinuity variables.' In the study to which Farrell refers, Prest (1949), says:

> It is of course true that we did not test all possible 'economic' influences, but nevertheless it does seem that the major part of the explanation must be attributed to the general nexus of socio-logical forces we group under the heading 'time'. It may be that to make further progress in 'explaining' variations in consumption we shall have to effect a vast improvement in our knowledge of these forces behind the growth and decay of tastes.

Similarly, Stone (1954) finds in the United Kingdom over the period 1920–38 that the residual trend coefficients were statistically significant for approximately one third‡ of the commodities for which the time series were analysed. This compares with slightly more than half of the commodities having significant elasticities with respect to their own prices.

However, it appears that the inclusion of extra explanatory variables in the form of the prices of related commodities increases the chances of finding a statistically significant trend coefficient.§ Of the 36 separate

† Real income per head of population and real price of the commodity.
‡ Sixteen of the 51 commodities for which time series analyses were carried out, not including the five aggregate commodities (fresh and cured fish; all food; tobacco as a whole; drink and tobacco; and all fuel) for which there are analyses of the constituent commodities.
§ Only 11 of the 51 commodities have significant residual trends if income and real price are the only other explanatory variables, compared with 16 commodities when various other prices are included as well.

food commodities† for which the total trend in consumption per head over the period 1920–38 can be broken down into the three influences, income, prices and residual, it is found that 15 commodities have large‡ total trends, of which six§ were associated with large trends in prices, eight‖ were associated with large residual trends, and one¶ was the effect of a large negative price trend outweighing a large positive residual. Of the 21 commodities with relatively small total trends in this period, it appears that five†† were due to the counterbalance of prices and residuals, while prices, incomes and residuals had little effect on the remaining 16 commodities.

The additional evidence presented by Stone's study of the relative importance of different influences on the demand for commodities, both from year to year and over a longer period, reinforces the Prest-Farrell view that a major part of the explanation of the variation in consumption must be found in influences outside prices and income.

Is it that these unexplained variations in consumption are largely due to technological changes in the consumption process? Theoretically, as has been shown, the introduction of new commodities can lead to significant changes in the pattern of consumption – not only being included as additional commodities in the budget but also making existing commodities outmoded or redundant.

In the real world of the demand analyst the effects of new commodities have not been closely investigated. One of the difficulties in the path of doing this is that there is no clear indication of which variable to use to represent the influence of the new commodity in the multiple-regression procedure adopted for isolating separate effects. If the diffusion of new commodities is, in general, a slow but steady process taking several decades or more to reach full effect, then, in those studies of new commodities which have 'time' as an explanatory variable,‡‡ the size of the coefficient of the 'time' variable will largely be the result of the strength of the diffusion of the new commodity. Similar results will follow for studies of outmoded commodities where 'time' is included as an explanatory variable.

There is also the possibility that much of the residual variation found in demand studies would be eliminated if the influence of past prices and income could be allowed for. Nerlove and Addison (1958) examine this hypothesis, and while there is some merit in the idea, the findings seem doubtful. This question will be taken up in chapter 10.

† See Stone (1954), table 109, p. 341.
‡ 'Large' throughout this paragraph refers to trends of 3% per annum or more.
§ Canned fruit; cream; bananas; chocolate and confectionery; cocoa; margarine.
‖ Canned vegetables; canned meat; eggs; oranges; butter; cured fish; flour; imported potatoes.
¶ Dried fruit.
†† Other fresh fruit; imported apples; imported beef; condensed milk; home apples.
‡‡ As a catch-all for changes in tastes and all other systematically moving variables.

10

6.2 EXPLICIT STUDIES OF NEW COMMODITIES

The demand analyses carried out by Prest (1949), Farrell (1952) and Stone (1954) were not undertaken as analyses of 'new' commodities, nor for that matter as analyses of 'old' commodities, but rather as analyses of 'established' or 'mature' commodities – commodities which were neither in a period of expansion or youthful growth, nor in a period of ageing or senile decline. However, some studies have viewed the commodity expressly as being in a period of growth.

The objectives of such studies have been rather different from those which view commodities as established. For new commodities, recognised as such, the demand analyst's primary concern has been with measuring the rate of growth of the demand for the commodity consequent upon its introduction. Early studies of the demand for automobiles, such as de Wolff (1938), and Roos and Szeliski (1939), and bicycles, Derksen and Rombouts (1937), and more recently the studies of the demand for television, Dernberg (1957) and Bain (1962), (1963) and (1964) have been particularly concerned with the growth in demand for the commodity, i.e. growth independent of growth in income or improvement in price.

In these studies the analyst has been certain, right from the start, that there has been something more behind demand than changes in income or in prices, and has considered other factors as being of major importance in the analysis. These few studies contrast sharply with the analyses oriented towards income and prices, where other factors are regarded more as of nuisance value. Although it may appear that the commodity with which the demand analyst is concerned is in a period neither of youthful growth nor of senile decay, he can rarely be sure that the expansion of demands for *other* commodities has not been responsible for changes in the demand for the commodity with which he is concerned.

6.3 REFERENCES TO NEW COMMODITIES

Apart from the few explicit studies of particular new commodities, there are some other references in economics to the importance of the appearance of new commodities on the market.

For Schumpeter (1934) both economic growth and cyclical fluctuations follow as a consequence of innovation – innovation in both the production and the consumption processes. In defining the process of development he says:

> Development in our sense is then defined by carrying out of new combinations.

This concept covers the following five cases: (1) The introduction of a new good – that is one with which consumers are not yet familiar – or of a new quality of a good. (2) The introduction of a new method of production, that is one not yet tested by experience . . . (3) The opening of a new market . . . (4) The conquest of a new source of supply . . . (5) The carrying out of the new organisation of any industry . . .†

Later in the same work, Schumpeter explains cyclical fluctuations in the following manner:

Why is it that economic development in our sense does not proceed evenly as a tree grows, but as it were jerkily; why does it display those characteristic ups and downs?

The answer cannot be short and precise enough: exclusively *because the new combinations are not, as one would expect according to general principles of probability, evenly distributed through time . . . but appear, if at all, discontinuously in groups or swarms.*‡

The overall effects of the introduction of new commodities on consumer behaviour are briefly examined by Duesenberry (1949).

Writing on the evidence in favour of the proposition that new products have caused a strong upward trend in consumption, Duesenberry concludes that although it appears that durables did seem to have this effect after 1909 in the U.S.A., they did not in the period from 1879 to 1909, when the proportion of income saved remained constant in spite of an increase in real income per consuming unit of 50 per cent. He puts it as follows:

Unless some set of important new goods in the non-durable classes can be shown to have influenced saving before 1909 we must conclude that the introduction of new goods does not provide an explanation of the stability of the percentage saved in the period before 1909.§

However, the evidence in the United Kingdom is that growth in consumption of a number of new *non-durable* commodities was important in the period before 1909. Similar evidence on consumption in the United States from Burns (1934) indicates that new non-durable commodities had similar importance in the period from 1870 (as far back as the evidence goes).

Thus Duesenberry was rather hasty in rejecting the hypothesis and it is probable that new commodities have been important in pushing up the consumption function over a long period of time.

On a rather less theoretical plane, Jefferys (1954) finds that much of the structural change in the organisation of retail trading in the United Kingdom over the period 1850 to 1950 was associated with

† Schumpeter (1934), p. 66.   ‡ Schumpeter (1934), p. 223. Italics in the original.
§ Duesenberry (1949), p. 61.

or caused by the introduction of new commodities. These changes were often associated with simultaneous changes in the nature of the production process. Jefferys says: 'The goods produced by these large-scale factory methods carried traditional names and served traditional purposes, but to the distributive trades they were virtually new products requiring new methods of sale and new types of outlet.'[†]

6.4 QUALITY CHANGES

At least one analysis of the effects of variation in the quality of a commodity has been made. This was Stone's analysis of the effect on consumption of changes in the alcoholic strength of beer. He finds that

> If the specific gravity of beer is introduced as a measure of its strength, there is obtained a significant partial regression of beer consumption on strength. This accords with the expectation that if stronger, and to that extent better, beer is obtainable at a given price, then more beer will be drunk.[‡]

Some analyses of quality differences in relation to the construction of price indexes have also been made by Griliches (1961), (1964), Adelman and Griliches (1961), and Dhrymes (1967). Nicholson (1967) discusses the problems of compiling index numbers brought about by changes in quality and the introduction of new commodities. In particular he discusses the difficulty of allocation of these changes between changes in prices and changes in real income. According to Griliches (1961) this problem was recognised by Levine (1960). Some earlier contributions regarding the difficulties of dealing with quality changes when constructing price indexes were made by Court (1939), Hofsten (1952) and Stone (1956).

6.5 SUMMARY

In measuring consumer behaviour, economists have been concerned with the analysis of data for a market in which the range and character of the goods in that market have been changing considerably.

There are some references to the influence of new commodities on such features of the economy as growth, cyclical fluctuations, shifts in the consumption function and the changing structure of retail trading. However, there have been only a few explicit studies of the phenomenon of diffusion following introduction. In general, the main demand studies have steered away from these commodities; or where analysts have accidentally come across them, they have been disturbed by the large residual trends which have been evident.

[†] Jefferys (1954), p. 8.   [‡] Stone (1954), p. 388.

7. NEW COMMODITIES IN THE
UNITED KINGDOM

An illustration of the succession of changes in the range of consumer goods can be obtained from various descriptions of the British consumer market and from an examination of the data on consumption in the United Kingdom. From this it is possible to discover which particular commodities have been introduced to the economy, and to obtain some idea of the relative importance of these commodities.

The first thing to do is to establish when these commodities were introduced.

7.1 A TIMETABLE FOR THE INTRODUCTION OF NEW COMMODITIES

An approximate timetable for the introduction of new consumer commodities into the United Kingdom market was compiled from various sources. An initial list of 28 new commodities was obtained from a study of Jefferys (1954) and Jewkes, Sawers and Stillerman (1958). This was supplemented by an examination of the consumption series in Prest (1954), Stone (1954), Jefferys and Walters (1955), some independent estimates of consumption based on official sources and on some of the series prepared for publication in the *Abstract of British Historical Statistics*, Mitchell and Deane (1962).

There is some difficulty in defining *the* date when a new commodity is introduced into an economy and thus the beginnings of the diffusion process. Is it defined as the date on which the first single item is sold? Even if this can be established, it may not be a very significant economic date since supplies at that time may not be sufficient to ensure anything like free-market conditions, with the result that the choice between buying or not buying the commodity is restricted to only a small portion of the market. Thus it may be better to define the date of introduction as the date when plentiful supplies are available.

However for most new commodities this would prove to be very difficult to establish without a detailed examination of the supply arrangements. The aggregate statistics of consumption or retail sales provide a record only of the actual transactions through time. Nevertheless, it might not be unreasonable to assume that, at the time when a 'take-off' or 'surge' in consumption occurs, sufficient supplies were available to allow the diffusion process to begin.

The problem then is to precisely identify the date of this take-off. Should this be done in absolute terms or in relative terms? This difficulty in deciding precisely when the 'take-off' in consumption of a commodity occurs can be seen by considering two graphs of consumption per head against time, the first on an arithmetic scale and the second on a logarithmic scale. For example, consider the consumption of ice-cream. From the arithmetic scale given in figure 7.1 the

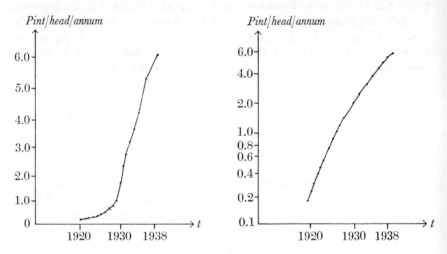

Figure 7.1. Time series charts for the consumption of ice-cream in the United Kingdom

take-off in ice-cream consumption in Britain would be regarded as taking place in the early 1930s; whereas from the logarithmic graph the take-off would be regarded as occurring earlier, at least in the 1920s, since the proportionate rate of growth was greater in the 1920s than in the 1930s. Similar difficulties in defining an exact take-off period arise with most other new commodities.

In preparing table 7.1 the 'introduction' of a new commodity has been taken as dating from the period of the 'take-off' in the upsurge of consumption. This take-off has been defined as the period in which there has been an acceleration in the rate of growth of consumption. This generally occurs at a slightly later period than the first sales of the commodity. For example, although the first shipment of bananas came to Britain in 1878, the 'take-off' in the consumption of bananas does not appear to have occurred until the 1890s. A counter-example is radios, where the take-off occurred immediately upon introduction in 1923.

The following timetable aims neither at being complete in covering all new commodities, nor at being exact in recording the period in which 'take-off' occurred.

TABLE 7.1   *New commodities: United Kingdom: timetable of their introduction*

Period of 'take-off'	Commodity
1630s	Tobacco (i)
1740s	Tea (i)
1780s	Cotton textiles
1810s	Coffee
1840s	Railways; tea (ii); oranges and lemons
1860s	Sewing machines; dry cleaning
1870s	Bicycles; perambulators; margarine
1880s	Telegrams; tramways; eating chocolate; pneumatic tyres; electroplate
1890s	Telephones; motor-cycles; canned and preserved foodstuffs; reliable bicycles; newspapers and periodicals; bananas
1900s	Proprietary medicines; plywood furniture; electric light; soft drinks
1910s	Cinema; photographic goods; milk chocolate; furniture suites; cigarettes; packaged tobaccos; safety razors
1920s	Motor-cars; radio; electric heating and cooking; wrapped bread; pasteurised milk; shorter skirts; grapefruit; zip fasteners; ice-cream
1930s	Rayon and artificial silk; refrigerators; bottled milk; sliced bread; crease-resisting fabrics
1950s	Television; nylon and terylene, etc. fabrics; detergents; frozen foods; motor-scooters; long-playing records; colour film; magnetic recording; ball-point pens; polythene

7.2   THE DURATION OF DIFFUSION PROCESSES

Having once found the new commodities and determined when they were introduced, the next task would be to attempt to determine whether the commodities had finished being absorbed by the market (i.e. whether their period of diffusion among consumers had ended). If not, can an estimate be made of the time when the absorption process will end? This might be done from a knowledge of the diffusion durations of other new commodities, from a knowledge of the diffusion durations of the same commodities in other countries (where the commodity may have been introduced at an earlier date) or finally from a knowledge of the process to date for the commodity in the United Kingdom.

The precise period of 'take-off' is difficult to establish. So also is the precise period of the completion of the diffusion process. For a number of the commodities listed in the timetable for the introduction of new commodities into the United Kingdom, statistics were obtained which

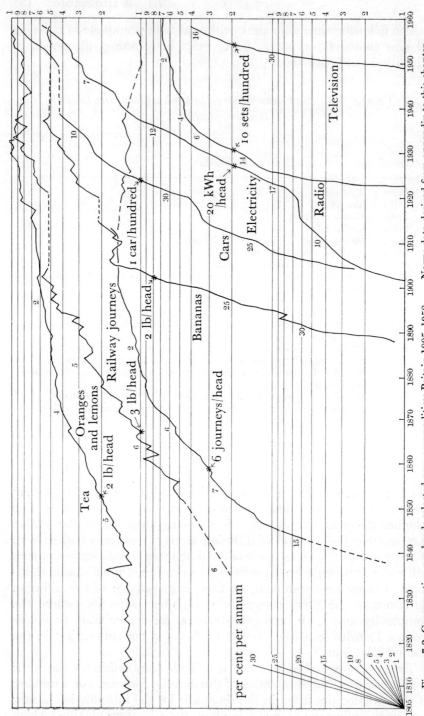

Figure 7.2. Consumption per head: selected new commodities: Britain 1805–1958   NOTE: data derived from appendix to this chapter.

enable approximate estimates to be made of the duration of the diffusion processes.

These statistics were expressed in terms of the annual consumption per head of population from the period of their introduction into the economy until after the world war II period. In figure 7.2, they are graphed on a logarithmic scale to indicate the shape of the rates of growth through the diffusion process and all shown on a common time scale so that the rates of growth of the different commodities can be compared. The numerals shown in the body of the graph indicate approximate annual percentage rates of growth at various stages in each diffusion process.

Not all new commodities have continued to grow without a pause. Some even declined, as did coffee in the period from 1850 to 1910, and rail passenger journeys after 1908. Nor are the rates of growth very even from year to year or from commodity to commodity. Tea seems to have been one of the slowest-growing commodities, whereas radio was among the fastest.

Table 7.2 shows the approximate duration of the diffusion processes for: (i) five commodities with apparently completed diffusion processes. and (ii) three commodities with apparently incomplete diffusion processes.

TABLE 7.2   *Diffusion of new commodities: United Kingdom*

Commodity	Approximate date of take-off	Approximate date of completion of diffusion	Approximate diffusion duration
Completed			
Tea	1840s	1920s	90 years
Railway passenger journeys	1840s	1900s	70 years
Oranges and lemons	1850s	1930s	70 years[a]
Bananas	1890s	1930s	50 years
Radio	1923	1950s	40 years
Incomplete			
Private cars	1920s	?(1990s)[b]	?(70 years)[c]
Electricity (home heat and power)	1930s	?(2000s)[d]	?(80 years)
Television	1950	?(1970)[e]	?(20 years)

[a] No increase from 1902 to 1922.

[b] Based on a comparison of the number in use per head of population in the U.K. compared with the probable saturation levels for U.S.A. and Canada.

[c] No increase from 1939 to 1949.

[d] A guess based on the strength of the diffusion process to date which has shown little sign of slackening.

[e] Based on an estimate of a saturation level of slightly more than the saturation level for radios in the U.K.

It will be seen that those with completed processes have tended to have shorter durations as time goes on, decreasing from 90 years to 40 years. However, there are two commodities with incomplete processes that, it would appear, will eventually have durations of 70 to 80 years. Although there is evidence for lengthy diffusion processes still proceeding, two hypotheses are suggested.

These are: (i) the rate at which new commodities are introduced into, and accepted by, the consumer market has increased and (ii) the rates of absorption of new commodities are faster now than they were a century ago. These hypotheses reinforce each other and are supported by the expectation that there is a greater current awareness on the part of producers of the opportunities for exploiting new products and on the other hand a greater degree of communication (between consumers and between producers and consumers – advertising and market research) today than formerly. Consumers at high incomes should also be more prepared to hazard the risk involved in buying an unknown new product than consumers at low incomes, so that, in so far as incomes have increased, it would be expected that there would be an increase in the amount of experimental purchases and thus the quicker discovery of suitable new commodities.

To test these hypotheses thoroughly would involve making a complete catalogue of the new products introduced to the consumer market and estimating the rates of growth in consumption for these commodities. As the bias of the quantity of available information on these commodities is towards recent periods, there would be a bias towards finding more new commodities in the most recent past than earlier. Even if this bias could be overcome in some way, the fact that the rate at which new commodities are introduced and accepted into the consumer market has increased does not mean that their importance has increased to the same degree. One major new commodity may be as important as 10 minor ones.

The task of making a more or less complete catalogue of the new commodities entering the British market would be gigantic. However, from the table and graphs, incomplete as they are,† it is seen that for many commodities, rates of growth in consumption per head, often well over 10 per cent per annum, have taken place for continuous periods of two or more decades, which by any standard must be regarded as phenomenal. The best example given is that of electricity, which after six decades of growth, much of which was at a rate of more than 15 per cent per annum, still grew in the 1960s at a rate of seven per cent per annum.

Parallel phenomena can be observed in other countries. For example,

---

† And indeed must be, having regard to the nature of technical change.   See the introduction to Jewkes, Sawers and Stillerman (1958).

Kuznets (1942) catalogues some of the changes in consumer expenditure on various categories in the United States and points out the growing importance of the proportion of consumer expenditure going to new commodities.

In making inter-economy comparisons of rates of consumption for new commodities,† it may make more sense to compare the rates of consumption at different chronological periods after the commodity's introduction, than to compare the rates of consumption at various levels of income per head.

7.3 SUMMARY

An approximate timetable has been established for the introduction into the United Kingdom of more than 60 new commodities or new forms of commodities. For some, the diffusion process appears to have been completed; for others, it is continuing. Although these processes sometimes appear to last for the comparatively short time of about 20 years, others take as long as 90 years. An important task for consumer-demand analysts would be not only to measure the length and strength of these processes, but also to try to ascertain why they occur with the strength and length that they do.

Although very little work has yet been done on consumer diffusion processes, a considerable and growing literature exists on producer diffusion processes. This includes work on machine tools by Jerome (1934); hybrid seed corn by Ryan and Gross (1943), Ryan (1948), and Griliches (1957); new drugs by Coleman, Katz and Menzel (1957); and various industrial processes by Mansfield (1961), (1963), and (1965). More general works concerned with the nature of diffusion processes, principally in the adoption of new producer processes and techniques, include Carter and Williams (1957), Rogers (1962) and Nelson and Phelps (1966). A useful summary of the recent literature on diffusion processes for both producer and consumer behaviour may be found in Nelson, Peck and Kalachek (1967).

Some of the problems encountered in analysing time series for aggregate consumption levels are examined in chapters 8 and 10. In particular, an experiment is tried using actual time series of these data to see whether the inclusion of lagged consumption as an explanatory variable can help to separate the diffusion process effects from the effects of price and income changes. This experiment forms the major part of the final chapter.

† For example the comparisons by Maizels (1959) for passenger cars, motor cycles, bicycles, radios, television sets, refrigerators and washing machines.

APPENDIX TO CHAPTER 7

TABLE 7.3.   *Consumption per head for selected commodities: United Kingdom, 1800–1958*

| | | | Coffee | |
Year	Tobacco U.K.	Tea U.K.	G.B.	U.K.
1800	1.24	1.48	0.08	
1	1.23	1.49	0.07	
2	1.06	1.58	0.08	
3	1.23	1.53	0.08	
4	1.14	1.34	0.10	
1805	1.08	1.45	0.11	
6	1.09	1.31	0.10	
7	1.01	1.39	0.10	
8	1.01	1.45	0.09	
9	0.96	1.19	0.78	
1810	1.18	1.37	0.44	
1	1.23	1.24	0.53	
2	1.21	1.34	0.66	
3	1.05	1.36	0.70	
4	0.94	1.29	0.50	
1815	0.86	1.35	0.47	0.34
6	0.95	1.16	0.57	0.40
7	0.93	1.24	0.65	0.47
8	0.90	1.32	0.59	0.42
9	0.81	1.24	0.54	0.38
1820	0.76	1.22		0.34
1	0.75	1.27		0.36
2	0.77	1.29		0.36
3	0.79	1.25		0.39
4	0.77	1.26		0.38
1825	0.85	1.31		0.50
6	0.79	1.29		0.58
7	0.82	1.31		0.68
8	0.80	1.26		0.74
9	0.81	1.25		0.83
1830	0.81	1.26		0.95
1	0.81	1.24		0.94
2	0.83	1.29		0.94
3	0.84	1.29		0.92
4	0.86	1.41		0.96
1835	0.88	1.46		0.93
6	0.88	1.93		0.98
7	0.88	1.19		1.03
8	0.91	1.25		0.99
9	0.88	1.34		1.02

Year	Tobacco U.K.	Tea U.K.	Coffee U.K.	Rail passengers G.B.	Oranges and lemons U.K.
1840	0.87	1.22	1.08	(1838 = 0.30)	
1	0.83	1.37	1.06	—	
2	0.83	1.38	1.06	—	
3	0.85	1.48	1.10	1.14	
4	0.89	1.50	1.14	1.31	
1845	0.94	1.59	1.23	1.56	
6	0.96	1.67	1.31	2.04	
7	0.95	1.66	1.34	2.40	
8	0.98	1.75	1.33	2.70	
9	1.00	1.81	1.24	2.83	
1850	1.00	1.86	1.13	3.26	
1	1.02	1.97	1.19	3.82	
2	1.04	1.99	1.27	3.92	
3	1.07	2.14	1.34	4.47	
4	1.10	2.24	1.35	4.84	1.75
1855	1.09	2.28	1.29	5.11	1.72
6	1.16	2.26	1.25	5.51	1.48
7	1.16	2.45	1.22	5.86	1.95
8	1.20	2.58	1.24	5.81	2.02
9	1.21	2.67	1.20	6.17	2.29
1860	1.22	2.67	1.23	6.69	2.38
1	1.20	2.69	1.21	7.03	3.00
2	1.21	2.69	1.18	7.24	2.08
3	1.13	2.89	1.11	8.09	2.72
4	1.28	2.99	1.06	9.08	2.57
1865	1.30	3.27	1.02	9.81	3.11
6	1.34	3.39	1.02	10.61	3.37
7	1.34	3.65	1.03	10.98	2.84
8	1.34	3.48	0.99	—	3.49
9	1.34	3.61	0.93	11.70	3.72
1870	1.32	3.76	0.97	12.47	3.67
1	1.35	3.91	0.97	13.75	4.47
2	1.37	4.01	0.98	15.34	4.45
3	1.41	4.10	0.99	16.35	4.26
4	1.43	4.22	0.96	16.96	4.39
1875	1.46	4.43	0.98	17.78	5.19
6	1.46	4.49	0.99	18.52	5.31
7	1.49	4.50	0.96	18.82	6.25
8	1.44	4.64	0.97	19.09	5.98
9	1.40	4.68	0.99	18.81	5.95

Year	Tobacco U.K.	Tea U.K.	Coffee U.K.	Rail passengers G.B.	Oranges and lemons U.K.
1880	1.42	4.57	0.92	20.28	6.27
1	1.41	4.58	0.89	20.42	6.52
2	1.42	4.69	0.89	21.13	7.12
3	1.43	4.82	0.89	21.84	7.51
4	1.45	4.90	0.90	21.96	8.23
1885	1.46	5.06	0.91	21.82	7.18
6	1.44	4.92	0.87	22.49	7.17
7	1.45	5.02	0.80	22.50	7.80
8	1.48	5.03	0.83	22.52	7.83
9	1.51	4.99	0.76	23.26	9.34
1890	1.55	5.17	0.75	24.30	9.11
1	1.61	5.35	0.76	24.86	8.14
2	1.64	5.43	0.74	25.13	10.53
3	1.62	5.40	0.69	25.07	8.76
4	1.66	5.51	0.68	25.88	12.06
1895	1.66	5.65	0.70	26.07	13.44
6	1.72	5.75	0.69	27.21	13.34
7	1.75	5.79	0.68	28.33	15.37
8	1.82	5.83	0.68	28.90	13.10
9	1.88	5.95	0.71	29.76	14.92
1900	1.95	6.07	0.71	30.38	14.79
1	1.89	6.16	0.76	30.88	15.42
2	1.93	6.07	0.68	30.97	18.10
3	1.94	6.04	0.71	30.84	17.07
4	1.96	6.02	0.68	30.62	16.18
1905	1.97	6.02	0.67	30.33	
6	1.99	6.22	0.66	31.08	
7	2.04	6.26	0.67	31.25	
8	2.04	6.24	0.66	31.43	
9	1.97	6.36	0.67	30.79	
1910	2.00	6.39	0.65	31.48	
1	2.06	6.48	0.62	31.68	
2	2.06	6.50	0.62	30.81	
3	2.10	6.69	0.62	34.47/29.04	
4	2.19	6.89	0.63	—	
1915	2.44	7.15	0.74	—	
6	2.35	6.91	0.66	—	
7	2.44	6.41	1.05	—	
8	2.51	7.21	1.11	—	
9	3.26	8.70	0.76	37.83	

Year	Bananas U.K.	Electricity U.K.	Private cars G.B.
1880	0.03		
1	0.03		
2	0.03		
3	0.03		
4	0.03		
1885	0.03		
6	0.03		
7	0.03		
8	0.03		
9	0.04		
1890	0.10		
1	0.14		
2	0.17		
3	0.23		
4	0.20		
1895	0.27		
6	0.41		
7	0.51		
8	0.60		
9	0.74		
1900	0.94	0.49	
1	1.62	0.91	
2	2.02	1.31	
3	2.20	1.71	
4	2.65	2.10	0.02
1905	4.04	2.48	0.04
6	4.45	2.86	0.06
7	4.18	3.34	0.08
8	4.20	3.54	0.10
9	3.91	3.85	0.12
1910	3.64	4.15	0.13
1	3.99	4.45	0.18
2	3.98	4.78	0.21
3	4.37	5.30	0.26
4	5.27	6.06	0.32
1915	5.44	6.35	0.35
6	4.23	6.48	0.36
7	1.60	6.57	0.28
8	0.53	6.60	0.20
9	3.43	6.62	0.27

Year	Tobacco U.K.	Tea U.K.	Coffee U.K.	Rail passengers G.B.	Oranges and lemons U.K.
1920	2.99	8.44	0.72	37.49	11.09
1	2.96	8.69	0.71	28.71	15.15
2	2.82	8.67	0.74	27.72	17.83
3	(2.90)	(8.68)	(0.79)	28.51	19.29
4	2.87	8.81	0.78	28.31	19.20
1925	2.96	8.85	0.79	28.14	19.96
6	3.00	8.91	0.77	24.31	20.58
7	3.04	9.03	0.80	26.61	20.03
8	3.11	9.16	0.78	26.98	19.33
9	3.24	10.16	0.76	27.82	23.20
1930	3.31	9.87	0.77	27.28	24.90
1	3.27	9.67	0.81	25.79	25.47
2	3.23	10.53	0.76	24.85	23.13
3	3.22	9.36	0.70	25.60	28.96
4	3.41	9.22	0.72	26.43	25.63
1935	3.51	9.42	0.70	27.00	24.81
6	3.72	9.31	0.72	27.44	22.47
7	3.87	9.19	0.72	28.20	28.66
8	4.00	9.09	0.72	26.77	24.77
9		—	—	26.37	
1940		8.6	1.2	21.61	
1		8.1	1.2	23.49	
2		8.2	1.2	28.33	
3		7.0	1.0	31.42	
4		7.4	1.2	31.70	
1945		8.2	1.2	32.21	
6		8.8	1.4	27.73	
7		8.5	1.6	24.32	
8		8.0	1.7	20.58	
9		8.3	1.8	20.38	
1950		8.5	1.5	20.05	
1		8.1	1.7	20.46	
2		8.5	1.5	20.15	
3		9.2	1.3	20.04	
4		9.7	1.3	20.65	
1955		9.4	1.3	20.05	
6		10.1	1.5	20.65	
7		9.8	1.6	22.00	

Year	Bananas U.K.	Electricity G.B.	Private cars G.B.	Radio U.K.	Television U.K.
1920	5.45	7.1	0.44	0.00	
1	6.21	7.4	0.57	0.01	
2	7.46	8.5	0.73	0.08	
3	8.13	10.5	0.89	1.34	
4	7.68	12.4	1.09	2.52	
1925	8.10	14.5	1.32	3.65	
6	9.12	17.1	1.56	4.82	
7	8.46	20.9	1.78	5.28	
8	8.52	24.8	2.00	5.77	
9	9.75	29.5	2.21	6.47	
1930	9.77	34.3	2.37	7.44	
1	10.60	39.6	2.42	9.40	
2	11.31	45.0	2.50	11.36	
3	10.50	50.7	2.66	12.84	
4	12.15	58.3	2.88	14.53	
1935	13.06	70.8	3.24	15.79	
6	13.12	86.5	3.59	16.91	
7	14.33	101.9	3.91	17.93	
8	13.27	116.0	4.21	18.76	
9	12.81	127.8	4.38	18.74	
1940	8.93	139.2	3.18	19.35	
1	0.06	152.4	3.45	19.23	
2	0.00	156.3	2.00	20.63	
3	0.00	157.9	1.69	21.55	
4	0.00	184.6	1.78	22.05	
1945	0.56	206.7	3.49	22.74	0.00
6	4.60	255.4	3.88	22.92	0.02
7	4.63	271.6	4.15	22.93	0.07
8	6.37	280.5	4.05	23.04	0.19
9	6.50	280.4	4.38	24.31	0.48
1950	5.34	304.6	4.61	24.53	1.15
1	6.92	346.2	4.86	25.05	2.31
2	7.03	343.8	5.11	25.49	3.75
3	10.92	359.4	5.61	26.22	5.84
4	12.13	386.2	6.28	27.32	8.18
1955	12.81	426.5	7.11	27.95	10.59
6	13.09	476.9	7.80	28.19	12.83
7	12.98	496.7	8.36	28.48	15.08
8	12.76	561.4	9.05	28.55	17.22

11

144 New commodities in U.K.

NOTES AND SOURCES:

Tobacco, tea and coffee: lb per head per annum.
1800–1938   Mitchell and Deane, *Abstract of British Historical Statistics* (1962).
1940–47   (tea and coffee) *Statistical Abstract for the United Kingdom*, nos. 85 and 95.

Rail passengers: Great Britain; passenger journeys per head per annum.
1838–1932   *Abstract of British Historical Statistics* (1962). Excludes season ticket holders.
1933–57   *Statistical Abstract for the United Kingdom* (various). Excludes all journeys on London Passenger Transport Board properties but includes mainline season ticket holders on basis of 600 journeys per annum.

Oranges and lemons: United Kingdom: lb per head per annum.
1854–1905   Statistics of imports from *Sessional Papers* less deduction of 10 per cent for wastage and oranges used in marmalade manufacture. Bushels taken as weighing 66 lb.
1920–38   Stone (1954), table 40, p. 133.

Bananas: United Kingdom: lb per head per annum.
1878–99   Estimated from statistics in *Sessional Papers* of imports of 'Fruit – unenumerated, raw' from Canary Is., Madeira and British West Indies.
1900–19   Prest (1954), table 33, p. 63, with correction to convert to lb figures of '000 bunches shown there as '000 cwt.
1920–38   Stone (1954), table 40, p. 133.
1939–58   *Statistical Abstract for the United Kingdom* (various). Imports less estimated 5 per cent wastage.

Electricity: Consumption by households and farms; kWh per head per annum.
1900–19   United Kingdom: Prest (1954), table 73, p. 112.
1920–58   Great Britain: *Ministry of Power Statistical Digest*, 1958, table 66, p. 91.

Private cars: Vehicles with licences current; private cars per hundred population.
1904–38   *Abstract of British Historical Statistics* (1962). Licences current in March (1904–20), August (1921–5) and September (1926–38).
1939–58   *Statistical Abstract for the United Kingdom* (various). Licences current at 31 August (1939–45) and at any time in September quarter (1946–58).

Radio: United Kingdom: Receiving licences current at end of year per hundred population.
1920–47   Coase R. H. (1950). *British Broadcasting*, Longmans, Green, London, p. 199.
1948–58   *Statistical Abstract for the United Kingdom*. Includes both sound and television licences.

Television: United Kingdom: Television licences current at end of year per hundred population.
Statistical Abstract for the United Kingdom, and *Monthly Digest of Statistics* (various).

8. NEW, ESTABLISHED AND OUTMODED COMMODITIES IN THE UNITED KINGDOM, 1920–38

'With the incessant introduction of new commodities and services, disappearance of old commodities, and shifts in the relative importance of continuing products, vast changes have occurred in the qualitative composition of national industry.'

A. F. Burns (1934), p. 49

The previous chapter presented some information about eight new consumer commodities which appear in the British economy during the last 150 years.

This chapter examines the comprehensive set of data concerning the entire range of consumer expenditure in the British economy during the period of approximately two decades stretching from 1920 to 1938. This data set provides details of the consumption levels for a number of new commodities. However, the average time for diffusion of the eight commodities examined in chapter 7 is about 60 years and thus the data from a fixed survey period of 19 years would not be expected to measure the complete diffusion process for any particular commodity unless it had a short diffusion period of less than 20 years.

Thus, in general, only a segment of a new commodity's diffusion process would be observed in the period 1920 to 1938. Some commodities such as radios, cars and electricity would be in early diffusion stages, others such as bananas and oranges in late diffusion stages and others such as tea and railway journeys would be in established or saturation situations. Moreover, some of the established commodities may be undergoing a reverse process to expansion with their consumption levels declining sharply because they have become outmoded or superseded by new commodities.

8.1 THE DATA

The most comprehensive sources of data on the consumption of commodities in Britain are the 1954 volume by Stone and the 1966 volume by Stone and Rowe, which between them present annual series of both quantities consumed and average retail prices for 220 commodities consumed in the United Kingdom over the years 1920–38.

The different sections of these volumes vary considerably in the amount of detail available. For example, 14 different types of fish and 24 different types of vegetables are separately distinguished, whereas there are no separate series for different types of furniture or household machinery, such as refrigerators and washing machines. Separate details are therefore unavailable for many commodities commonly recognised as the most important new commodities. However, the most expensive new commodity of all, the motor car, is separately distinguished as is electricity, the power needed to run the new types of household machinery.

8.2 NEW, ESTABLISHED AND OUTMODED COMMODITIES

All commodities must have been new at some time or other. Therefore, the question arises: 'For how long can a commodity be called new?' Obviously if it is just appearing on the market for the first time, it would certainly be called new. For example, the telephone would fall into this category in Britain in the 1900s, and so would bananas in Britain in the 1880s. These newly introduced commodities could continue to be called 'new' commodities in a particular economy until they reached the stage where they had been completely diffused through the market of consumers with all potential consumers using the commodity to the full. This could be called the stage of saturation, but it would seem difficult to ascertain it precisely, and there is always the possibility that a particular commodity might become outmoded by another new commodity before it managed to become fully diffused. For example, in some countries, radios may be partly outmoded by television before they reach full saturation.

There are other commodities which do not fall into the 'newly introduced' category, but would appear to go through a long stage with little change, consumption remaining at a fairly low level. The commodity may be consumed by only a few, or by many on only rare occasions. Then for some reason, perhaps a small change in quality or a promotion campaign, the diffusion process gets under way and the consumption of the commodity spreads widely through the body of consumers. Tea seems to have followed this pattern in Britain from 1840, after having been through a long period with a low stationary consumption level. A similar process was apparently taking place with some other commodities – notably wine, eggs, cream, poultry, lamb, and various vegetables – in Britain in the inter-war period.

Both these categories – the newly introduced commodities and what might be called the 'resurgent' commodities – eventually reach a stage sometimes called 'the stage of mass consumption'. During their diffusion stages it would seem appropriate to label both groups of commodities 'new'.

'Established' commodities will be those with more or less stationary consumption levels and 'outmoded' commodities will be those with declining consumption levels, in most cases being outmoded by some newly introduced commodity or by some resurgent commodity.

The procedure for the remainder of this chapter will be to classify the data for consumption as well as possible in the three categories 'new', 'established' or 'outmoded'.

The commodities belonging to each of three groups – new commodities, established commodities and outmoded commodities, will also be ranked within each group. New commodities will be ranked from the earliest to the latest stages of growth. Established commodities will be ranked according to whether they are showing slight growth tendencies, are very stable, or are perhaps tending to decline. Outmoded commodities will be ranked according to whether they are in the early, middle or final stages of a decline. This will produce a spectrum of commodities ranked from those in very early stages of growth to those in the final stages of decline.

This classification and ranking was made by examining the time series of the levels of consumption. To assist this the time series of the levels could be graphed on logarithmic scales (as in the preceding chapter for eight new commodities). An alternative method of presenting the movements is to plot the annual observations of consumption per head on the two dimensional space $Ox_t x_{t-1}$, the points being labelled by the current year. The resulting scatter of points can be called the 'lag-sequence' graph.

8.3 LAG-SEQUENCE GRAPHS

This method shows up the difference between established, new and outmoded commodities more strikingly than the usual time series graph of x_t against time. For established commodities the lag-sequence graphs show the observations crowded around a single point instead of a fluctuating line. For new and outmoded commodities the lag-sequence graphs show points, either above (for new) or below (for outmoded) the 45° line, which when connected give a ray for outmoded commodities which has the reverse direction to the ray for the new commodities. In the usual time-series graphs, such rays have the same direction and are only distinguished by their slopes.

Figure 8.1 shows how the lag-sequence graph collapses the observations for an established commodity to a single point, thus becoming truly stationary; the time-series graph for an established commodity gives a false impression of movement. Similarly figure 8.1 shows how the lag-sequence graph reverses the direction of movement for an outmoded commodity. The lag-sequence graph seems to take the time out of a time series when time is irrelevant.

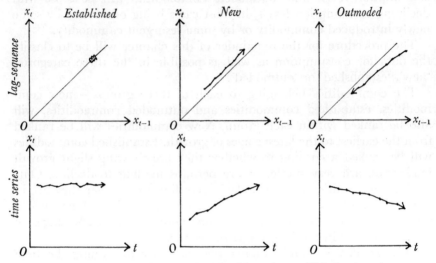

Figure 8.1. Lag-sequence and time-series graphs: established, new and outmoded commodities

The annual observations of consumption per head plotted in the two-dimensional space $Ox_t x_{t-1}$ show that the typical 'life cycle' for a commodity takes the pattern shown in figure 8.2 going through a sequence of stages 1 to 8.

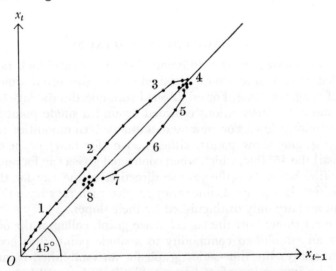

Figure 8.2. Lag-sequence graph for stages of growth and decline

   During a period when a strong upward surge in consumption of a commodity is taking place, the points of the lag-sequence graph will lie along a line approximately through the origin with a slope somewhat greater than one (stage 1 of the figure), early observations lying near the origin and successively getting further and further apart. This pattern is typified by the observations for canned vegetables in the United Kingdom during the period 1920 to 1938, which are plotted in figure 8.3.
   During the middle period of a commodity's acceptance into the market when the rate of growth is steady, the distribution of points in the $Ox_t x_{t-1}$ space would lie along a line slightly above and parallel

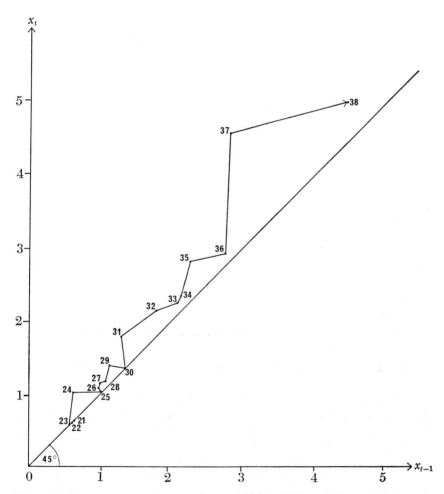

Figure 8.3. Lag-sequence graph: canned vegetables (tons/000 equivalent adults/annum): United Kingdom

to the line $x_t = x_{t-1}$ through the origin (stage 2). Early observations are closer to the origin than later ones, which are fairly evenly spaced along the line. This pattern is typified by the observations for the steady growth in the consumption of cigarettes in the United Kingdom during the period 1924–38, which are shown in figure 8.4.

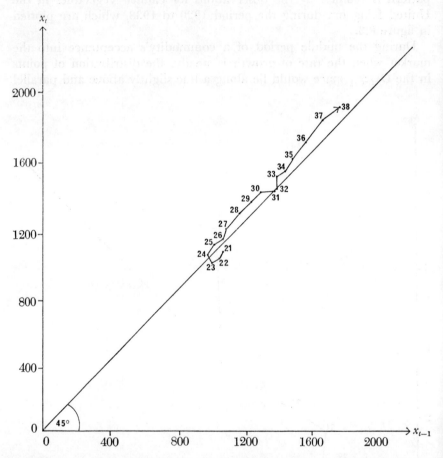

Figure 8.4. Lag-sequence graph: cigarettes (number/adult/annum): United Kingdom

During a third period, (stage 3), when the commodity moves towards a saturation level, the observations would tend to lie along a line with a slope of less than one and which intersects the line $x_t = x_{t-1}$ at the saturation level (stage 4), later observations being further from the origin and closer together. This pattern is typified by the consumption of oranges in the United Kingdom during the period 1920–38. This pattern is shown in figure 8.5.

During the period when consumption is relatively stable, the observa-

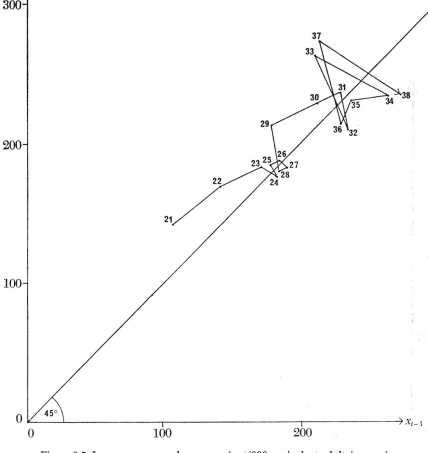

Figure 8.5. Lag-sequence graph: oranges (cwt/000 equivalent adults/annum):
United Kingdom

tions of the lag-sequence graph will be clustered round a point on line $x_t = x_{t-1}$, with very little spread (stage 4) as typified by bread in the United Kingdom over the period 1920–38, or with somewhat greater spread as typified by potatoes in the same economy over the same period. These patterns are shown in figures 8.6 and 8.7. These commodities during this period in this economy can be regarded as established commodities.

Sometimes commodities enter a stage of decline (stage 5). This can occur as the result of the appearance of a more efficient substitute, as took place with gas lighting when electric light was introduced. Since the timing of the decline will depend on the timing of the introduction

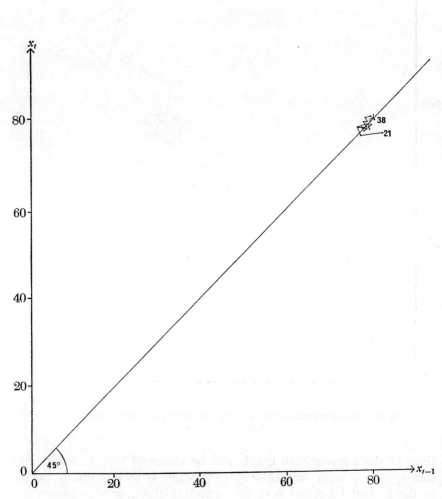

Figure 8.6. Lag-sequence graph: bread (tons/000 equivalent adults/annum):
United Kingdom

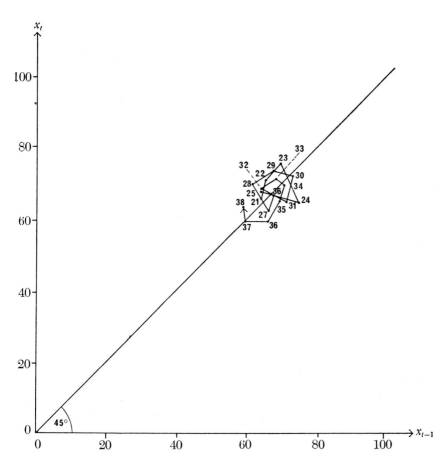

Figure 8.7. Lag-sequence graph: potatoes (home and imported) (tons/000 equivalent adults/
annum): United Kingdom

of the more efficient substitute, it can occur after the commodity has become well established or before this stage has been reached.

Figure 8.8 for pipe tobacco in the United Kingdom over the 1920–38 period typifies the pattern for a commodity undergoing a fairly steady

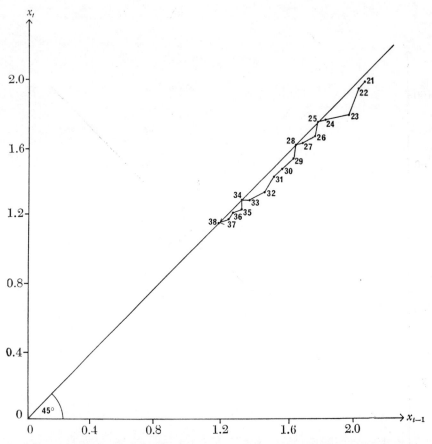

Figure 8.8. Lag-sequence graph: pipe tobacco (lb/adult/annum): United Kingdom

decline, while figure 8.9 for spirits in the same economy for the same period typifies a commodity declining (stage 6) to a new lower stable level of consumption (stages 7 and 8), the points in the $Ox_t x_{t-1}$ space lying along a line with slope less than one, early points being further from the origin and later points clustering around a new equilibrium level. Figure 8.10 for margarine shows a full stage adjustment from a high equilibrium level over the years 1921 to 1929 to a lower equilibrium level reached in 1934 – the adjustment taking five years to complete.

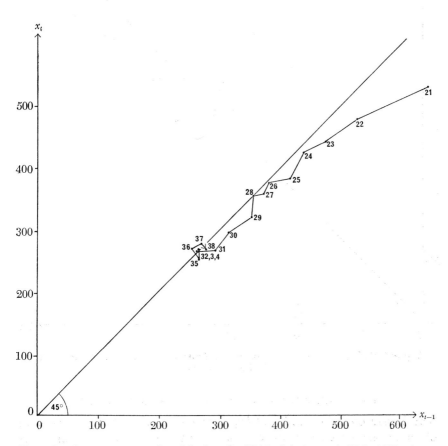

Figure 8.9. Lag-sequence graph: spirits (proof gal/000 adults/annum): United Kingdom

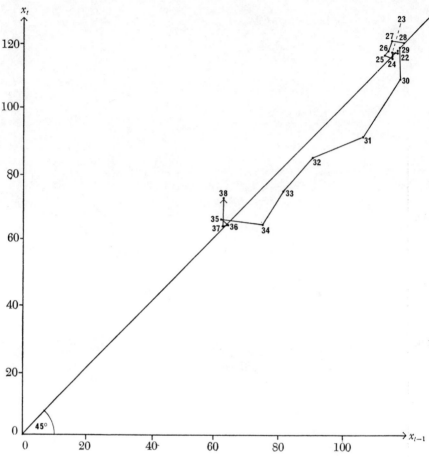

Figure 8.10. Lag-sequence graph: margarine (cwt/000 equivalent adults/annum):
United Kingdom

8.4 THE STAGES OF GROWTH AND DECLINE

The linear equation, $x_t = a + bx_{t-1}$, when fitted to the lag-sequence
observations for a commodity in just one stage of the commodity life-
cycle will have values of the constant, a, and slope, b, as follows:

Stage	Constant	Slope
1: Early new	$a = 0$	$b > 1$
2: Middle new	$a > 0$	$b = 1$
3: Late new	$a > 0$	$b < 1$
4: and 8: Established	$a = \bar{x}_t$	$b = 0$
5: Early outmoded	$a < 0$	$b > 1$
6: Middle outmoded	$a < 0$	$b = 1$
7: Late outmoded	$a > 0$	$b < 1$

TABLE 8.1. *Stages of growth and decline: commodities in the United Kingdom: 1920 to 1938*

Commodity and annual rate of per capita growth (per cent)	Constant a	Slope b
Early new stage (slope significantly greater than one with strong positive growth)		
Trolley vehicles (30.2)	−0.05	1.40
Ice-cream (22.7)	0.05	1.20
Canned vegetables (11.9)	−0.09	1.18
Electricity (16.3)	−0.04	1.17
Cigarettes (4.0)	−7.45	1.12
Health services (2.1)	−5.79	1.12
Telephone services (9.6)	0.01	1.09
Biscuits (6.0)	0.06	1.06
Soap flakes, powders, etc. (4.2)	−0.15	1.06
Rubber footwear (7.3)	0.02	1.05
Middle new stage (slope not significantly different from one with strong positive growth)		
Personal effects (3.0)	−9.50	1.14
Breakfast cereals (7.6)	−0.02	1.10
Table waters (4.1)	−0.45	1.09
British wine (8.4)	0.00	1.08
Chocolate and chocolate confectionery (3.6)	−0.80	1.07
Buses and coaches (9.4)	2.41	1.03
Motor vehicle running costs (11.4)	3.11	1.02
Air travel (15.2)	0.03	1.02
Postal services (2.1)	0.50	1.02
Soft drinks (7.8)	0.06	1.01
Hairdressing, etc. (4.9)	0.49	1.01
Grapefruit (20.9)	0.15	1.00
Bicycles, accessories and repairs (6.1)	0.34	1.00
Cakes (3.0)	1.60	0.99
Radio, etc. licences (11.4)	0.33	0.99
Fresh cod (4.9)	0.11	0.98
Drycleaning, laundry and dyeing (4.1)	1.20	0.98
Eggs (5.7)	3.40	0.98
Cream (6.5)	0.38	0.96
Motor vehicles (7.9)	3.52	0.93
Insurance (3.7)	5.30	0.93
Coke (4.5)	0.34	0.93
Green vegetables and legumes (3.9)	2.06	0.92
Bananas (4.7)	0.91	0.91
Furniture and furnishings (3.8)	17.98	0.91
Miscellaneous services (2.1)	4.17	0.91
Betting (7.4)	2.28	0.90
Lamb (4.5)	6.43	0.89
Canned fruit (6.9)	1.15	0.84
Sugar confectionery (1.9)	5.04	0.80
Canned fish (4.1)	1.77	0.79
Hardware, hollow ware, etc. (2.4)	18.74	0.72
Honey (5.0)	0.20	0.68

Commodity and annual rate of per capita growth (per cent)	Constant a	Slope b
Late new stage (slope significantly less than one with strong positive growth)		
Poultry (3.6)	1.59	0.90
Oranges (3.6)	4.66	0.66
Canned meat (5.4)	2.26	0.64
Lemons (2.4)	0.89	0.59
Salmon (3.5)	0.53	0.58
Raspberries (10.4)	0.20	0.55
Established stage		
Butter (5.3)	1.32	0.87
Cider and perry (2.7)	0.23	0.92
Bacon and ham (1.8)	30.22	0.66
Other recreation (1.8)	1.19	0.99
Sugar (1.7)	9.84	0.59
Public entertainments (1.5)	1.76	0.98
Private education (1.4)	1.10	0.96
Rent, rates and water (1.3)	−34.39	1.09
Domestic service (1.2)	0.32	1.01
Apples and pears (1.1)	16.74	0.31
Reading matter (0.9)	3.84	0.94
Other household services (0.9)	5.51	0.90
Cheese (0.9)	4.20	0.77
Leather footwear (0.8)	−1.89	1.04
Cooking fats and oils (0.8)	10.62	0.21
Offal (0.7)	8.49	0.66
Gas (0.7)	7.22	0.82
Imported wine (0.7)	9.04	0.60
Toys, travel and sports goods (0.8)	7.61	0.65
Apparel and dress materials (0.8)	172.81	0.51
Condensed milk (0.7)	5.70	0.19
Fish and chips (0.7)	8.95	0.54
Tea (0.5)	11.42	0.77
Beef and veal (0.5)	138.47	−0.06
Fresh milk (0.5)	3.78	0.64
Nuts (0.4)	1.12	0.29
Coal (0.4)	121.26	−0.17
Syrup and treacle (0.3)	1.13	0.28
Coffee (0.2)	1.83	0.64
Railways (0.2)	31.77	0.40
Bread (0.2)	49.51	0.25
Matches, polishes, etc. (0.1)	7.53	0.67
Rabbits and game (−0.03)	5.55	0.23
Meat essences and extracts (−0.2)	5.48	−0.08
Jam and marmalade (−0.3)	6.83	0.56
Pottery and glassware (−0.5)	19.32	−0.03
Rice, barley and oatmeal (−0.6)	4.57	0.47
Pork (−0.9)	7.94	0.67
Telegrams (−1.2)	0.18	0.76
Cured fish (−1.4)	4.39	0.34
Margarine (−4.5)	0.91	0.73

Commodity and annual rate of per capita growth (per cent)	Constant a	Slope b
Middle outmoded stage (slope not significantly different from one with strong negative growth)		
Tramways (−1.5)	−4.10	1.18
Hard soap (−1.2)	−0.32	1.02
Taxis and hire cars (−7.3)	−0.69	0.97
Candles (−2.8)	0.02	0.96
Pipe tobacco (−2.8)	0.50	0.96
Snuff, cigars, etc. (−2.9)	0.29	0.89
Gooseberries (−4.4)	0.16	0.89
Shell fish (−1.7)	0.32	0.80
Kerosene (1928–38) (−0.4)	1.22	0.80
Steamboats and ferries (−2.8)	3.06	0.77
Late outmoded stage (slope significantly less than one with strong negative growth)		
Horse drawn vehicles (−15.7)	−0.15	0.93
Religion and charity (−0.5)	3.06	0.87
Cocoa (−2.4)	0.55	0.81
Spirits (−4.1)	15.90	0.76
Mutton (−4.6)	3.49	0.77
Beer (−1.9)	65.72	0.67
Sago, tapioca and arrowroot (−1.9)	0.29	0.44
Flour (−2.0)	12.67	0.56
Minor tobacco products (−1.2)	0.88	0.62
Dried legumes (−2.5)	2.26	0.06
Dried fruit (−1.5)	6.96	−0.04

On the basis of estimates of the constant and slope of the lag-sequence graphs, 113 commodities were grouped into stages of growth and decline. The results are shown in table 8.1, which also shows the exponential rate of growth of consumption for each commodity.

Chapter 9 examines the extent to which the diffusion of new commodities changed the pattern of consumption in the United Kingdom over the years 1920–38.

9. THE EXTENT OF DIFFUSION

'Time may be also wanted for the growth of habits of familiarity with the new commodities and the discovery of methods of economizing them. For instance . . . when petroleum first became plentiful few people were ready to use it freely; gradually petroleum and petroleum lamps have become familar to all classes of society: too much influence would therefore be attributed to the fall in price which has occurred since then, if it were credited with all the increase of consumption.'

A. Marshall (1890), 8th edn 1920, pp. 110–11

The grouping of commodities into stages of growth and decline provides the key to an approximate estimate of the overall importance of the diffusion of new consumer commodities in the inter-war period.

Of the 113 commodities listed in table 8.1, 50 were classified as new, 42 as established and 21 as outmoded. But a mere counting of numbers will not be very helpful, for in terms of consumer expenditures the commodities are of greatly different importance. In 1938 consumers spent only £0.5 million on air travel but over £56 million on railway journeys.

9.1 THE GROSS DIFFUSION EFFECT

A summation of expenditures for the commodities in each category will be more relevant.

Taking figures for expenditure in constant 1938 prices for the terminal years, the 50 commodities classified as new were 19 per cent of the total in 1920 and 33 per cent in 1938. The relative importance of the new commodities changed dramatically in 18 years. The rise of £842 million in real expenditure on them represents 78 per cent of the total rise of £1,083 million in real expenditure. But this attributes too much to the diffusion process. An element of the increase must be attributed to the 8.6 per cent growth in population in the period. Deducting an amount of £55 million (8.6 per cent of the 1920 level) gives a diffusion effect of £780 million. This can be called the 'gross' diffusion effect. From this some allowance should be made for the offsetting negative diffusion of outmoded commodities. The relationships between various new and outmoded commodities are worth further examination.

9.2 OFFSETTING AMOUNTS BETWEEN NEW AND
OUTMODED COMMODITIES

Outmoded and new products can best be considered together when grouped according to a system of wants which brings out the relationships between their relevant qualities. When put together in this way the statistics for the associated outmoded and new commodities can be used to see whether any new commodity is merely offset by an outmoded one or whether there is any positive net diffusion effect.

The series for expenditure on each of the 113 commodities were grouped together under ten headings representing ten major wants or uses. These were:

> Snack and breakfast foods
> Main course foods
> Sweet course foods
> Drinks
> Tobacco products
> Clothing, housing and household operation
> Transport
> Communications
> Entertainment and recreation
> Health and other personal services

This provided a framework for considering the degree to which each new product was merely supplanting an outmoded product. For example the degree to which the diffusion of manufactured cakes and biscuits was offset by a fall in sales of flour; or the degree to which the diffusion of motor transport was offset by a fall in horse-drawn transport.

Snack and breakfast foods

There were two major diffusion processes operating in this group of products in the 1920–38 period. The first was the spread of manufactured cakes and biscuits, which also resulted in a rapid decline in purchases of flour and dried fruit for the baking of cakes and biscuits in the home. The second major diffusion process was that for manufactured confectionery, particularly chocolate and chocolate confectionery.

The net diffusion effect was a real increase (in 1938 prices) of £29 million for cakes and biscuits and an increase of £25 million for chocolate and sugar confectionery.

Although real consumption of breakfast cereals quadrupled in the period the net effect was small, only £3 million.

Main course foods

There were two major diffusion processes occurring in this group. Lamb was being introduced and was pushing mutton out of the main course diet. However the largest diffusion process, in terms of value, in the group at this time was that for eggs. In constant 1938 prices, the value of egg consumption grew from £23.3 million in 1920 to £67.6 million in 1938. Other minor diffusion processes occurring were those of poultry, green vegetables, and the canned foods—meat, fish and vegetables. The introduction of frozen main course foods had not yet begun.

Sweet course foods

Increases in the consumption of ice-cream, canned fruit, oranges and bananas were the main diffusion processes occurring among sweet course foods in the 1920s and 1930s. For oranges and bananas it was the tail end of processes begun much earlier. Ice-cream was just beginning and canned fruit was in a relatively early stage of growth. Unlike the two previous groups, where the diffusion of new foods led to the substantial decline of established products, in the sweet course foods there was no major decline of an established food. Thus in this group the diffusion processes were almost entirely additional consumption.

Drinks

Although there were some minor diffusion processes occurring with soft drinks, table waters and British wine, the major change taking place among drinks was the decline of consumption of beer and spirits. The net effect was a decline of almost £100 million in real consumption of drinks over the eighteen-year period. The explanation for the decline of beer and spirits consumption is apparently to be found in the rise of consumption of products outside the group. One hypothesis is that as conditions at home were improved through the introduction of electric light and radio and as the attractiveness of other entertainments – principally the cinema – grew, the relative attractiveness of the public house declined. A small increase in the hours spent at home or at the cinema could have led to a large decline in the hours spent at the public house with consequent substantial decline in the consumption of alcoholic drinks.

Tobacco products

The diffusion of the smoking habit was taking place at a rapid rate during the 1920s and 1930s. Cigarettes dominated this growth at the expense of pipe-tobacco and other products, such as snuff and cigars, which declined substantially.

Clothing, housing and household operation

The statistics for this group are not as finely divided as would be desirable to separately distinguish all new commodities. For example there is just one item for 'furniture and furnishings' which includes items such as carpets, linoleum, radios, gramophones, mattresses and beds for which strong diffusion processes would be expected to be occurring at this time. Similarly lawnmowers, sewing machines, refrigerators, and other electrical goods such as cookers, vacuum cleaners, irons, lamps and fittings are included with items such as cutlery, brooms and cooking utensils in the item 'hardware and hollow ware'. Again a range of new products, such as cameras, photographic materials, watches, cosmetics and toilet requisites, is included in the omnibus item 'other personal effects', along with established items such as pens and pencils, stationery, jewellery, clocks and leather goods.

Although some other new commodities, such as rubber footwear, various new types of soap, dry cleaning and laundry services and electricity itself, are separately distinguished, the separation of new commodities from the established and outmoded commodities of this group is only very approximate. The detectable decline of outmoded products in this group is limited to three products – hard soap, candles and (after 1927) kerosene.

Transport

The dramatic changes in modes of transport through the diffusion of motor vehicles – in both the private and the public sectors – are clearly discernible from the statistics. The introduction of trolley vehicles and the beginnings of air transport are also shown.

Railway passenger transport, which had diffused rapidly in the second half of the nineteenth century, was well established and hardly suffered any decline throughout the 1920s and 1930s. However tramways, ferries, taxis and hire-cars and horse-drawn vehicles declined rapidly, the last mentioned almost disappearing entirely.

Communications

The continued diffusion of postal services and the dramatic growth in telephone services in this period is apparent from the statistics. Telegrams remained a static and very minor form of personal communication.

Entertainment and recreation

Unfortunately cinema entertainment is separately distinguished from other public entertainments for only the last five years of the period. In 1938 cinemas provided about two-thirds of all public entertainment. In 1920 the proportion would have been very much less, since the popularity of the cinema was helped greatly by the introduction of the 'talkies' at the beginning of the 1930s.

The diffusion of gambling, particularly with the introduction of the 'tote' and football pools in 1927, and of radio is shown by the figures of expenditure on 'betting' and on 'licences'.

The aggregate nature of the series in this group prevents any accurate distinction between new, established and outmoded products and consequently the figures give only a very rough approximation.

Health and other personal services

The diffusion of additional health services resulted in an increase of fifty per cent per head in the level of provision of these services between 1920 and 1938. Most other personal services also increased rapidly. This was particularly true of insurance and hairdressing. Although the figures for religion and charity fall in the error classes of 'rough estimate' and 'conjecture', it appears that in this period these services were outmoded slightly by the growth of other services. In 1920 religious and charitable organisations provided about one fifth of personal services; by 1938 they provided less than one tenth.

9.3 THE NET DIFFUSION EFFECT

Table 9.1 provides an aggregate measure of the magnitude of the gross and net diffusion effects of the introduction of new products in the period. New commodities grew from £637 million in 1920 to £1472 million in 1938, a growth of 131 per cent in 18 years (an exponential growth of 4.7 per cent per annum). After subtracting an element of

TABLE 9.1. *Gross and net diffusion effects: all commodities (£ million, 1938 prices)*

| | Level 1920 | Growth 1920–38 | | | Level 1938 |
		Population	Diffusion	Other	
New	637.5	54.7	779.5	—	1471.7
Outmoded	633.9	53.6	—277.2	—	400.3
Established	2140.6	183.7	—	288.7	2612.8
Total	3402.0	292.0	502.3	288.7	4484.8
Percentage growth	—	8.6	14.8	8.5	—

£55 million for population growth, the gross diffusion effect of new commodities was £780 million. This was offset by a decline in out-moded products of £277 million, after allowing for population growth, to give a net diffusion effect of £502 million. This is a growth of almost 40 per cent on the total 1920 level of consumption of new and out-moded products, or of almost 15 per cent on the 1920 level of consumption of all products. The growth of 15 per cent compares with a growth of less than 9 per cent due to population and 9 per cent due to other factors.

10. A SAMPLE EXPERIMENT

'Research workers, therefore, have to accustom themselves to the fact that in many branches of research the really critical experiment is rare, and that it is frequently necessary to combine the results of numbers of experiments dealing with the same issue in order to form a satisfactory picture of the true situation.'

F. Yates (1951), p. 33

Although the previous chapter isolates the diffusion process effects for the whole range of consumption, it does it in a very rough way. Moreover, the procedure does not provide estimates of the effects on consumption of changes in incomes and in prices. This chapter attempts to isolate the diffusion process effects from the effects of changes in prices and incomes for a sample group of commodities and compares the results of this analysis with earlier analyses of the same commodities. The chapter also discusses the results of aggregating new and outmoded commodities with others when measuring consumer reactions and tries to come to some conclusions about the possibilities of measurement of consumer behaviour from annual time series.

10.1 TWENTY-FIVE COMMODITIES

With modern computing machines such as Cambridge University's EDSAC II it would have been possible to analyse all the commodities covered by Stone's volumes, and given further resources it would have been possible to calculate for other commodities or even to analyse commodities for longer periods. However, it was thought that the most manageable procedure would be to select a sample of say 20 or so commodities and to use these for the experiment.

The selection of this reasonably-sized sample could have been done randomly, say by drawing from a hat, or purposefully. It was thought desirable to be able to compare the results with those of Stone (1954). So that he could make use of budget study estimates of income elasticity, Stone combined the data for 135 of these commodities by chain indexes to give data for 26 commodity groups, and he left the data for 25 commodities in their original form. These 25 were chosen for analysis.

This sample is not a very promising set in the sense that it does not include many strikingly new commodities. Nevertheless it can be expected, from the survey in chapter 8, that some of these commodities would be in fairly strong stages of growth.

The commodities are:

New commodities:	Canned vegetables
	British wine
	Cigarettes
	Bananas
	Canned meat
	Canned fish
	Oranges

Established commodities:	Imported wine
	Sugar
	Coffee
	Tea
	Bread
	Potatoes, home and imported
	Apples, home and imported
	Beef, home and imported

Outmoded commodities:	Dried fruit
	Dried legumes
	Flour
	Margarine
	Pipe tobacco
	Spirits
	Cocoa

The extreme movements in consumption for the home and import components of potatoes, apples and beef suggested that it would have been better to have considered these as aggregates rather than separately. When aggregated, the consumption patterns tended to stabilise. Margarine goes through a full stage of downward adjustment in the period, and thus was classified as 'outmoded' for the analysis.

Simple transformations of the data were made so that quantities were expressed per equivalent adult† for the 20 food commodities and per adult‡ for the five drink and tobacco commodities. The series are shown in table 10.1.

† See Stone (1954), p. 416, for the weights of the sex–age groups.
‡ Aged 15 years and over.

TABLE 10.1.   *Consumption and price variables*

Year	Canned vegetables	British wine	Cigarettes	Bananas	Canned meat	Canned fish	Oranges
			a. Consumption rate per annum				
	ton per 1,000 eq. adults	gal. per 100 adults	number per adult	cwt per 1,000 eq. adults	cwt per 1,000 eq. adults	cwt per 1,000 eq. adults	cwt per 1,000 eq. adults
1920	0.6566	52.36	1105.1	58.25	7.852	23.86	105.64
1921	0.6525	40.88	1066.2	66.34	12.126	19.63	141.14
1922	0.6481	46.41	1011.2	79.69	21.388	22.12	168.62
1923	0.6184	52.13	1000.6	87.01	18.553	17.69	182.76
1924	1.0139	56.52	1029.2	82.20	22.252	28.94	175.56
1925	1.0069	61.69	1087.6	86.35	31.876	23.85	181.29
1926	1.0526	64.21	1120.1	96.95	27.290	24.11	186.61
1927	1.1230	78.73	1188.4	89.58	27.474	24.50	182.06
1928	1.1948	81.74	1264.3	90.05	27.558	30.73	177.35
1929	1.3950	81.01	1327.3	102.71	25.730	31.59	212.43
1930	1.3344	81.95	1395.1	102.69	35.643	34.15	226.64
1931	1.7857	79.19	1410.5	111.28	35.153	31.30	234.23
1932	2.0781	89.85	1410.3	118.60	23.923	31.73	209.55
1933	2.1942	106.37	1474.7	109.99	27.743	26.68	260.95
1934	2.2859	112.74	1510.7	127.18	31.223	38.63	232.68
1935	2.7930	136.31	1593.0	136.28	31.372	37.43	228.28
1936	2.8734	160.21	1692.8	136.56	32.599	37.48	211.64
1937	4.5298	169.21	1790.0	148.92	33.653	40.94	271.54
1938	4.9486	170.95	1880.2	137.85	35.228	38.61	233.39
			b. Average real (1938) price				
	d/lb	s/pint	d/ten	d/lb	d/lb	d/lb	d/lb
1920	4.77	0.81	3.24	7.39	19.47	17.47	4.88
1921	4.16	0.90	3.55	7.11	14.63	15.59	4.00
1922	5.35	1.11	4.32	5.96	11.59	16.61	3.83
1923	5.00	1.17	4.53	6.00	10.04	14.97	3.50
1924	4.34	1.16	4.49	6.24	9.18	14.35	3.56
1925	4.13	1.15	4.46	6.29	10.81	15.68	3.99
1926	4.16	1.18	4.57	5.89	10.96	15.95	3.71
1927	4.40	1.21	4.73	6.14	11.54	16.01	4.28
1928	4.54	1.41	4.81	5.92	12.02	15.68	4.04
1929	4.53	1.43	4.88	5.23	12.55	15.22	4.28
1930	4.76	1.48	5.05	5.43	12.14	14.71	3.95
1931	4.81	1.59	5.41	5.29	10.68	14.59	4.12
1932	5.04	1.62	5.50	4.22	10.94	13.97	3.90
1933	5.19	1.67	5.61	4.90	10.25	14.37	3.68
1934	5.16	1.66	5.59	4.32	11.84	14.38	3.76
1935	5.02	1.64	5.48	3.93	11.24	13.96	3.93
1936	5.28	1.59	5.31	3.61	11.46	14.01	3.82
1937	4.81	1.62	5.05	3.44	10.93	13.26	2.93
1938	4.83	1.60	4.96	3.50	10.80	13.40	3.30

T<small>ABLE</small> 10.1. (*contd.*)

Year	Imported wine	Sugar	Coffee	Tea	Bread
		a. Consumption rate per annum			
	gal. per 1,000 adults	tons per 1,000 eq. adults	cwt per 1,000 eq. adults	cwt per 1,000 eq. adults	tons per 1,000 eq. adults
1920	429.9	19.48	9.220	90.21	82.82
1921	307.8	19.77	9.108	93.94	77.11
1922	345.4	24.84	9.722	93.63	76.96
1923	382.3	20.68	10.056	91.58	78.54
1924	439.4	22.52	9.979	94.21	79.56
1925	487.0	24.48	9.989	94.33	77.61
1926	504.0	25.05	10.026	94.71	78.95
1927	503.5	23.69	10.045	95.61	79.76
1928	397.0	25.38	10.286	96.81	78.86
1929	420.7	26.19	10.282	97.16	77.96
1930	397.1	26.61	10.444	100.64	77.44
1931	393.7	29.64	10.918	101.10	76.53
1932	355.7	26.28	10.365	100.56	77.83
1933	372.3	25.25	9.382	98.03	79.27
1934	401.4	27.05	9.721	96.56	79.40
1935	410.8	25.84	9.501	98.31	78.38
1936	431.5	27.64	9.735	96.93	77.86
1937	441.1	26.49	9.675	95.52	80.01
1938	411.2	26.09	9.652	94.44	79.18

			b. Average real (1938) price		
	s/pint	d/lb	d/lb	d/lb	d/4 lb loaf
1920	3.38	7.20	22.72	21.60	7.67
1921	3.66	5.18	23.25	21.39	9.14
1922	4.00	4.90	25.82	24.50	8.31
1923	3.59	6.05	28.06	27.34	7.84
1924	3.47	4.90	28.33	25.62	8.02
1925	3.46	3.32	30.30	25.92	9.08
1926	3.44	3.17	31.08	26.50	9.06
1927	3.54	3.49	32.31	26.77	9.08
1928	3.76	3.29	32.58	27.23	8.45
1929	3.90	2.85	32.05	24.49	8.32
1930	4.05	2.71	33.36	23.44	8.39
1931	4.23	2.64	34.25	23.52	7.40
1932	4.22	2.71	32.27	22.74	7.85
1933	4.34	2.51	32.86	23.95	8.36
1934	4.43	2.49	32.97	25.73	8.30
1935	4.36	2.45	31.09	25.64	8.46
1936	4.24	2.39	28.75	26.26	8.75
1937	4.05	2.53	26.62	26.31	9.61
1938	3.90	2.50	26.90	27.50	9.00

TABLE 10.1.   (*contd.*)

Year	Potatoes			Apples			Beef and veal		
	Home	Imported	Total	Home	Imported	Total	Home	Imported	Total

a. Consumption rate per annum

	ton per 1,000 eq. adults			cwt per 1,000 eq. adults			cwt per 1,000 eq. adults		
1920	56.91	8.400	65.31	48.70	104.02	152.72	331.7	237.6	569.3
1921	60.63	5.302	65.93	95.05	99.95	195.00	310.6	281.8	592.4
1922	66.27	4.186	70.46	65.24	111.26	176.50	322.0	253.8	575.8
1923	70.21	5.432	70.64	79.70	151.14	230.84	332.4	312.1	644.5
1924	54.24	9.685	63.92	154.62	154.62	225.75	329.8	305.9	635.7
1925	57.58	10.493	68.17	129.60	131.66	261.26	317.8	298.0	615.8
1926	59.21	7.184	66.39	55.68	189.11	244.79	311.7	323.9	635.6
1927	56.02	6.137	62.16	120.81	140.50	261.31	314.0	317.4	631.4
1928	59.40	9.948	69.35	85.25	140.88	226.13	324.5	294.3	618.8
1929	67.27	6.071	73.34	131.90	132.63	264.53	326.8	277.7	604.5
1930	66.00	5.953	71.95	106.80	140.31	247.11	312.1	274.8	586.9
1931	47.55	17.143	64.69	53.65	160.69	214.34	293.4	284.1	577.5
1932	52.20	15.864	68.06	61.07	171.67	232.74	273.3	267.8	541.1
1933	66.81	4.010	70.82	71.75	165.42	237.17	281.3	264.2	545.5
1934	66.59	3.115	69.70	145.89	135.24	281.13	286.0	277.4	563.4
1935	61.45	3.840	65.29	71.45	160.60	232.05	304.7	272.3	577.0
1936	52.56	6.317	58.88	113.85	127.87	241.72	308.2	274.0	582.2
1937	54.75	4.407	59.16	85.20	119.57	204.77	288.4	289.8	578.2
1938	59.02	2.866	61.89	46.86	148.26	195.12	283.5	286.7	570.2

b. Average real (1938) price

	d/7 lb	d/7 lb	d/7 lb	d/lb	d/lb	d/lb	d/lb	d/lb	d/lb
1920	8.20	16.78		6.95	5.57		13.27	9.20	
1921	7.18	18.84		3.31	5.45		15.18	9.18	
1922	6.65	22.66		2.73	5.28		14.48	8.35	
1923	5.83	14.70		4.39	4.39		14.79	8.52	
1924	9.62	14.52		4.28	4.54		14.70	8.38	
1925	8.15	11.52		3.46	4.87		14.62	8.59	
1926	6.70	13.14		4.71	4.53		14.68	8.52	
1927	7.63	17.04		3.54	4.66		14.43	8.38	
1928	7.51	13.05		4.13	5.16		14.55	8.83	
1929	6.28	13.98		3.80	5.04		14.74	9.22	
1930	5.63	12.34		3.55	5.13		15.11	9.57	
1931	8.67	11.94		4.97	4.97		15.33	9.51	
1932	8.66	10.83		4.98	4.87		14.73	9.21	
1933	6.24	15.82		4.12	4.68		14.37	9.13	
1934	6.86	20.36		2.99	4.76		14.27	9.07	
1935	7.31	21.49		5.67	4.91		13.53	8.73	
1936	7.96	14.01		3.40	4.77		12.94	8.49	
1937	7.69	14.07		4.25	4.15		13.05	8.60	
1938	6.80	19.00		5.70	4.10		13.40	9.00	

TABLE 10.1.   (*contd.*)

Year	Dried fruit	Dried legumes	Flour	Margarine	Pipe tobacco	Spirits	Cocoa
			a. Consumption rate per annum				
	cwt per 1,000 eq. adults	ton per 1,000 eq. adults	ton per 1,000 eq. adults	cwt per 1,000 eq. adults	lb per adult	proof gal. per 1,000 adults	cwt per 1,000 eq. adults
1920	79.73	2.052	51.14	172.37	2.038	646.8	11.710
1921	41.52	6.145	39.64	119.09	2.003	529.9	10.984
1922	60.95	3.970	45.21	117.74	1.935	473.7	10.073
1923	66.79	4.786	45.36	117.24	1.791	438.7	9.599
1924	67.00	5.176	45.91	114.19	1.766	430.7	9.765
1925	54.13	3.789	35.80	115.53	1.752	416.2	9.486
1926	57.11	3.079	36.76	116.84	1.677	377.1	9.105
1927	60.46	3.500	37.55	120.66	1.634	372.8	8.827
1928	58.94	4.234	34.52	119.48	1.608	354.8	8.390
1929	60.63	4.495	34.51	118.83	1.552	351.1	8.060
1930	53.81	2.977	37.90	107.26	1.485	317.0	7.750
1931	48.90	3.520	43.06	90.82	1.425	292.4	7.806
1932	66.50	3.041	39.10	83.63	1.339	263.3	7.856
1933	53.32	3.228	34.33	74.65	1.288	266.9	7.793
1934	48.13	2.989	36.12	63.30	1.291	260.6	7.184
1935	51.12	2.843	32.99	64.84	1.251	257.2	6.783
1936	44.14	3.765	32.57	63.91	1.212	270.5	7.506
1937	42.88	1.846	29.25	63.52	1.172	277.2	7.090
1938	50.64	2.376	28.49	72.02	1.152	264.9	7.398

			b. Average real (1938) price				
	d/lb	d/lb	d/7 lb	d/lb	d/oz	s/proof pint	d/lb
1920	10.14	2.98	13.77	8.51	5.63	9.58	29.48
1921	11.45	1.77	16.91	6.69	6.21	11.18	31.88
1922	11.84	2.58	14.70	5.96	7.67	13.80	34.42
1923	10.13	2.04	13.90	6.01	8.07	14.52	24.30
1924	8.82	1.99	14.26	5.97	8.02	14.43	24.50
1925	8.33	2.36	16.61	6.65	7.89	14.35	22.95
1926	8.34	2.84	16.53	7.25	7.97	14.68	23.83
1927	9.22	2.77	16.53	7.08	8.47	15.08	24.67
1928	8.17	2.54	15.49	7.04	8.71	15.21	24.51
1929	8.08	2.38	14.98	7.13	8.72	15.41	24.92
1930	7.60	2.28	15.05	7.21	9.02	15.99	25.07
1931	8.35	1.91	12.16	7.50	9.65	17.12	25.90
1932	8.45	2.43	12.73	7.26	10.26	17.54	27.08
1933	8.80	2.34	13.65	6.80	10.49	18.05	24.84
1934	8.08	2.10	13.55	6.20	10.38	17.93	23.02
1935	7.53	1.69	13.91	5.67	10.22	17.67	22.58
1936	7.53	1.60	14.32	6.05	9.93	17.19	23.87
1937	7.19	1.99	16.19	6.48	9.47	16.39	21.76
1938	6.50	1.80	15.25	6.50	9.40	16.20	21.00

10.2   THE COURSE OF INCOME AND PRICES

In the analyses of the next sections, the income variable used was the real total consumer expenditure in 1938 prices as shown in *The London and Cambridge Economic Bulletin* or in Stone and Rowe (1957). The consumption series were expressed as quantities per equivalent adult (for foods) and per adult (for drinks and tobaccos). Total real consumer expenditure was similarly transformed.

TABLE 10.2.   *Price, population and income variables*

Year	All consumer prices	Population		Real (1938) total consumer expenditure		
		Equivalent adults	Adults	Total	Per equivalent adult	Per adult
	1938 = 1.000	million	million	£ million	£	£
1920	1.597	36.55	31.40	3332	91.36	106.34
1921	1.449	36.78	31.70	3143	85.73	99.46
1922	1.173	37.03	32.04	3267	88.14	101.87
1923	1.116	37.19	32.38	3363	90.43	103.86
1924	1.123	37.48	32.84	3452	91.78	104.75
1925	1.129	37.74	33.10	3540	93.27	106.34
1926	1.103	38.00	33.39	3505	92.45	105.21
1927	1.074	38.29	33.66	3657	95.35	108.47
1928	1.065	38.50	34.01	3704	96.31	109.03
1929	1.052	38.71	34.28	3781	97.83	110.47
1930	1.013	38.97	34.62	3838	98.56	110.95
1931	0.946	39.20	34.88	3900	98.95	111.21
1932	0.923	39.46	35.17	3854	97.77	109.70
1933	0.898	39.65	35.33	3944	99.75	111.94
1934	0.904	39.81	35.48	4061	102.26	114.74
1935	0.917	40.10	35.97	4201	104.17	116.12
1936	0.942	40.37	36.39	4313	106.42	118.05
1937	0.988	40.62	36.76	4392	107.61	118.91
1938	1.000	40.82	37.07	4394	107.64	118.53

The all-price index used for deflating the individual prices is the Ministry of Labour's cost of living index as published by Chapman (1953). Over the 19-year period this index follows very closely the average value index published in *The London and Cambridge Economic Bulletin*.

10.2.1   *The course of income*

Real income per head increased fairly steadily throughout the period, although it remained practically steady for two years (1931 and 1938) and decreased in another two (1926 and 1932). At the end of the 18-year period, real income was running at a rate some 26 per cent per head higher than at the beginning.

10.2.2 *The course of relative prices*

New commodities. For one commodity, bananas, the relative price declined continuously to less than 50 per cent of its initial level; for two commodities, cigarettes and British wine, prices rose continuously to reach more than one and a half times their initial level by the 13th year of the period (1933), cigarette prices then declined while British wine prices remained fairly steady. The relative prices of the remaining new commodities varied within a smaller range of approximately ± 20 per cent of the mean levels with no trend except for canned fish, where there was a distinct drop half-way through the period.

Established commodities. For one commodity, sugar, the relative price declined almost continuously to less than 40 per cent of its initial level; for three others – home potatoes, import potatoes and home apples – relative prices fluctuated widely, with peak prices being approximately double the trough prices. For other established commodities, prices moved less sharply with no trends except for coffee, where there was a continuous rise until the 11th year (1931), and then a continuous fall back to the initial level, and home beef, which was fairly steady for 14 years, and then showed a discontinuous drop to a lower level for the remaining four years.

Outmoded commodities. For one commodity, dried fruit, the relative price declined continuously to less than 60 per cent of the initial level; for two commodities, pipe tobacco and spirits (as with the two related new commodities, cigarettes and British wine) prices rose more or less continuously to reach more than one and a half times their initial level by the 13th year of the period (1933), then both prices declined slightly. For other commodities in the group, flour and cocoa prices were fairly steady, dried legume prices fluctuated fairly widely and margarine prices were at a higher level for the middle seven years.

Summary. For bananas, sugar and dried fruit, relative prices moved continuously downward throughout the period; canned fish and home beef prices experienced a discontinuous drop about half way through the period; cigarettes, pipe tobacco, spirits and British wine all moved continuously upward to reach, in the 13th year (1933), a peak of approximately 70 per cent higher than the initial prices and then declined somewhat; the price of coffee moved similarly with a peak in the eleventh year (1931). Prices of home and imported potatoes, home apples and dried legumes fluctuated widely with no marked trends; prices for other commodities were relatively steady.

10.2.3   *The broad relationship between consumption, price and income levels*

New commodities. For new commodities, consumption levels tend to alter strongly upwards *regardless of price and income*. Whether the prices of new commodities move up or down seems to depend mainly on the market conditions of supply. For two commodities in the sample, cigarettes and British wine, prices rose markedly and almost continuously. For another, bananas, prices fell continuously by more than 50 per cent. The movement in the consumption level did not appear to be checked or accelerated in these cases.

Established commodities. Quantities remained fairly stationary for established commodities. However, where supply depends on agricultural harvests, it seems that the quantities consumed in any one year will be mainly determined by the success or failure of the harvest. Prices in these conditions show a marked movement in the opposite direction to consumption, thus rationing the available supplies and tending to equalise the returns to the producers. This mechanism seems to occur with two of the commodities in our sample, namely home apples and home potatoes, where good and bad harvests seem to alternate. Import supplies of these commodities tended to even out the fluctuations in the home supplies, with the prices of the imported again moving in the opposite direction to the quantities sold.

For other established commodities, not dependent on harvest uncertainties, consumption levels remained fairly static, regardless of price and income changes, unless the price of a close substitute got out of step with the price of the established commodity; then, depending on which way the price ratio moved, the consumption level either increased or decreased significantly. For example, although the price of sugar declined markedly and the price of coffee rose markedly and then fell, the consumption levels of these commodities remained fairly static, sugar consumption rising slightly and coffee consumption rising and falling slightly.

Outmoded commodities. For outmoded commodities, consumption levels tended to alter strongly downwards *regardless of price or income*. The conditions of supply seem mainly to determine whether the prices of these commodities move up or down. For two outmoded commodities, pipe tobacco and spirits, prices increased, but these prices kept more or less in step with the rise in the prices of the related new commodities, cigarettes and British wine. Again, for another outmoded commodity, dried fruit, the relative price declined markedly during the period. In this instance the price decline may well have prevented consumption declining further than it did.

The movements in consumption, income and prices provide an outline of the broad relationships, or lack of them, which appear to exist. Attention will now be directed to the regressions of current consumption on lagged consumption, current price and current income, to see whether this technique can separate the diffusion process effects from the effects of price and income changes.

10.3 THE REGRESSIONS

Consider fitting a linear regression to the observations on the $Ox_t x_{t-1}$ plane. Provided these observations all belong to only one of the three periods of growth, or to a period of decline, then the regression can be expected to fit the data well. However, in so far as observations belonging to periods of stability, or observations belonging to several of the three periods of growth, are included in the regression, then the fit of a linear equation cannot be expected to be good. In particular, if the observations refer to a period of stability alone, as for bread and potatoes in figures 8.6 and 8.7, the fit will be extremely poor.

10.3.1 *The equations*

Seven regressions were calculated for each commodity, using current consumption as the dependent variable and using linear equations in the plain variables, i.e. not transforming the observations by taking logarithms or first differences. These equations are numbered (1) to (7). An eighth regression was calculated using logarithms of the variables. The eight equations are:

(1) $x_t = b_{10} + b_{11} p_t + \varepsilon_{1t}$

(2) $x_t = b_{20} + b_{22} y_t + \varepsilon_{2t}$

(3) $x_t = b_{30} + b_{33} x_{t-1} + \varepsilon_{3t}$

(4) $x_t = b_{40} + b_{41} p_t + b_{42} y_t + \varepsilon_{4t}$

(5) $x_t = b_{50} + b_{51} p_t + b_{53} x_{t-1} + \varepsilon_{5t}$

(6) $x_t = b_{60} + b_{62} y_t + b_{63} x_{t-1} + \varepsilon_{6t}$

(7) $x_t = b_{70} + b_{71} p_t + b_{72} y_t + b_{73} x_{t-1} + \varepsilon_{7t}$

(8) $\log x_t = b_{80} + b_{81} \log p_t + b_{82} \log y_t + b_{83} \log x_{t-1} + \varepsilon_{8t}$

The first three equations used one explanatory variable; equations (4), (5) and (6) used two explanatory variables; and equations (7) and (8) used all three explanatory variables. These calculations were done in the University of Cambridge Mathematical Laboratory on the EDSAC II computer.

Problems which are not considered here are:

(i) Multi-collinearity – which could be examined by confluence analysis or also by examining the standard errors of the regression coefficients.

13

(ii) Identification – in other words, supply is assumed infinitely elastic, following Stone (1954).

(iii) Serial correlation of the residuals – the Durbin–Watson test is available to examine this problem.†

TABLE 10.3. *Coefficients of previous consumption*

				Equation		
				With price and Income		Trend coefficient
Commodity	Alone (3)	With price (5)	With income (6)	Plain (7)	Log (8)	Stone (1954)
New						
Canned vegetables	1.18[c]	1.20[c]	0.95[c]	0.96[c]	0.63[b]	0.106[b]
British wine	1.08[c]	0.99[c]	0.75[c]	0.68[c]	0.31[d]	0.057[b]
Cigarettes	1.11[c]	1.08[c]	0.81[c]	0.79[c]	0.74[d]	0.048[c]
Bananas	0.90[c]	0.21	0.87[c]	−0.09	0.12	0.011
Canned meat	0.62[b]	0.61[b]	0.26	0.23	0.33	0.056
Canned fish	0.76[c]	0.40	−0.24	−0.26	−0.24	0.016
Oranges	0.63[c]	0.58[c]	0.10	0.12	0.23	0.015
Established						
Imported wine	0.57[a]	0.47[a]	0.55[a]	0.12	0.02	−0.010
Sugar	0.55[b]	0.02	0.18	−0.01	−0.03	−0.004
Coffee	0.62[b]	0.40	0.63[c]	0.38	0.37[a]	−0.015
Tea	0.71[c]	0.66[c]	0.77[c]	0.55[b]	0.54[a]	0.005
Bread	0.00	−0.17	0.02	−0.12	−0.12	−0.001
Potatoes: home	0.18	0.15	0.16	0.13	0.07	−0.006
import	0.37	0.08	0.35	0.03	−0.12	−0.052
Apples: home	−0.28	−0.04	−0.31	−0.10	−0.12	−0.027
import	0.30	0.26	0.29	0.30	0.37	−0.012
Beef: home	0.76[c]	0.81[c]	0.64[b]	0.65[b]	0.65[d]	−0.012
import	0.36[a]	0.27	0.36	0.28	0.26	0.009
Outmoded						
Dried fruit	0.01	−0.07	−0.29	−0.41	−0.31	−0.049
Dried legumes	0.11	0.19	−0.26	−0.11	−0.02	−0.039
Flour	0.60[b]	0.62[b]	0.09	−0.10	−0.13	−0.028
Margarine	0.73[c]	0.73[c]	0.52[b]	0.40	0.84[b]	−0.026
Pipe tobacco	0.96[c]	0.86[c]	0.96[c]	0.74[c]	0.90[c]	−0.019[c]
Spirits	0.77[c]	0.62[c]	0.73[c]	0.34	0.99	−0.033[c]
Cocoa	0.82[c]	0.84[c]	0.66[c]	0.67[b]	0.51[a]	−0.023[a]

[a] Significantly different from zero at the 5% level.
[b] Significantly different from zero at the 1% level.
[c] Significantly different from zero at the 0.1% level.
[d] Significance of coefficient not calculated due to a computer programming fault.

† Except that they state that the test is not applicable to cases where the explanatory variables include lagged values of the dependent variable and hence the test cannot be used with equations (3), (5), (6), (7) and (8).

10.3.2 *The regression coefficients*

The coefficients of the explanatory variables and their standard errors were obtained from the regressions. The coefficients of previous consumption (x_{t-1}), income (y_t) and own price (p_t), (income and price coefficients expressed as elasticities at the mean) are shown in tables 10.3 to 10.6, together with the trend coefficients and income and price

TABLE 10.4. *Mean income elasticities*

				Equation		
				With price and previous consumption		
			With previous Con-	Plain	Log	Stone
Commodity	Alone (2)	With price (4)	sumption (6)	(7)	(8)	(1954)
New						
Canned vegetables	9.09c	9.30c	2.14	2.36	4.06b	0.70b
British wine	8.16c	10.70c	2.77a	3.90a	6.12d	1.70b
Cigarettes	3.72c	4.09c	1.14c	1.40c	1.42d	0.13
Bananas	0.42	1.16b	0.75	1.40a	1.29	0.95c
Canned meat	2.74c	2.62c	1.92a	1.96a	1.71	0.27
Canned fish	3.46c	2.95c	4.23c	3.64c	3.92c	0.76b
Oranges	2.10c	1.99c	1.84a	1.67a	1.41a	0.92b
Established						
Imported wine	0.52	1.98b	0.37	1.79a	2.13b	1.40b
Sugar	1.01c	0.06	0.79	0.05	−0.08	0.09a
Coffee	−0.13	−0.13	−0.65	−0.11	−0.11	1.42
Tea	0.18	0.26b	−0.05	0.07	0.08	0.04
Bread	0.07	0.06	0.07	0.05	0.05	−0.05
Potatoes: home	−0.38	−0.33	−0.35	−0.31	−0.30 ⎫	0.21b
import	−1.53	−1.61	−0.99	−1.56	−2.46a ⎬	
Apples: home	0.15	1.80	0.57	1.88	1.64 ⎫	1.33c
import	0.32	−0.12	0.10	−0.35	−0.29 ⎬	
Beef: home	−0.53b	−0.75a	0.18	−0.42	−0.39d ⎫	0.34c
import	−0.25	−0.18	−0.25	−0.20	−0.19 ⎬	
Outmoded						
Dried fruit	−1.00	−2.02a	−1.45a	−3.11b	−2.69a	0.75
Dried legumes	−3.25c	−4.10c	−3.74c	−4.23c	−3.92c	−0.15
Flour	−1.61c	−1.90c	−1.44a	−2.09c	−2.15c	0.18
Margarine	−3.16c	−3.08c	−1.08	−1.53	−0.04	−0.16
Pipe tobacco	−3.24c	−2.25c	−0.005	−0.36	−0.02	−0.04
Spirits	−4.24c	−1.88a	−0.26	−1.03	0.63	0.60c
Cocoa	−1.98c	−1.99c	−0.42	−0.47	−0.86	−0.10

[a] Significantly different from zero at the 5% level.
[b] Significantly different from zero at the 1% level.
[c] Significantly different from zero at the 0.1% level.
[d] Significance of elasticity not calculated due to a computer programming fault.

elasticities derived by Stone (1954). In the main, Stone's income elasticities are from the 1937–9 budget surveys.

A table showing the proportion of the variance in consumption explained by each of the equations for each commodity is also included. This statistic shows how good the fit or explanation is in each case.

TABLE 10.5.   *Mean own-price elasticities*

	Equation					
			With previous con-sumption	With previous consumption and income		
Commodity	Alone (1)	With income (4)	sumption (5)	Plain (7)	Log (8)	Stone (1954)
New						
Canned vegetables	2.93	−0.34	−0.32	−0.49	−0.43	−0.96[a]
British wine	2.01[c]	−0.86[a]	0.28	−0.23	−0.10[d]	−0.31
Cigarettes	1.26[c]	−0.25	0.06	−0.12[a]	−0.07[d]	−0.48[c]
Bananas	−1.02[c]	−0.69[c]	−0.81[c]	−0.71[c]	−0.49[a]	−0.67[a]
Canned meat	−0.63	−0.28	−0.07	−0.16	−0.15	−0.76
Canned fish	−2.79[c]	−0.35	−1.75[a]	−0.43	−0.21	−0.24
Oranges	−0.78	−0.24	−0.43	−0.25	−0.22	−0.93[b]
Established						
Imported wine	−0.63	−1.40[c]	−0.33	−1.25[a]	−1.39[b]	−0.60
Sugar	−0.24[c]	−0.23[b]	−0.23[c]	−0.22[b]	−0.31[b]	−0.42[a]
Coffee	0.27[b]	0.29[b]	0.14	0.17	0.17	0.27
Tea	−0.19[a]	−0.27[b]	−0.14[a]	−0.17[a]	−0.17	−0.19[a]
Bread	0.08	0.07	0.10	0.08	0.08	−0.08
Potatoes: home	−0.63[c]	−0.62[c]	−0.62[c]	−0.62[c]	−0.63[c]	−0.57[c]
import	−1.73[b]	−1.73[b]	−1.65[b]	−1.70[b]	−1.97[c]	−1.48[b]
Apples: home	−1.11[b]	−1.34[c]	−1.09[b]	−1.30[b]	−1.25[b]	−1.17[c]
import	−0.74	−0.79	−0.66	−0.80	−0.76	−1.16
Beef: home	0.37	−0.40	−0.11	−0.45	−0.39[d]	−0.11
import	−0.65	−0.60	−0.48	−0.41	−0.40	0.55
Outmoded						
Dried fruit	0.23	−0.50	0.25	−0.72	−0.66	−0.69
Dried legumes	−0.12	−0.80[b]	−0.27	−0.73[a]	−0.58	−1.58[c]
Flour	−0.44	−0.79[c]	−0.51	−0.82[c]	−0.83[c]	−0.79[b]
Margarine	0.88	0.69	0.03	0.32	−0.06	0.26
Pipe tobacco	−1.23[c]	−0.48[b]	−0.16	−0.19[a]	−0.12	−0.08
Spirits	−2.07[c]	−1.37[c]	−0.43	−0.80	0.08	−0.57[c]
Cocoa	0.69[b]	−0.01	−0.03	−0.05	−0.05	0.07

[a] Significantly different from zero at the 5% level.
[b] Significantly different from zero at the 1% level.
[c] Significantly different from zero at the 0.1% level.
[d] Significance of elasticity not calculated due to a computer programming fault.

TABLE 10.6.   *Proportion of variance in consumption explained by various factors*

Commodity	Price alone (1)	Income alone (2)	Previous consumption alone (3)	Price and income (4)	Price and consumption (5)	Income and consumption (6)	Price income and consumption Plain (7)	Log (8)
New								
Canned vegetables	0.13	0.81	0.92a	0.81	0.92	0.93a	0.93	0.96
British wine	0.61	0.91	0.96a	0.94	0.96	0.97a	0.98	.b
Cigarettes	0.47	0.92	0.98a	0.93	0.98	0.995a	0.996	.b
Bananas	0.96a	0.19	0.89	0.98a	0.97	0.89	0.98	0.93
Canned meat	0.08	0.64a	0.55	0.65	0.55	0.68a	0.68	0.74
Canned fish	0.58	0.84a	0.55	0.84	0.66	0.85a	0.86	0.83
Oranges	0.17	0.71a	0.57	0.72a	0.62	0.71	0.73	0.81
Established								
Imported wine	0.18	0.05	0.32a	0.58a	0.37	0.35	0.59	0.66
Sugar	0.72a	0.51	0.39	0.72	0.72a	0.52	0.72	0.74
Coffee	0.40	0.00	0.43a	0.44	0.49a	0.44	0.52	0.52
Tea	0.22	0.19	0.64a	0.59	0.75a	0.65	0.77	0.51
Bread	0.14a	0.12	0.00	0.23a	0.20	0.11	0.26	.b
Potatoes: home	0.73a	0.06	0.03	0.78a	0.76	0.08	0.80	0.78
import	0.48a	0.03	0.13	0.51a	0.48	0.14	0.51	0.73
Apples: home	0.47a	0.00	0.08	0.57a	0.47	0.09	0.58	0.55
import	0.13a	0.02	0.11	0.14	0.21a	0.11	0.23	0.28
Beef: home	0.09	0.36	0.58a	0.41	0.58	0.60a	0.66	.b
import	0.19a	0.06	0.18	0.22	0.27a	0.25	0.31	0.28
Outmoded								
Dried fruit	0.06	0.21a	0.00	0.28	0.07	0.29a	0.44	0.29
Dried legumes	0.01	0.58a	0.01	0.76a	0.03	0.64	0.77	0.70
Flour	0.09	0.60a	0.43	0.86a	0.55	0.60	0.86	0.92
Margarine	0.09	0.73	0.79a	0.78	0.79	0.81a	0.82	0.89
Pipe tobacco	0.83	0.93	0.99a	0.97	0.99a	0.99	0.991	0.99
Spirits	0.91	0.82	0.96a	0.97a	0.97	0.96	0.97	0.91
Cocoa	0.42	0.88	0.93a	0.88	0.93	0.94a	0.94	0.93

a Best proportion at level of one explanatory variable or at level of two explanatory variables.
b Proportion of variance explained not calculated due to a computer programming fault.

10.3.3   *The results of the analyses*

The experiment is to determine whether the inclusion of the level of consumption lagged by one period ('previous consumption') in the variables explaining current consumption, can isolate the diffusion process effects. The aim is to establish the circumstances in which significant† coefficients of previous consumption are obtained, and to

† Throughout this section, 'significant' coefficients or elasticities mean those 'significantly different from zero at the 5% level'.

ascertain the effects of the inclusion of this variable on the values obtained for the price and income elasticities.

Most attention will be paid to the coefficients derived from equations (7) and (8), for it is in these equations that the influences of income and own-price have also been taken into account (in so far as this is possible with the multiple regression technique). However, the coefficients obtained from equations (1) to (6) are also discussed, for there is some benefit to be gained from observing the results of including different variables in the explanation.

For each commodity there are a large number of regression coefficients and it would be tedious to examine these coefficients individually for each commodity in turn. First the commodities for which there are significant coefficients of previous consumption will be examined.† It is expected that this coefficient will be significant for both new and outmoded commodities but not for established commodities.

10.3.4   *The coefficients of previous consumption*

In equation (7) and probably also in (8), three of the new commodities – canned vegetables, British wine and cigarettes – have significant coefficients of previous consumption. Thus in these cases a strong diffusion process is associated with a significant coefficient of previous consumption, after allowing for the effects of changes in income and own-price.

However, the four 'less new' commodities – canned meat, canned fish, bananas and oranges – do not have significant coefficients of previous consumption in equations (7) and (8). Perhaps these four were no longer undergoing a diffusion process in the period 1920–38.

These commodities all have income elasticities in excess of 1.00 in equations (7) and (8). For canned fish and canned meat these are implausibly high income elasticities in view of the values calculated by Stone from the 1937–9 budget studies. Thus it appears that the regression technique tends to give to the income variable a larger importance than it probably has.

For bananas, where prices declined almost continuously, a significant own-price elasticity is found in equations (7) and (8). Although this, together with a moderately high income elasticity, offers an alternative to the diffusion process as an explanation for the growth in consumption, it might well be the case that the multiple regression technique has given too much importance to the decline in banana prices.

Among the established commodities only tea, home beef and coffee have significant coefficients of previous consumption in equations (7) and (8). Thus for eight of the 11 established commodities, the results agree with the expectation that the coefficients would not be significant.

† See table on page 176.

Perhaps tea and coffee should have been classified as new commodities and home beef as outmoded.

It seems that, until about half-way through the period, tea was still in the final stages of the diffusion process begun in 1840, and therefore could have been classified as a new commodity. For coffee there is a negative income elasticity instead of the rather high positive one found by Stone. Here the regression technique seems to have allotted to income a perverse effect, which may well have resulted in making significant the coefficient of previous consumption. Coffee also has a small positive own-price elasticity which is statistically significant in equations (1) and (4) but is clearly unacceptable. This positive elasticity is due to prices moving steadily upward more or less in line with consumption for the first 11 years and falling together in 1932. However, although this suggests a strong positive relationship, the largest decrease in coffee prices occurred in the years 1935, 1936 and 1937, over which period consumption remained practically constant. It seems likely that the variation of coffee prices has had very little influence on the consumption of coffee. The parallel movements in consumption and prices for the first 12 years may well have been co-incidental.

For home beef, equations (7) and (8) show a moderate negative income elasticity in conflict with the highly significant positive elasticity found by Stone. However, in this case it seems that even if the multiple regression technique had given to income a positive co-efficient, the coefficient of previous consumption would still have been significant.

Thus among the 11 commodities classified as established, it seems that on the basis of the regression results tea should have been classified as new (at least for the first half of the 1920–38 period) and home beef as outmoded.

Among the outmoded commodities, pipe tobacco and cocoa have significant coefficients of previous consumption in both equations (7) and (8) and thus agree with expectations. Margarine does in (8) but not in (7). The coefficient for spirits is very large in equation (8) but not significant. The small positive own-price elasticity in this equation looks odd. Similarly the large negative income elasticity in equation (7) for spirits may be the cause of the low and non-significant value of the coefficient of previous consumption.

The very large and significant negative income elasticities for dried fruit, dried legumes and flour are quite implausible in view of the values found by Stone. Here again it seems that the regression technique gives to the income variable a larger importance than it has in reality.

It is to be noted that the regression coefficients of previous consumption in equation (3) are significant for all new commodities, for most outmoded commodities, but for only just over half of established commodities; and, although these coefficients fall in value and tend to become non-significant as income and own-price are introduced into the explanation, for pipe tobacco, canned vegetables, British wine and cigarettes, the coefficients of previous consumption are significantly different from zero at the 0.1 per cent level in equation (7).

The six commodities for which Stone finds significant residual trends turn out to be three of the new and three of the outmoded commodities in table 10.3. The coefficient b_{73} of x_{t-1} picks out five of these six, failing to give a statistically significant coefficient for spirits. Despite the fact that two of the established commodities also turn up with significant coefficients, there is a strong degree of association between finding a significant coefficient of x_{t-1} and finding a significant residual trend.

10.3.5   *The price and income elasticities*

The more important effects of the inclusion of previous consumption on the values obtained for the price and income elasticities can be seen by considering the distributions of these measures for the three groups – new commodities, established commodities and outmoded commodities.

Table 10.7 shows the distribution of the income elasticities. The

TABLE 10.7.   *Distribution of income elasticities*

Range of income elasticity	New commodities Equation						Established commodities Equation						Outmoded commodities Equation					
	(2)	(4)	(6)	(7)	(8)	(9)	(2)	(4)	(6)	(7)	(8)	(9)	(2)	(4)	(6)	(7)	(8)	(9)
5.00 ——	2	2	–	–	1	–	–	–	–	–	–	–	–	–	–	–	–	–
2.00 to 4.99	4	3	3	3	2	–	–	–	–	–	1	–	–	–	–	–	–	–
1.00 to 1.99	–	2	3	4	4	1	1	2	–	2	1	4	–	–	–	–	–	–
0.00 to 0.99	1	–	1	–	–	6	5	3	5	3	2	6	–	–	–	–	1	3
−0.01 to −0.99	–	–	–	–	–	–	4	5	6	5	6	1	–	–	3	2	3	4
−1.00 to −1.99	–	–	–	–	–	–	1	1	–	1	–	–	3	3	3	2	–	–
−2.00 to −4.99	–	–	–	–	–	–	–	–	–	–	1	–	4	4	1	3	3	–
Total	7	7	7	7	7	7	11	11	11	11	11	11	7	7	7	7	7	7
Significant	6	7	5	6	6[a]	5	2	3	–	1	2[a]	8	6	7	3	3	3	1

[a] At most

distributions of those found by Stone are shown for comparison in columns (9). The final row of figures in the table shows the number of cases in which the elasticity was significantly different from zero at the 5 per cent level.

For new commodities the income elasticities calculated here are in practically all cases greater than unity and in over 40 per cent of the cases are greater than 2.00. This contrasts strongly with the findings of Stone (1954) that, although positive, 85 per cent (six of the seven) had income elasticities of less than unity. For the five† commodities for which Stone finds significant positive elasticities significant elasticities are found also here, but these are invariably much greater in strength (except for bananas in the equations (2) and (6), where prices are omitted).

For established commodities, instead of finding, with Stone, that these tend to have significant positive income elasticities, it is found that these tend to be distributed more or less evenly round a zero elasticity and that very few are significantly different from zero.

In this study outmoded commodities tend to have fairly large and significant negative income elasticities. On the other hand, Stone found the income elasticities for the commodities in this group to be distributed round a zero elasticity – only one, spirits, with a positive elasticity of 0.60, being significantly different from zero.

Thus, broadly speaking, this study finds a much wider distribution of values for the income elasticities than the distribution reported by Stone (1954). As he estimated only five of the income elasticities (those for drinks and tobacco) on the basis of the time-series observations, the majority being determined from the 1937–9 budget data, it follows that the differences between the distributions of the income elasticities found in the two studies reflect the differences between those income elasticities found from analysis of aggregate time-series data and those found from the analysis of budget-study data.

In so far as increases in real income are largely the sum of the

TABLE 10.8. *Distribution of own-price elasticities*

Range of own-price elasticity	New commodities Equation (1) (4) (5) (7) (8) (9)						Established commodities Equation (1) (4) (5) (7) (8) (9)						Outmoded commodities Equation (1) (4) (5) (7) (8) (9)					
2.00 ——	2	-	-	-	-	-	-	-	-	-	-	-	-	-	-	-	-	-
1.00 to 1.99	1	-	-	-	-	-	-	-	-	-	-	-	-	-	-	-	-	-
0.00 to 0.99	-	-	2	-	-	-	3	2	2	2	2	2	3	1	2	1	1	2
−0.01 to −0.99	2	7	4	7	7	7	6	6	7	6	6	6	2	5	5	6	6	4
−1.00 to −1.99	1	-	1	-	-	-	2	3	2	3	3	3	1	1	-	-	-	1
−2.00 ——	1	-	-	-	-	-	-	-	-	-	-	-	1	-	-	-	-	-
Total	7	7	7	7	7	7	11	11	11	11	11	11	7	7	7	7	7	7
Significant	4	2	2	2	1	4	6	7	5	6	5	5	3	4	-	3	1	3

† Canned vegetables, British wine, bananas, canned fish and oranges.

increases in consumption of new products less the decreases in consumption of outmoded products, changes in individual components of this aggregate would be expected to be highly correlated with changes in the aggregate itself. And since, for a new commodity, either its quality or consumer's estimates of its quality are likely to be changing rapidly, it is unlikely that a single cross-section budget study made during this process can throw much light on the dynamics of the process itself.

The distribution of the values of the own-price elasticities found in this study are shown in table 10.8. Those found by Stone are shown in columns (9). The final line of the table shows the number of cases in which the elasticity was significantly different from zero at the 5 per cent level.

Stone finds that for half of the commodities the own-price elasticity is statistically significant. While this proportion of significant own-price elasticities is found among the established commodities, the proportion is somewhat less for both new and outmoded commodities. There is fairly close agreement between this and Stone's studies in the values of the own-price elasticity. The significant, but unacceptable, positive elasticities found for some new commodities all become negative when income and previous consumption are included as explanatory variables. The significant positive own-price elasticity for the established commodity, coffee, while not becoming negative, does lose its significance when previous consumption is included as an explanatory variable.

10.3.6   *The proportion of variance explained*

Table 10.6 above shows the proportion of the variance in current consumption of each commodity explained by each regression equation. Table 10.9 shows, for new, established and outmoded commodities, the distributions of the proportion of variance explained by equations (1) to (7). The distributions for equation (8) are not shown since the proportion was missing on four occasions. With minor exceptions, the

TABLE 10.9.   *Distribution of proportion of variance explained*

Range of R^2	New commodities Equation							Established commodities Equation							Outmoded commodities Equation						
	(1)	(2)	(3)	(4)	(5)	(6)	(7)	(1)	(2)	(3)	(4)	(5)	(6)	(7)	(1)	(2)	(3)	(4)	(5)	(6)	(7)
0–0.33	3	1	–	–	–	–	–	6	9	7	3	3	6	3	4	1	2	1	2	1	–
0.34–0.67	3	1	3	1	3	–	–	3	2	4	6	5	5	5	1	2	1	–	1	2	1
0.68–0.83	–	2	–	2	–	2	2	2	–	–	2	3	–	3	1	2	1	2	1	1	2
0.84—	1	3	4	4	4	5	5	–	–	–	–	–	–	–	1	2	3	4	3	3	4
Total	7	7	7	7	7	7	7	11	11	11	11	11	11	11	7	7	7	7	7	7	7

proportion explained by equation (8) was very similar to that in equation (7).

For new commodities, previous consumption (equation (3)), tends to give higher values of R^2 than price or income, though there is not much to choose between previous consumption and income. A similar situation exists with the outmoded commodities. For established, commodities, own-price (equation (1)), tends to give higher values of R^2 than previous consumption or income. However, the proportion of variance explained is never very high, the highest being 0.73 for home potatoes.

For any commodity, the proportion explained by all three variables – equation (7) – should be no less than the proportion explained by any two of the variables – equations (4), (5) and (6). Similarly, for any commodity, R^2 should, in equation (4), be no less than R^2 in either equation (1) or (2), and so on. This is because as variables are added in the equations, more opportunity is given for 'explaining' the variation in current consumption. If the value of R^2 increases a great deal when a variable is included, then the extra variable adds a lot to the explanation.

For example, for sugar, when price is included as well as previous consumption, R^2 rises from 0.39 to 0.72, and thus price helps considerably in explaining the variation in consumption. For the equation with price alone, R^2 is also 0.72, so that previous consumption adds nothing to the explanation offered by price alone.

For established commodities, own-price adds considerably to the explanation offered by income or previous consumption. For new and outmoded commodities, own-price adds much to the explanation in only one instance, bananas. For most new and outmoded commodities, previous consumption adds considerably to the explanation offered by price alone. Income also has this effect, but for established commodities neither income nor previous consumption adds much to the explanation provided by own-prices.

These movements in the level of R^2 are in line with the movements in the values and significance of the regression coefficients that were discussed in the previous section.

It must be realised, of course, that for the new and outmoded commodities, there is to be explained a large amount of variation in consumption in relation to the mean consumption level. For the established commodities while some, such as potatoes and apples, have relatively large variations in consumption, others, notably coffee, tea and bread, have very little variation.

The 'relative error in prediction'† in equation (7) is less than 5 per

† Defined as $100 \times$ the ratio of the standard error of estimate to the mean value of consumption.

cent for cigarettes, bananas, coffee, tea, bread, home beef, pipe tobacco, spirits and cocoa and greater than 20 per cent for import potatoes and home apples. For bread, while R^2 only reaches 0.26 in equation (7), the 'relative error in prediction' is only 1.3 per cent. This value of R^2 for bread reflects the fact that none of the coefficients of the determining variables was found to be significant. Nevertheless, as consumption of bread was practically constant, anyone could have predicted its level with a high degree of accuracy without a knowledge of current price or current income.

10.4 AGGREGATING NEW OR OUTMODED COMMODITIES WITH OTHERS

When new commodities are introduced to a market and find acceptance by the consumers buying in that market, the consumption per head of the new commodity increases over time and the growth curve of consumption tends to have a sigmoid shape.

Suppose a new commodity is a new type of a particular class of commodity, for example, as bananas were a new type of fruit, or grapefruit a new type of citrus fruit, or television a new type of entertainment. Suppose the demand analyst has the relevant data on the incomes of the consumers and on the consumption per head, and prices, of the new commodity and of the other commodities in its class, for a series of say 20 or more years. In this situation he can make several types of analysis.

The new commodity can be aggregated with the others of its class so as to obtain details of the consumption per head, and prices of the aggregate commodity (fruit, citrus fruit, or entertainment) and on the usual hypotheses involved, an analysis of the influence of incomes and prices on the consumption of the aggregate commodity can be made through a regression or confluence analysis.†

Some attention will have to be paid to the manner of aggregating the new commodity with the others in its class. Will the analyst follow Marshall (1890) in taking a given amount of the new commodity, expressed in some physical unit as weight or number, as equivalent to‡ given amounts of the other commodities in its class, also expressed in some physical unit? Or will he use some form of quantity index, such as the chained 'ideal' index used by Stone (1954) and the ideal index advocated by Bergstrom (1955)? In either event the new commodity will tend to be swamped by the others in its class and there is a sacrifice of available data.

† The influence of income may be separately determined from the cross-section data from a budget study.
‡ '. . . in such a case of course some convention must be made as to the number of ounces of tea which are taken as equivalent to a pound of coffee.' Marshall (1890), 8th edn, p. 100, n. I.

To get around these difficulties, the analyst can subject the new commodity and each of the several other commodities in its class to a similar regression or confluence analysis as he did with the aggregate commodity. Often, it seems to be the case that the only change of any magnitude in the consumption rates and in the prices of the several commodities is that the consumption rate of the new commodity has increased fairly steadily with increases of the order of 10 to 20 per cent per annum over a period of 15 to 20 years.

In this situation, the growth in consumption could be attributed to the increase in the average consumer's estimates of the want satisfying powers of the new commodity, as described in chapter 4. But whether the growth is regarded as occurring because the new commodity does what the previous commodities did but in a more efficient manner, or because it does other things that the previous commodities were unable to do, or for a combination of the two reasons, seems to depend on whether the new commodity merely replaces some of the consumption of the existing commodities in the group, is an addition to aggregate consumption, or is partly both. In other words, it seems to depend on whether the aggregate commodity group shows no increase, an increase fully equal to the increase in consumption of the new commodity, or some increase in between these extremes.

In terms of the analysis of chapters 2 and 3, the new commodity may merely provide a more efficient means of satisfying the supra-marginal wants of consumers, and hence just replace an existing commodity in the budget, releasing some purchasing power for the purchase of other commodities. Alternatively, it may not only provide a means of satisfying the marginal wants of consumers, but also at the same time satisfy some supra-marginal wants – so releasing some purchasing power from existing commodities for the purchase of the new.

The data for the aggregate class of commodities and the data for the individual commodities can in this way complement each other in helping the demand analyst arrive at a sensible explanation of what has occurred. Differences between the interpretations of the results of analyses of data for aggregated groups of commodities and the interpretation of the results of similar analyses of the individual commodities comprising these groups may well be eliminated under the conceptual scheme outlined above. The discussion between Nerlove and the author in the *Journal of Farm Economics*† reveals some of the difficulties in interpretation of results in such a case.

Nerlove and Addison (1959) suggest that a significant coefficient of previous consumption in a regression model such as equation (7) or (8) can be interpreted as a significant lag in the response of consumers to

† Vol. 41, August 1959, pp. 626–40.

changes in incomes and prices. Using Stone's data for group commodities, they find significant coefficients in 12 out of 13 cases. In the discussion with Nerlove, it was suggested that the large changes in the rates of consumption of a few of the commodities comprising the groups were 'mainly due to changes in the preferences of consumers for these commodities',† and factors such as changes in fashion, increase in advertisement, and an increase in the proportion of women working in industry were suggested as the possible causes of these changes. These factors may well have had some influence in assisting the diffusion process.

However, it seems that in general the individual commodities making up these groups do not have significant coefficients of previous consumption unless they are at the extremes of the commodity spectrum – new commodities in an early stage of growth or outmoded commodities in a stage of strong decline. And, although tests have not been made for all possible relevant variables such as the prices of close substitutes, it would seem that for the individual commodities the significant coefficients of previous consumption should not be interpreted as lags in the adjustment of the consumers to *changes in prices and incomes*, but as reflecting the time taken for the knowledge of new commodities to spread and the diffusion of consumption to be effected.

10.5   Conclusions

Over 100 individual commodities were examined and grouped from those new commodities in early stages of diffusion through to those outmoded commodities in the final stages of decline. Twenty-five commodities were subjected to further analysis to see whether the regression technique of including the level of consumption lagged by one period ('previous consumption') in the variables explaining current consumption could isolate the diffusion process effects. It was expected that this coefficient would be significant for all new and outmoded commodities but not for established commodities.

The method gives significant coefficients to the previous consumption variable for those new commodities in early stages of growth and for those outmoded commodities in a strong decline. The method also tends to produce income and own-price elasticities more in line with expectations than would be the case if previous consumption was excluded from the regression.

Comparison of these results with those of Stone showed that in quite a few cases the multiple regression technique gives to the income variable a larger importance than it has been found to have in budget studies. Fairly close agreement was found between the values for the own-

† Ironmonger (1959), p. 630.

price elasticities obtained in this and in Stone's study. There tends to be a higher proportion of significant own-price elasticities among the established commodities than among the new and outmoded.

An alternative interpretation of the regression model involving previous consumption in the determining variables has been examined by Nerlove and Addison, using Stone's data for groups of commodities. There are difficulties involved in using observations for commodity groups and, although all relevant variables have not been tested, it would seem that for *individual* commodities, the significant values of the coefficient of previous consumption should not be interpreted as lags in the adjustments of consumers to price and income changes. They reflect conditions of an early period of growth for a new commodity or a strong period of decline for an outmoded commodity.

The classification of commodities according to whether they are new, established or outmoded provides a useful method of organising the study of demand for consumer goods, and some progress has been achieved in sorting out diffusion process effects from price and income changes. Although much has been done in measuring consumer behaviour – one of the oldest econometric problems – more efforts need to be made in measuring consumer reactions to innovation.

REFERENCES

Adelman, Irma and Z. Griliches (1961). 'On an index of quality change', *Journal of the American Statistical Association*, **56**, 535–48.

Aitchison, J. and J. A. C. Brown (1957). *The Lognormal Distribution*, University of Cambridge Department of Applied Economics Monograph no. 5, Cambridge University Press.

Allen, R. G. D. (1932). 'The foundations of a mathematical theory of exchange', *Economica*, **12**, 197–226.

Allen, R. G. D. (1934). 'A reconsideration of the theory of value', *Economica*, N.S. **1**, 196–219.

Allen, R. G. D. (1936). 'Professor Slutsky's theory of consumer's choice', *Review of Economic Studies*, **3**, 120–9.

Allen, R. G. D. (1938). *Mathematical Analysis for Economists*, Macmillan, London.

Allen, R. G. D. and A. L. Bowley (1935). *Family Expenditure*, King and Son, London.

Bailey, M. J. (1956). 'A generalized comparative statics in linear programming', *Review of Economic Studies*, **23**, 236–40.

Bailey, N. T. J. (1950). 'A simple stochastic epidemic', *Biometrika*, **37**, 193–202.

Bain, A. D. (1962). 'The growth of television ownership in the United Kingdom', *International Economic Review*, **3**, 145–67.

Bain, A. D. (1963). 'The growth of demand for new commodities', *Journal of the Royal Statistical Society*, A, **126**, 285–99.

Bain, A. D. (1964). *The Growth of Television Ownership in the United Kingdom since the War*, University of Cambridge Department of Applied Economics Monograph no. 12, Cambridge University Press.

Beckman, M. J. (1956). 'Comparative statics, linear programming and the Giffen paradox', *Review of Economic Studies*, **23**, 232–5.

Bergstrom, A. R. (1955). 'The use of index numbers in demand analysis', *Review of Economic Studies*, **23**, 17–26.

Brown, J. A. C. (1954). 'An experiment in demand analysis: The computation of a diet problem on the Manchester computer', paper no. 6 in *Conference on Linear Programming May 1954*, Ferranti Ltd, London.

Brown, J. A. C. (1959). 'Seasonality and elasticity of the demand for food in Great Britain since derationing', *Journal of Agricultural Economics*, **13**, 1–12.

Burns, A. F. (1934). *Production Trends in the United States since* 1870, National Bureau of Economic Research, Publication no. 23, New York.

Carter, C. and B. Williams (1957). *Industry and Technical Progress: Factors Governing the Speed and Application of Science*, Oxford, London.

Chapman, Agatha L. (assisted by Rose Knight) (1953). *Wages and Salaries in the United Kingdom, 1920–1938*, Studies in the National Income and Expenditure of the United Kingdom, volume 5, Cambridge University Press.

Chipman, J. S. (1960). 'The foundations of utility', *Econometrica*, **28**, 193–224.

Coleman, J., E. Katz, and H. Menzel (1957). 'The diffusion of an innovation among physicians', *Sociometry*, **20**, 253–70.

Court, A. T. (1939). 'Hedonic price indexes with automotive examples' in *The Dynamics of Automobile Demand*, General Motors Corporation, New York.

Croxton, F. E. and D. J. Cowden (1939). *Applied General Statistics*, Pitman, London.

Dantzig, G. B. (1963). *Linear Programming and Extensions*, Princeton University Press.

Debreu, G. (1954). 'Representation of preference ordering by a numerical function', 159–65, in *Decision Processes*, eds. R. M. Thrall, C. H. Coombs, and R. L. Davis, New York, John Wiley and Sons.

Derksen, J. B. D. and A. Rombouts (1937). 'The demand for bicycles in the Netherlands', *Econometrica*, **5**, 295–300.

Dernberg, T. F. (1957). *Consumer Response to Innovation: Television*, Cowles Foundation Discussion Paper no. 36.

Dhrymes, P. J. (1967). 'On the measurement of price and quality changes in some consumer capital goods', *American Economic Review*, **57**, 501–18.

Dorfman, R., P. A. Samuelson, and R. M. Solow (1958). *Linear Programming and Economic Analysis*, McGraw-Hill, New York.

Duesenberry, J. S. (1949). *Income, Saving and the Theory of Consumer Behaviour*, Harvard, Cambridge Mass.

The Economist, **189** (1958). 'Motors in the lead', supplement to issue of 25 October 1958.

Farrell, M. J. (1952). 'Irreversible demand functions', *Econometrica*, **20**, 171–86.

Farrell, M. J. (1954). 'Some aggregation problems in demand analysis', *Review of Economic Studies*, **21**, 193–202.

Fisher, I. (1892). *Mathematical Investigations in the Theory of Value and Prices*, reprinted (1925) from the *Transactions of the Connecticut Academy*, **9.**

14

Georgescu-Roegen, N. (1954). 'Choice, expectations and measurability', *Quarterly Journal of Economics*, **68**, 503–34.

Griliches, Z. (1957). 'Hybrid corn: an exploration in the economics of technological change', *Econometrica*, **25**, 501–22.

Griliches, Z. (1961). 'Hedonic price indexes for automobiles: An econometric analysis of quality change', in *The Price Statistics of the Federal Government*, National Bureau of Economic Research, New York.

Griliches, Z. (1964). 'Notes on the measurement of price and quality changes', in *Models of Income Determination*, National Bureau of Economic Research, Princeton.

Harsanyi, J. (1954). 'Welfare economics of variable tastes', *Review of Economic Studies*, **21**, 204–13.

Hausner, M. (1954). 'Multidimensional utilities', ch. 12 in *Decision Processes*, eds. R. M. Thrall, C. H. Coombs and R. L. Davis, John Wiley and Sons, New York.

Hicks, J. R. (1934). 'A reconsideration of the theory of value', *Economica*, **1**, 52–76.

Hicks, J. R. (1937). *La Théorie Mathématique de la Valeur*, Hermann, Paris.

Hicks, J. R. (1939). *Value and Capital*, 2nd edn, 1946, Clarendon, Oxford.

Hicks, J. R. (1956). *A Revision of Demand Theory*, Clarendon, Oxford.

Hofsten, E. von (1952). *Price Indexes and Quality Changes*, Bokförlaget Forum, Stockholm.

Ironmonger, D. S. (1959). 'A note on the estimation of long-run elasticities', *Journal of Farm Economics*, **41**, 626–32.

Jefferys, J. B. (1954). *Retail Trading in Britain 1850–1950*, National Institute of Economic and Social Research, Economic and Social Studies 13, Cambridge University Press.

Jefferys, J. B. and Dorothy Walters (1955). 'National income and expenditure of the United Kingdom *1870–1952*', *Income and Wealth Series*, **5**, 1–40.

Jerome, H. (1934). *Mechanization in Industry*, National Bureau of Economic Research, New York.

Jewkes, J., D. Sawers and R. Stillerman (1958). *The Sources of Invention*, Macmillan, London.

Keynes, J. M. (1930). *A Treatise on Money*, 2 volumes, Macmillan, London.

Kuznets, S. (1942). *Uses of National Income in Peace and War*, National Bureau of Economic Research, Occasional Paper no. 6, New York.

Lancaster, K. J. (1966). 'A new approach to consumer theory', *Journal of Political Economy*, **74**, 132–57.

Levine, H. S. (1960). 'A small problem in the analysis of growth', *Review of Economics and Statistics*, **42**, 225–8.

Maizels, A. (1959). 'Trends in world trade in durable consumer goods', *National Institute Review*, November 1959.

Malmquist, S. (1948). *A Statistical Analysis of the Demand for Liquor in Sweden*, Appelbergs Boktryckerieaktiebolag, Uppsala.

Mansfield, E. (1961). 'Technical change and the rate of imitation', *Econometrica*, **29**, 741–66.

Mansfield, E. (1963). 'Intrafirm rates of diffusion of an innovation', *Review of Economics and Statistics*, **45**, 348–59.

Mansfield, E. (1965). 'Innovation and technical change in the railroad industry', in *Transportation Economics*, National Bureau of Economic Research, New York.

Marschak, J. (1939). 'Personal and collective budget functions', *Review of Economics and Statistics*, **21**, 161–70.

Marshall, A. (1890). *Principles of Economics*, 8th edn 1920, Macmillan, London.

Mitchell, B. R. (with the collaboration of Phyllis Deane) (1962). *Abstract of British Historical Statistics*, Cambridge University Press.

Morgenstern, O. (1948). 'Demand theory reconsidered', *Quarterly Journal of Economics*, **62**, 165–201.

Nelson, R. R. and E. S. Phelps (1966). 'Investment in humans, technological diffusion, and economic growth', *American Economic Review*, **56**, 69–75.

Nelson, R. R., M. J. Peck and E. D. Kalachek (1967). *Technology, Economic Growth and Public Policy*, Brookings, Washington.

Nerlove, M. (1958). 'Distributed lags and estimation of long-run supply and demand elasticities: Theoretical considerations', *Journal of Farm Economics*, **40**, 301–11.

Nerlove, M. (1959). 'On the estimation of long-run elasticities: A reply', *Journal of Farm Economics*, **41**, 632–40.

Nerlove, M. and W. Addison (1958). 'Statistical estimation of long-run elasticities of supply and demand', *Journal of Farm Economics*, **40**, 861–80.

Nicholson, J. L. (1967). 'The measurement of quality changes', *Economic Journal*, **77**, 512–30.

Pareto, V. (1892–3). 'Considerazioni sui principii fundamentali dell'economia politica pura', *Giornali degli Economisti*, **5**, 415 and **7**, 297. (Mentioned by G. J. Stigler (1950), 'The development of utility theory', *Journal of Political Economy*, **58**, 307–27 and 373–96.)

Pearce, I. F. (1964). *A Contribution to Demand Analysis*, Clarendon, Oxford.

Pigou, A. C. (1913). 'The interdependence of different sources of demand and supply in a market', *Economic Journal*, **23**, 19–24.

Prais, S. J. and H. S. Houthakker (1955). *The Analysis of Family Budgets*, University of Cambridge Department of Applied Economics Monograph no. 4, Cambridge University Press.

Prescott, R. B. (1922). 'Laws of growth in forecasting demand', *Journal of the American Statistical Association*, **18**, 471–9.

Prest, A. R. (1949). 'Some experiments in demand analysis', *Review of Economics and Statistics*, **31**, 33–49.

Prest, A. R. (assisted by A. A. Adams) (1954). *Consumers' Expenditure in the United Kingdom* 1900–1919, Studies in the National Income and Expenditure of the United Kingdom, volume 3, Cambridge University Press.

Pyatt, F. G. (1964). *Priority Patterns and the Demand for Household Durable Goods*, University of Cambridge Department of Applied Economics Monograph no. 11, Cambridge University Press.

Robbins, L. (1932). *An Essay on the Nature and Significance of Economic Science*, Macmillan, London.

Robinson, Joan (1956). *The Accumulation of Capital*, Macmillan, London.

Rogers, E. M. (1962). *The Diffusion of Innovations*, Glencoe, New York.

Roos, C. F. and V. S. von Szeliski (1939). 'The concept of demand and price elasticity – the dynamics of automobile demand', *Journal of the American Statistical Association*, **34**, 652–64.

Roy, R. (1943). 'La hiérarchie des besoins et la notion de groups dans l'économie de choix', *Econometrica*, **11**, 13–24.

Roy, R. (1952). 'Les élasticities de la demande relative aux biens de consommation et aux groupes de biens', *Econometrica*, **20**, 391–405.

Ryan, B. (1948). 'A study of technological diffusion', *Rural Sociology*, **13**, 373–85.

Ryan, B. and N. C. Gross (1943). 'The diffusion of hybrid seed corn in two Iowa communities', *Rural Sociology*, **8**, 15–24.

Samuelson, P. A. (1946). 'Comparative statics and the logic of economic maximizing', *Review of Economic Studies*, **14**, 41–3.

Schumpeter, J. A. (1934). *The Theory of Economic Development*, Harvard, Cambridge Mass.

Slutsky, E. E. (1915). 'Sulla teoria del bilancio del consummatore', *Giornale degli Economisti*, **51**, 1–26. (Reprinted (1952) in an English translation by Olga Ragusa, as 'On the theory of the budget of the consumer', in *Readings in Price Theory*, Irwin, Chicago.)

Stigler, G. J. (1945). 'The cost of subsistence', *Journal of Farm Economics*, **27**, 303–14.

Stone, R. (assisted by D. A. Rowe, W. J. Corlett, Renee Hurstfield and Muriel Potter) (1954). *The Measurement of Consumers' Expenditure and Behaviour in the United Kingdom, 1920–1938*, vol. I, Studies in the National Income and Expenditure of the United Kingdom, Cambridge University Press.

Stone, R. (1956). Ch. IV in *Quantity and Price Indexes in National Accounts*, Organisation for European Economic Cooperation, Paris.

Stone, R. and D. A. Rowe (1966). *The Measurement of Consumers' Expenditure and Behaviour in the United Kingdom, 1920–1938*, vol. II, Studies in the National Income and Expenditure of the United Kingdom, Cambridge University Press.

Stone, R. and D. A. Rowe (1957). 'The market demand for durable goods', *Econometrica*, **25**, 423–43.

Thrall, R. M. (1954). 'Applications of multidimensional utility theory', ch. 13 in *Decision Processes*, eds. R. M. Thrall, C. H. Coombs and R. L. Davis, John Wiley and Sons, New York.

Tobin, J. (1952). 'A survey of the theory of rationing', *Econometrica*, **20**, 521–53.

Wold, H. (in association with L. Jureen) (1953). *Demand Analysis: A Study in Econometrics*, Wiley, New York.

Wolff, P. de (1938). 'The demand for passenger cars in the United States', *Econometrica*, **6**, 113–29.

Wolff, P. de (1941). 'Income elasticity of demand: A micro-economic and a macro-economic interpretation', *Economic Journal*, **51**, 140–5.

Yates, F. (1951). 'The influence of *Statistical Methods for Research Workers* on the development of the science of statistics', *Journal of the American Statistical Association*, **46**, 19–34.

INDEX

AUTHORS

SUBJECTS

(*see p.* 199 *for 'Commodities'.*)

COMMODITIES

(see p. 198 for 'Subjects'.)